HER OWN WOMAN

The Life of Mary Wollstonecraft

DIANE JACOBS

An *Abacus* Book

First published in the United States of America by Simon & Schuster in 2001
First published in Great Britain by Abacus in 2001

Copyright © 2001 by Diane Jacobs

The moral right of the author has been asserted.

A CIP catalogue record for this book
is available from the British Library.

ISBN 0 349 11461 7

Typeset in Baskerville by M Rules
Printed and bound in Great Britain by Clays Ltd, St Ives plc

Abacus
A division of
Little, Brown and Company (UK)
Brettenham House
Lancaster Place
London WC2E 7EN
www.littlebrown.co.uk

For Masha

and in memory of Rose

CONTENTS

Prologue, 11

PART ONE The Old Regime, 13
PART TWO Revolution, 77
PART THREE The New Order, 187

Epilogue, 277
Postscript, 287
Notes, 289
Select Bibliography, 315
Acknowledgments, 321
Index, 323

HER OWN WOMAN

PROLOGUE

At the height of the French Revolution, a thirty-three-year-old Englishwoman arrived in the port of Calais. She was a foreign correspondent, commissioned by a famous London publisher to write about all the momentous events since the fall of the Bastille. The watchwords of the Revolution—liberty, fraternity, equality—spoke to her own deepest desires. Since childhood, she'd battled injustice: from her father, who had prepared only his male children for meaningful futures; from her mother, who had clearly favored her older brother, Ned. She was tall and pretty but had no dowry or inheritance; only her courage and tenacity pushed her forward. Everything she knew she had taught herself, and she had fought to succeed in the man's world of professional writing. She had made herself a philosopher and could hold her own with friends like Thomas Paine. A year before, she had become internationally famous when she had published *A Vindication of the Rights of Woman*, demanding liberty for the female sex. Now she was eager to see what freedom had brought to the French people. And what would she find for herself?

At Calais, Mary Wollstonecraft stepped into a carriage heading inland to Paris. The winter countryside was bleak, the two-day trip exhausting. She caught a debilitating cough. And for every liberty tree she passed, she saw a sign demanding the head of King Louis XVI, who was now in jail, waiting to be tried for treason. When she arrived at her hosts' house in Paris, only the servants were home. And though Mary could read and write French, the spoken language completely escaped her. She sensed danger in the Paris streets and may have been tempted to return to the safety of King George's London. But she was not in the habit of turning back. She climbed down from the carriage. The greatest adventure of her life lay ahead.

PART ONE

The Old Regime

CHAPTER ONE

*A*lmost a century before, in the early 1700s, Mary's grandfather, Edward Wollstonecraft, came down from Lancashire to make his fortune in London. Perhaps because he knew someone there or perhaps just by chance, Edward settled in Spitalfields, one of the indigent communities pushing the borders of London eastward. Then as now, Spitalfields had winding, narrow streets, spindly buildings, and an exotic air. The roads were cluttered and dirty. In the eighteenth century, Spitalfields was the center of London's weaving industry. Most of the weavers were French Huguenots who'd fled persecution after the Edict of Nantes was revoked in France. Spitalfields was, and still is, a cynosure for the unwanted: Baptists, Quakers, Jews, and Moslems all have fled there in their time. A mosque stands today on a site formerly occupied by a nineteenth-century synagogue, which began, in Edward's time, as a Protestant church.

But there's nothing to indicate that Edward was any sort of an outcast. He was Anglican and British. He was also clever and deft with his hands. Quickly, he apprenticed himself to a weaver, probably a

Frenchman. The average silk weaver earned even less than jewelers or chair makers. So for little pay, Edward worked long days in a Georgian brick building, weaving silk at a garret window built high to capture all the available light. He was a pious man and must have stopped often at Christ Church, which to this day towers over the splaying market like a Chinese carriage with four chunky pillared legs and a soaring spire.

Soon Edward bought a small house on Primrose Street. He married a woman named Jane and had several children, became a master weaver, began acquiring property, and rose in the world. Jane died, and their only surviving child, a girl named Elizabeth Ann, married a man named Isaac Rutson. Edward himself took a second wife. But she died, and again only one child lived into full adulthood. This time it was a boy named Edward John.

By now, the senior Edward was rich. He owned many houses on Primrose Street. He could have moved anywhere he liked; so the fact that he chose to build his new house right in the heart of Spitalfields, on Hanbury Street, says something about his character. At the very least, he felt comfortable in a world dominated by immigrants. Maybe he was also more the nonconformist than he seemed. In the deeds for the new house, Edward describes himself as a "gentleman": he'd acquired a good name.

When Edward Wollstonecraft died in 1765, he left a large estate, two-thirds of which was to be divided equally between his only son, Edward John, and his seven-year-old grandson, Ned. Thanks to primogeniture, by which the eldest son inherits everything, nothing went to Ned's younger siblings, five-year-old Mary, three-year-old Henry, and baby Eliza. Besides, under English law girls could not own property; they *were* property, first of a father and then, if they were lucky, of a spouse.

Yet, for reasons we can only surmise, Edward decided to leave nearly a third of his estate to the daughter of his first marriage, Eliza-

beth Ann, and nothing to her husband. In fact, Edward was so determined that he went through the elaborate motions of setting up a
bank trust jointly in her and her husband's names. The income from
the trust would be received yearly by *both* partners, but it could be
"employed" (Edward's executors were instructed in no uncertain language) only by Elizabeth Ann: "for her sole distinct peculiar and separate use and benefit exclusive of her said husband and so as that the
same shall not be subject to . . . intermeddling control."[1]

Edward's stipulation that the money should be for Elizabeth Ann's
"peculiar" use hints, even in its eighteenth-century context, at something unusual. Indeed, Edward's will was a peculiar document. It ad-
hered to the *letter* of English law by bequeathing dividends to both
the Rutsons, but attacked the *spirit* by forbidding his son-in-law to
spend a cent. Unfortunately, there are no records to show what became of the Rutsons and their money. Maybe Isaac Rutson was so
embittered by his father-in-law's chicanery that he defied the executors and kept all the dividends himself. After all, according to English
law, everything his wife owned was his. Or maybe the will and its executors prevailed. Maybe Elizabeth Ann tasted freedom. But however it turned out, Edward Wollstonecraft had made a statement. And
if it's a bit presumptuous to claim he'd made a feminist statement, he
had transgressed a code oppressive to the female sex. It would be
pretty to think that he did this in the name of abstract justice. But his
motives were probably personal. Most likely, he took all this trouble
because he loved his daughter or hated her spouse. But no matter:
many enlightenments begin with love and hate. Or so it would
seem if one traces the journey of Edward's granddaughter Mary
Wollstonecraft.

Mary Wollstonecraft was born on April 27, 1759, in her grandfather's Primrose Street house in Spitalfields. She was her family's
second child and the first female. Her father, Edward John Wollstonecraft, was a young weaver. Her Irish mother, Elizabeth

Dickson, had come down from Ballyshannon to marry him—which is all we know of her past.[2] It was the era of George III, who loved his wife and sang the praises of domestic life. But the Wollstonecrafts did not support his theme.

Mary remembered her parents as unequal warriors, her mother weak and pretty, her father a sentimental tyrant who fawned over his family one moment, then beat them the next because he was drunk or out of sorts. Often Mary threw herself between her parents to protect Elizabeth. But Mary's mother could be as brutal as Edward John in her more devious ways. She devised a particularly cruel method of punishing talkative young Mary—insisting that she sit still and absolutely silent for three or four hours while her parents conversed.[3] Mary could bear any discipline, she later said, provided that the cause was just. But she despised Elizabeth's unfairness: what her mother let pass one day, she pounced on the next. Worst of all, though Mary's mother bore seven children—first Ned, then Mary, then Henry, Eliza, Everina, James, and finally Charles, she suckled and indulged only Ned, her firstborn, who, according to the laws of primogeniture, would inherit all the family wealth. From her earliest years, Mary knew she was stronger, smarter, and more trustworthy than her coddled brother. Her first ardent struggle was to convince her mother to love her best.

When Mary was a year old, the 1760 *Complete Guide to . . . the City of London* listed her father, Edward John, as a master weaver, but he lacked his father's zeal for work. The Industrial Revolution, drawing hordes to London, eluded him. He wanted to travel in the opposite direction: to live in the country and rise in the social world. So in 1763, Edward John moved his family to a farm in Epping Forest, on the periphery of London, though he knew nothing about crops or livestock. And when the elder Edward died in February 1765, leaving Edward John a large share of his fortune, the Wollstonecrafts moved to a farm nearby in posher Barking, where Mary's parents could boast of dining in manors with the upper class.

Mary's earliest memories are of Barking: Elizabeth's well-kept garden, the bustling wharf, the acres of fields, where her mother—for once scorning conventional wisdom, which favored dolls and dress-up for female children—urged her to exercise her tall, well-built body and run off angry moods. At six, Mary had fair hair and regular features. She bore a chip on her shoulder because her mother still favored Ned, but she was learning to turn to God for approval. *He* cared nothing about first sons or rich neighbors; he spoke of righteousness and the struggle to be good. There was an afterlife where justice triumphed, the Anglican Church consoled Mary, and until then there were flowers and birds and clouds and sunsets. If nothing could divert Mary's parents from their petty squabbles, nature, Mary discovered, could fill *her* with "sublime ideas."[4]

The Wollstonecrafts remained just three years in Barking before either the farm failed or restless Edward John lost patience with staying in one spot. In 1768, they were off again, this time north to a farm in Yorkshire outside Beverley, where they remained just long enough for Charles, the last Wollstonecraft child, to be born. Then, when Mary was ten, in 1769, Edward John left his land for a house in Wednesday's Market inside the town of Beverley, which Mary always spoke of as her childhood home.

In the mid-eighteenth century, Beverley was an affluent community, filled with doctors and lawyers, living in neat rows of Dutch-style tile-roofed houses on long cobblestone streets. It boasted a lively theater, a grammar school, a handsome Assembly Room for concerts and dances, a circulating library, and a charity school for the poor. Outside town lay a wooded park with a racecourse. And overhead towered a majestic cathedral—the Beverley Minster—which appealed to Mary's love of Gothic grandeur as well as her longing for a world elsewhere. There was a pretty market cross bearing the arms of Queen Anne on one end of the town in Saturday's Market and an obelisk at the other end in Wednesday's Market, which was the smartest section of town.[5]

Certainly, this fashionable address gratified Edward John's vanity, but at a high price. Mary remembers her father's "extravagance," inciting talk and dire predictions among the neighbors. He must have lost much of his father's fortune, for no one gossips about a rich man spending his wealth.

By the time they reached Beverley, Edward John was already the blackguard husband, boozing and gambling; Elizabeth was the passive martyr complaining of vague symptoms and spending hours in bed. The children too began falling into niches. Mary was the boss, Eliza (born four years later) the beauty, and their youngest sister, Everina (born two years after Eliza), had the most common sense. Mary describes Ned as aloof and conceited, while Henry, James, and Charles blend together in her account of these early years. It was time for the older children to be educated, so Ned and Henry began studying what all boys learned—literature, classical languages, mathematics—at the Beverley Grammar School, while, at the local girls' school, Mary and her sisters learned to sew, add simple numbers, and read just enough to please a spouse.

While sought after in French salons, learned females were ridiculed in Great Britain. "If you happen to have any learning, keep it a profound secret," one father implored his daughters in a popular book of the times.[6] And women writers were no less vigilant—insisting that wives parrot their husbands' opinions (this from the poet-moralist Hester Chapone) and predicting old maidhood for girls who could think. (Lady Mary Wortley Montagu warned her granddaughter, a gifted mathematician, to "conceal whatever learning she attains with as much solicitude as she would hide crookedness or lameness.")[7]

Ridiculous, thought Mary, who seems to have been born avid for knowledge and envied her brothers, and even her new Beverley friend Jane Arden, because *her* father, a lecturer on science and literature, taught his daughters as if they were boys. Mary yearned for a father like Jane's and also longed for Jane's friendship. One of the first letters she ever composed was to Jane Arden, and it is so revealing of the ardent and exasperating young Mary that it is worth quoting in full:

Miss Arden.— Before I begin I beg pardon for the freedom of my style.— If I did not love you I should not write so;—I have a heart that scorns disguise, and a countenance which will not dissemble:— I have formed romantic notions of friendship.— I have once been disappointed:— I think if I am a second time I shall only want some infidelity in a love affair, to qualify me for an old maid, as then I shall have no idea of either of them.— I am a little singular in my thoughts of love and friendship; I must have the first place or none.— I own your behaviour is more according to the opinion of the world, but I would break such narrow bounds.— I will give you reasons for what I say;—since Miss C—— has been here you have behaved in the coolest manner.— I once hoped our friendship was built on a permanent foundation:— We have all our failings—I have more than usual, but I thought you might mildly have corrected me as I always loved you with true sisterly affection. If I found any faults I should have told you but a lady possessed of so many accomplishments as Miss A—— cannot find any loss in your humble Servant.— I would not have seen it, but your behaviour the other night I cannot pass over;—and when I spoke of sitting with you at Church you made an objection, because I and your sisters quarrelled;—I did not think a little raillery would have been taken in such a manner, or that you would have insinuated, that I dared to have prophaned so sacred a place with idle chit-chat.

I once thought myself worthy of your friendship;—and I thank you for bringing me to a right sense of myself.— When I have been at your house with Miss J—— the greatest respect has been paid to her; every thing handed to her first;—and in short, as if she were a superior being.— Your Mama too behaved with more politeness to her.

I am obliged to your Papa and Mama and desire you will give them my complimentary thanks, and as I have spent many happy hours in your company, shall always have the sincerest esteem for Miss A.——.— There is no accounting for the imbecility of human nature—I might misconstrue your behavior, but what I have written flows spontaneously from my pen and this I am sure. I only desire to be done by as I do;—I shall expect a written answer to this,—

and am yours
M.W.

Don't tell C—— to you I have told all my failings . . . ;—I would not be so mean as to shew only the bright side of the picture;—I have reason to think you have not been so ingenuous to me.—I cannot bear the recollection that that when Miss R—— comes I should have less of your company.— After seeing you yesterday, I thought not to have sent this—(but you desire it) for to see you and be angry, is not in my power.— I long for a walk in my darling Westwood. Adieu.

Mary Wollstonecraft[8]

Mary's Bevèrley of the 1770s comes to life in this passage. We see the Minster full of girls torn between piety and the urge to gossip. Who sits next to whom is a matter of great concern, and one's first loyalty is to one's siblings: if they're insulted, you're insulted too. We read of Mary's "darling Westwood" park, where the great problems of adolescence can be walked away, and of visits from out-of-towners like the dreaded Miss C—— from Hull. We discover how Miss J—— shows up at the Arden house to further distract Jane's attention from Mary.

Mary is insecure about her family's status in the community. Miss J——'s background, she intimates, is wealthier or more respectable, making her the socially "worthier" friend. But "I have a heart that scorns disguise, and a countenance which will not dissemble." Mary is her own woman and proud of it. She has "romantic notions of friendship." Her mother's preference for Ned has not reconciled her to an inferior position: she must be loved best or not at all. In her "romantic ideas" and determination to break "narrow bounds," we get an early glimpse of the champion of the French Revolution. Mary threatens that she will break with the Ardens and their snobbery. But then again, maybe not. "There is no accounting for the imbecility of human nature," she writes. Perhaps she has misconstrued Jane's behavior, and then too it is hard to see a person you love and remain angry for long. Mary makes it clear she doesn't *want* to be friendless or an "old maid." By her last paragraph, she is on the verge of forgiving her tormentor; then she remembers Jane's friend Miss R—— from York will soon come between them. How much can a person bear?

Jane was not, it seems, intentionally goading Mary. She values her mercurial young friend, but won't give up everyone else she knows. Reluctantly, Mary accepts the relationship on Jane's terms. The girls make up, and in her next letter Mary tells Jane she may favor Miss R——, though not, she implores, Miss C——! "Love and jealousy are twins," Mary concedes. And: "I have a heart too susceptible for my own peace."

This is not Mary's first jealous outburst. Mary has fought with Miss R—— and refused to apologize first.[9] Mary felt snubbed at Miss J——'s, where Jane's "behaviour . . . hurt me extremely, and not answering my letter shews that you set little value on my friendship.— If you had sent to ask me, I should have gone to the play, but none of you seemed to want my company."[10] So Mary stayed home and sulked. She cannot be bothered, it seems, to befriend any girl but Jane. Yet her letters reveal an interest in Jane's scholarly father, who lends her an essay on friendship, and in a clergyman from Derbyshire, a "worthy Philosopher,"[11] who teaches Mary some math. All Mary's letters to Jane abound in literary references—to Pope and Dryden and Gray. She must have been borrowing books from someone and educating herself.

And when Mary wasn't brooding over her position in Jane's hier-archy, they spent "many agreeable days together" and "eagerly told every girlish secret of our hearts."[12] There were dances and concerts and beaux to mull over. And deaths and marriages, of course. In one letter to Jane, Mary tells of the lucky Miss N——s, whose uncle passed away and left them a fortune; in another, she herself "expects a great deal of pleasure" from going out to the Beverley theater to see a play.[13] "The oddest mortal that ever existed" is courting Miss C——, Jane informs Mary. What's worse, to please her parents, Miss C—— submits. "The contrast will be very entertaining," Mary cat-tily responds to Jane's description. "Her over-giddiness, and his over-graveness must be superlatively ridiculous;—in short you must allow me to laugh." She knows Jane would never tolerate "such nonsense." As for herself, Mary has just attended a "very agreeable" party: "all the world was there."[14]

In one letter, Mary prints out a song praising Beverley; in another she sends Jane a satire by a local poet deriding the marriageable women they know. "I am sorry I am not older to have had my name inscribed in such divine poetry," Mary remarks. And though she mocks the verse, Mary may indeed anticipate the day when she'll dance at the Beverley Assembly and be courted by eligible men.[15]

In the fall of 1774, she may even have deluded herself that her family was improving when in fact they were sinking down in the world. Her father could no longer afford his elegant Wednesday's Market address. Besides, a "commercial speculation"[16] beckoned him, he said. The decision to move was probably quick because Mary never wrote to inform Jane Arden; or maybe she was too embarrassed to write, or too sad. For she had a deep love for Beverley and the Yorkshire countryside. "When my heart is warm," she wrote years later, "pop come the expressions of [Yorkshire] into my head." These were tuneful expressions like "lightsome" and "go badly with me." She would hold them vividly in her mind as she would hold the Minster and the Assembly and the theater and Westwood and all the Ardens. Despite Miss C—— and Miss R—— and her distressing family, Mary would remember her days in Beverley as tranquil times.

NOW, IN 1795, Mary's father was racing after some new business scheme in the London environs. He settled the family in Hoxton, which boasted an esteemed academy founded by religious Dissidents who were barred from Oxford and Cambridge because they rejected the Anglican faith. But Hoxton was also known for its almshouses, insane asylums, and noisy pubs. At dusk, thieves gathered in Hoxton Field to pounce on city workers passing through on their way to the nicer suburbs—Islington or Highbury.

Ned Wollstonecraft, now seventeen, had a job at a London law firm. Fourteen-year-old Henry was apprenticed to a surgeon-apothecary, while Eliza and Everina finished their girls' education and James and Charles enrolled in primary school. At sixteen, Mary was beyond school age, so she languished at home with her miserable parents. "Reason as well as religion convinces me that all has happened for the best . . . for I am persuaded misfortunes are of the greatest service," Mary wrote unconvincingly when she resumed her correspondence with Jane Arden.[17] Deprived and bored, she threw her energies into defying propriety—letting her shiny, thick hair hang limp, wearing dull, rough clothes, and refusing all but the most meager portion of food and eating almost no meat. She showed early signs of her lifelong tendency to depression, complaining to her sisters about "gloom," violent headaches, and "nervous" fevers. She was grappling with the great question of adolescence—Who am I?—and had an easier time deciding what she was not—not powerful, not free to choose, not loved or happy or valued at her worth.

Matters improved somewhat when Mary met her new neighbor, an odd, reclusive scholar who was physically deformed and said to have worn the same pair of shoes for fourteen years. His name was Mr. Clare, and he singled her out as intellectually gifted, though ignorant. He and his friendly wife invited Mary to come study and live with them. She accepted and began visiting for as long as a month at a time. And whereas in Beverley she'd chosen books randomly, now she followed Mr. Clare's regime, reading well-thought-of works like *The Seasons,* James Thomson's tome on nature, and *The Complaint; or, Night Thoughts on Life, Death, and Immortality,* Edward Young's elegy for his perished wife, as well as the Bible, Swift, Shakespeare, Milton, and philosophy. Milton's Satan particularly thrilled her, while Locke's insistence that the world was ameliorable challenged her sullen conviction that nothing changed.

Still, Mary was unprepared for her own transformation when one day Mr. Clare took her to meet another girl he tutored—Fanny Blood. It was love at first sight, Mary later said. Fanny was slightly older than Mary and not just pretty and smart, but delicate and talented: superior to anyone Mary had ever met. Even her poverty seemed romantic. When Mr. Blood lost jobs, he had no inheritance to fall back on; and Mrs. Blood exhausted herself struggling to support her hungry brood. All summer long, she hunched over her needlework from four in the morning until it was too dark to see at night, and Fanny worked loyally beside her, though the long hours were disastrous for her health. Fanny was an artist. She played piano and drew so well that people bought her paintings. In addition, while Mary still strained to tame her wild sentences, Fanny knew grammar and could organize her ideas.

Those ideas seemed at first to coincide ideally with Mary's. Fanny too was sad and solitary. Her mother, while kind, exasperated everyone with her endless chatter, and Mr. Blood thought of nothing but his ambition to go home to Ireland, which was highly impractical considering he could barely afford food. Fanny seemed dreamy and reflective. She was in the early stages of tuberculosis and unhappy because her fiancé kept putting off their wedding date since his family looked down on hers. The fiancé was Hugh Skeys, whom Fanny had met studying at the Clares' house. Now he was planning to start a business in Portugal, to which he promised to take Fanny—but not soon.

Meanwhile, Mary ignored Skeys and began planning for eternal friendship with Fanny. "I could dwell for ever on [Fanny's] praises," Mary wrote Jane Arden, "and you wod not wonder at it, if you knew the many favours she has conferred on me, and the many valuable qualifications she possesses."[18]

At fourteen, Mary had confided in Jane her "romantic notions of friendship." Now she loved Fanny "better than all the world besides."[19] Suddenly, Mary had a goal: to forge what the eighteenth century called a "romantic friendship"—a relationship between two women that could be as tempestuous as any love affair, but only rarely involved sex. The most famous romantic friendship of the day was between two genteel women named Sarah Ponsonby and Eleanor Butler, the "ladies of Llangollen." But there was also the clergyman's daughter Miss Carter, who called a female friend "almost my passion"; the writer Henrietta Bowdler, who worshiped the poet

Elizabeth Smith; and the famous bluestocking Mrs. Montagu, who consoled herself for a dreary marriage by loving a succession of women friends.

For men, the term "romantic friendship" conjured images of pale females reading Richardson out loud while watching the sun set; but the aggressiveness of these relationships was unsettling, contradicting the comforting notion that women were passive beings. Mary hoped for a friendship as consuming as any heterosexual relationship and with the advantage that, unlike married couples, she and Fanny held equal power under the law, though their goals were not identical. Fanny loved Mary, but still wanted a husband, while Mary claimed she would never marry. "I know this resolution [not to marry] may appear a little extraordinary," she told Jane Arden, "but in forming it I follow the dictates of reason as well as the bent of my inclination."[20] Perhaps. But since Mary had neither a respectable dowry nor dazzling beauty, bachelors as interesting as Fanny were unlikely to ask for her hand. Better to reject *them* than give them the chance to snub her. Besides, "Like a true woman," Mary later admitted, "[I] rail at what I don't possess."[21]

That Mary did not possess any semblance of stability was driven home once again when, soon after she met Fanny, her father whisked her and all the younger children off to a farm he'd gotten it into his head to buy in Laugharne, Wales. Laugharne was ravishingly beautiful,[22] Mary told Jane Arden, and she wrote constantly to Fanny, who instructed her about nouns and verbs as well as sending news from home and love. Their separation was short because Edward John's latest pipe dream failed quickly, and, a year after they left, the Wollstonecrafts trudged back to outer London, taking a house in Walworth near Fanny's family in Walham Green.

So Mary and Fanny now walked and read and talked together whenever they liked. Fanny became a sister to Eliza and Everina, and Fanny's parents and their money woes were now Mary's as well.

"Our mother," Mary called Mrs. Blood, and she sat through so many meals listening to Mr. Blood pining to return to Ireland that she began singing that country's praises herself. Fanny's brother George became Mary's pet. "The Princess," he dubbed her, raising her above their ignoble fathers and the less remarkable younger Wollstonecrafts and Bloods.

Even Fanny, George knew, lacked Mary's originality and penetrating intellect. His sister loved stories with a comforting moral, but couldn't fathom the theories of Locke or Rousseau, which Mary was always quoting. And Fanny was content to bear life as she found it, while Mary was determined to assert her will. And she followed through on her impulses. For instance, in the spring of 1778, just before her nineteenth birthday, Mary announced that she was going to find a way to earn money so she and Fanny could afford to live on their own—even if this meant leaving Fanny in the short run. Teaching, governessing, and playing companion to demanding old women were the few jobs women without fortunes could hope to procure. Since a lady's companion seemed less horrible than the two other options, Mary accepted a job with a widow named Mrs. Dawson, who lived most of the year in Bath.

Mary took off for Bath in high spirits, which were soon deflated by her gruff and imperious boss. "My health is ruined, my spirits broken, and I have a constant pain in my side that is daily gaining ground," Mary, in a letter to Jane, enumerates the effects of her first job. Still, she stuck it out, accompanying ungrateful Mrs. Dawson on a holiday to Southampton during the summer of 1779 and to visit her class-conscious sister in Windsor the following fall. Here Mary rode in the forest, went "constantly" to the Cathedral, and gossiped to Jane about offensive high society and all the "poor girls" mooning after the prince.

Mary was twenty-one and still in Windsor with Mrs. Dawson in August of 1780 when a puzzling letter from her sister Eliza arrived.

Eliza's letter is lost, but Mary's reply gives the first hint of the complicated relationship between them. "There is an irony through your whole epistle that hurts me exceedingly," writes Mary, and she alludes to her sister's false compliments and cutting wit. Clearly, Eliza has had complaints to air, for Mary is on the defensive, protesting that she *has* written her father and is sorry that Everina was sick. "You don't say a word of my mother. I take it for granted she is well," Mary adds.[23] But their mother was not well. She was slowly dying of what the doctors called dropsy, or edema, a painful engorgement of body tissues caused by liver or kidney disease. Dropsy patients require constant care, and with Edward John so feckless and Mary in Windsor, the burden fell on Eliza and Everina. It was usual for Eliza to make Mary guess at the cause of her resentment. But Mary soon grasped the predicament and abruptly left her outraged employer to hurry home to her mother's side.

For two years, Mary (with help from her sisters) devoted herself to caring for Elizabeth Wollstonecraft, while her father was off seducing a younger woman named Lydia and Ned, now a married lawyer, rarely came around. Still, Elizabeth experienced no deathbed revelation: to the end she preferred Ned. And her last words were typically submissive: "A little patience and all will be over." These words had a profound effect on her far more courageous daughter. Mary too would seek freedom from pain in death.

ONCE HIS WIFE was buried, Edward John lost no time proposing to his new lover, Lydia. The Wollstonecraft children snubbed her. She married their prospectless father nonetheless and cheerfully endured his black moods in the velvety green town he chose from all the places he'd passed through—Laugharne, Wales. Of the children, only Charles accompanied Edward John and Lydia to Wales after

Elizabeth's death. Henry was now out of the picture: in *A Different Face,* biographer Emily Sunstein persuasively hypothesizes that he had an emotional breakdown in adolescence and was committed to a madhouse for the rest of his life.[24] Meanwhile, James was at sea. Ned grudgingly took Eliza and Everina into his household on St. Katherine Street, while Mary went to Fanny at Walham Green near Putney Bridge. Often, Mary strolled across that bridge, staring down at the gray water and feeling as if she were already wrinkled and old.[25] What troubled twenty-three-year-old Mary was not just her mother's death, but the fact that she had not found perfect happiness with Fanny. Was it that Fanny was less wonderful than she'd imagined at first, or was there some deficiency in herself?

Still, Mary did not yearn for a husband, even when six months after her mother's death, on October 20, Eliza married a man named Meredith Bishop, a shipbuilder from Bermondsey, across the Tower Bridge from Ned. Mary exalted him a bit in a letter announcing the news to Jane Arden. Bishop was "a worthy man whose position in life is truly enviable,"[26] she said. This was Mary's last letter to Jane Arden. The obsessions of adolescence—love, family, the neighborhood—no longer bound them as strongly as they were pulled apart by different fates, and they went their separate ways. For years, Jane was an exemplary teacher. She did not marry until 1797, the year Mary died. After her death, Jane became the subject of an adoring book by her daughter, *Recollections of a Beloved Mother*—a celebration of the conventional woman, which was everything the first, radical biography of Mary was not. Although Mary emerges as the needier girl throughout their correspondence, it was Jane, not Mary, who saved her friend's letters for twenty years. They are unusual letters, a first outlet for Mary Wollstonecraft's frustrations and bold ideas. Awkward at times, always emotional, the letters to Jane are filled with observations that will be refined in her early books.

. . .

DURING THE FALL of 1782, Eliza and her new husband settled into married life. Bishop got to know Mary, Everina, Ned, and their companions; when the Bloods were penniless at Christmas, Bishop lent them the handsome sum of twenty pounds.[27] Eliza was pregnant in November and in August gave birth to a healthy girl. They named her Elizabeth Mary Francis Bishop. The Bishops seemed well on their way to a complacent married future when, shortly after the birth, Bishop urgently summoned Mary to their Bermondsey home. Her sister, he said, had gone mad.

Mary rushed to Bermondsey, where she indeed found Eliza raving and delirious. At first, Mary pitied Bishop, who must have had strong feelings for Eliza to have married her in the first place without a dowry, and now to call in her sister rather than march Eliza out of the house. (Brief or permanent stays at insane asylums were the common treatment for mental breakdowns in the eighteenth century; the writer Mary Lamb, for example, was frequently escorted to madhouses by her loving brother Charles.)

But as Eliza grew more cogent, she insisted that her husband had mistreated her. Exactly what wrong he'd done her, and when, can only be inferred from Mary's cryptic letters to Everina, which suggest that Bishop wanted sex and Eliza did not. Eliza's aversion may have emerged out of the blue, as Bishop seemed to believe, after the birth of the baby, in which case there was an obvious catalyst. Or, as Eliza insisted, the disgust may have started much earlier. Maybe Bishop was a clumsy, rough, or even brutal lover. Perhaps he was rough and volatile out of bed. A friend of Bishop's told Mary that Bishop was either a "lion or a spannial," which is much the way Mary describes her father. Mary could see that Bishop had a "weak mind"; Eliza was sharp and curious. So her disgust for Bishop's body may have begun with scorn for his intellect. Or maybe her alarm was at the marital state itself.

Mary moved into the Bishops' house, and in her second letter to

Everina confessed: "I don't know what to do— Poor Eliza's situation almost turns my brain—I can't stay and see this continual misery— and to leave her to bear it by herself without any one to comfort her is still more distressing."[28] So Mary soldiered on, sighing all the while, growing attached to the baby, whom they were calling Mary, and struggling to be fair. One minute she was swayed by Bishop. "My heart is almost broken with listening to B. while he *reasons* the case,"[29] she lamented to Everina. But no sooner did "B." leave the room than Eliza would appear and do something outrageous or just look tragically sad, and Mary would be convinced that her sister could never recover her sanity until she was bodily removed from her house. Which, of course, wasn't her house, as, under eighteenth-century law, the baby wasn't her baby: there was the real problem. For, if Eliza left, Elizabeth Mary Francis would have to stay behind since the British father had absolute rights to his child.

Along with Everina and Mary, Fanny was now involved in Eliza's affairs, as was Fanny's fiancé, Hugh Skeys, who was speaking seriously about marriage again, and Ned, of course. At first, it seemed as if everything rested on Ned, the only solvent Wollstonecraft. Mary hoped to prevail upon him to take Eliza under his roof. Ned didn't absolutely refuse. But—being stingy, conservative, and having a wife already resentful of Everina's presence—he did not encourage the plan either. Skeys, meanwhile, sided with Bishop, who, in Mary's words, was drawing "fixed conclutions from general rules." Presumably, he argued that like any sensible woman Eliza would regain her commitment to their marriage once her fits of madness passed.

But as Mary saw it, the saner Eliza felt the more she despised Bishop. She blamed him for her breakdown and declared she'd lose her mind entirely if she stayed his wife. By this time, Eliza must have been thinking practically because she informed Mary she'd do anything, even teach, rather than stay in Bermondsey. And Mary believed her and prepared an escape. Action was a relief after all this waiting, but while Mary was not intimidated by men individually, she feared their collective power under British law.

"Miracles don't occur now,"[30] she cautioned Everina. Still, Mary was obviously hoping God would make an exception and transform Bishop or at least resign Eliza to her fate. For England's marriage laws were so one-sided that, while men could leave their wives on the flimsiest pretext, it literally required an act of Parliament for a woman to obtain a divorce and a miracle indeed for her to see her child without the father's consent. Mary's correspondence with Everina shows she had few illusions about Eliza's future prospects. Eliza would merely be free. And indeed Mary often sounds as if she's liberating a slave rather than seeking a better life for an intelligent woman.

Escape plans were held up because Bishop got sick. Days passed, and he hung around the house. Eliza grew "so harrassed with the fear of being discovered and the thought of leaving the child that she could not have stood it long."[31] Finally, Bishop went out. Eliza and Mary threw their clothes into suitcases, which they gave Fanny to deliver to Everina at Ned's. Eliza filled a last traveling bag with some dresses but forgot the linen, while Mary ran out for a coach. Eliza grew increasingly agitated as the time approached when she would have to part with the baby. She lingered, but in the end joined Mary, who, agitated herself and familiar with Gothic novels, got the idea that they should change coaches midway to their destination—Hackney, near London Fields—to throw Bishop off the trail. Meanwhile, Eliza "bit her *wedding ring* to pieces"[32]—a fitting farewell to domesticity. There were other portents of a breakdown, but it did not come.

At last, Mary and Eliza pulled up at a Mrs. Dodd's rooming house on Church Street in Hackney, where, assuming the name "Miss Johnson," Mary had booked them a room. Both sisters were trembling and weak. Eliza fell into bed, but Mary sat wide awake, imagining that every carriage rolling by was Bishop's, expecting him to stride through the door and demand his wife back. Mary began a letter to

Everina. Could Bishop force Eliza to return? she wondered, and she went on to report the surprising news that she, Mary Wollstonecraft, almost wished for a husband, so desperate was she for support.[33]

The day after their carriage ride, both sisters slept. The following day, they ached in every muscle, and Mary's stomach roiled. Once, Eliza went deaf for hours, which was exactly how her earlier insanity had begun—so Mary was terrified. There were endless worries about money, and there was the great sorrow for Eliza that her child was elsewhere. Bishop did not, as Mary had predicted, pursue or harass Eliza; he went immediately to her elder brother and tried honorably to woo her back. And he assured Hugh Skeys that he would now "endeavour to make Mrs. B. happy."[34] But rather than accept that offer, Eliza chose permanent separation, whereby Bishop forbade her to see her daughter and refused to give her a cent.

Eliza improved steadily as the weeks passed. She never broke down again, though she also never found a way to speak of Elizabeth Mary Frances, who died, probably of neglect, before her first birthday, in August of 1784. Eliza's lifetime correspondence is filled with sardonic references to marriage in general, but she refers to her own just once in the middle of a letter to Everina four years after the escape to Hackney: "I can not make myself understood here," she complains of her current teaching situation. "Had I an inclination to do so, praying is their only amusement, not forgetting eating and [marrying] . . . , and so on— The idea of parting from a husband one could never make them comprehend, I could much sooner persuade them that a stone might speak. . . ."[35] So she did not repudiate her decision to leave home.

For Mary, this incident with Eliza was crucial. By taking action, she discovered the un-Christian joy of asserting her will. Against the male sex, no less, and not just in a *will* like her grandfather the weaver, but out in the streets of London. Mary had to leap to many conclusions in order to assist Eliza to leave her husband: that patriarchy was pregnable, that you could defy a social covenant, that things could improve. Over the next eight years, events in the greater world would make clear to Mary Wollstonecraft the need for a whole new theory about women and happiness. But the idea for her great work, *A Vindication of the Rights of Woman*, was born the day Eliza fled.

CHAPTER TWO

*B*ut in the winter of 1784, *Vindication* lay nearly a decade in the future. For now, Mary and Eliza were two high-strung young women living on top of each other in a cold, dreary Hackney boardinghouse. Mary had caught Bishop's cold and fever, and Eliza's head ached perpetually. They had only three guineas between them and few visitors. Eliza's momentous decision appalled (and doubtless threatened) many of their friends like "new married" Mrs. Brooks, who "with grief of heart gave up my friendship," Mary scoffed in a letter to Everina, though plainly the rejection hurt. Worse, none of the Wollstonecraft girls had future prospects. And while Mary's old champions the Clares sent them wine and pie from Hoxton, it took a bolder new friend to find them work.

That friend (whom Mary probably met through the Clares) was bustling Mrs. Burgh, widow of a well-known Dissident educator. A champion of personal freedom, James Burgh called marriage "that most perfect of all friendships" and depicted the ideal wife as intelligent, cheerful, and convinced of the superiority of men.[1] Teaching was an honorable career, in Mrs. Burgh's opinion, and she persuaded

Mary, Eliza, Everina, and even reticent Fanny that the answer to their troubles was to open a school. Of course, intellectual courses were out of the question; they'd have to pinch their curriculum to suit parents like their own. Jane Austen claimed she could think of "nothing worse" than being a schoolteacher, but Mary started out hoping for the best, especially when Mrs. Burgh quickly rustled up twenty-odd students and found them a house near her in Newington Green.

Just outside of London, Newington Green was a pastoral community filled with orchards, cornfields, and splendid seventeenth-century mansions surrounding a pretty green. On the north corner of the green stood the Unitarian church, defiant in its plainness. Like Hoxton, Newington Green abounded in religious Dissenters, ranging from fervid Millennialists, preoccupied with the literal scripture, to Unitarians, who rejected miracles and demanded social change. They gave up sugar, for instance, to protest slavery. Though they scorned pleasure for its own sake, Dissenters—as much as Anglicans—valued success and affluence. The Dissident academies were England's finest. Dissident scholars became lawyers or businessmen or doctors, or they opened newspapers to spread their ardor for change.

So Mary began meeting people bent on social improvement, from Mrs. Burgh and her outgoing nephew Mr. Church (whom Mary dubbed "Friendly Church")[2] to the neighborhood celebrities: Unitarian clergyman and philosopher Richard Price; Quaker doctor and philanthropist John Coakley Lettsome; Anglican clergyman and author John Hewlett. Everyone welcomed the bright new teachers, particularly Mary, who made a point of distinguishing herself from the rest.

Mary's most famous early admirer was Dr. Price, a modest, kindly man in his mid-sixties who was revered throughout Britain as a disciple of John Locke. He mumbled his sermons, but wrote eloquently.[3] For Price, love of God meant attacking injustice. He was among the first to speak up for American independence and would soon further infuriate the English government by endorsing the rebellious French. Scorning male exclusivity, he joined one of the few London clubs that admitted female intellectuals. And while he did not convert Mary from her Anglican resignation, he did impel her, some Sundays, to miss her own church service and come sit on a stiff wooden pew in his stark Unitarian chapel, listening to him expound about happiness on earth.

Mary got a touch of literary glamour when someone from the Green took her to visit the great Dr. Samuel Johnson on his deathbed, while her young author friend John Hewlett insisted that she had so many ideas, she should write herself. After all, England had a history of literary females: from philosopher Mary Astell and playwright Aphra Behn during the Restoration to historian Catharine Macaulay and essayist-poet Anna Laetitia Barbauld in Mary's day. But what Hewlett imagined for Mary was a far more audacious step than Mrs. Barbauld's writing on the side while her husband supported her. He wanted Mary to defy the tabu against professional female writers and pursue a literary career.

For the moment, though, Mary was preoccupied balancing school accounts. Emboldened by Mrs. Burgh's initial success with enrollments, she had rushed to rent a larger schoolhouse and now had to take in boarders to make ends meet. Every child who quit the school created a financial crisis. And Eliza, now that she was freed of Bishop, had lost all humility and was mocking the very parents who paid their bills. "Eliza still turns up her nose and ridicules," Mary complained to Fanny's brother, George Blood.[4] Meanwhile, Fanny herself grew sicker. Doctors said her only hope was a warmer climate, so when Hugh Skeys, off in Portugal, at last proposed marriage in the fall of 1784, even Mary urged Fanny to go ahead. Fanny was married in Lisbon on February 24, 1785.

And then Mary suffered. Recently, she'd taken Fanny for granted.

Now her old passion returned, and she missed all Fanny's endearing habits—the sad songs she sang, her soothing encouragements. Mary's charm might win her new friends, but only Fanny loved her as much when she was spiteful as when she was clever. Lonesome for Fanny, Mary grew depressed, physically ill, and morbid. "My harrassed mind will in time wear out my body,"[5] she informed Fanny's brother. And: "I have no creature to be unreserved to, Eliza and [Everina] are so different that I could as soon fly as open my heart to them."[6]

Twenty-eight-year-old Fanny, on the other hand, was apparently thriving. Her health improved. By summer, she was pregnant. Though Fanny makes light of her happiness, there's no mistaking it in her single remaining letter (addressed to Eliza and Everina), where she describes Skeys as "a good sort of creature. He has been a dreadful flirt . . . but I have completely metamorphosed [*sic*] him into a plain man—and I am sorry to add that he is much too inclined to pay more attention to his wife than any other woman—but 'tis a fault that a little time, no doubt, will cure."[7]

But how much time was there left for Fanny? Not much, perhaps, given the difficulty of childbearing for a consumptive mother, which was all the more reason for Mary to hurry to Lisbon to be with her friend when the baby came. This meant abandoning the schoolhouse for at least three months around the Christmas holidays. A neighbor named Mrs. Cockburn threatened to scare away Mary's boarders if she left affairs to her sisters, insisting Eliza was unstable and Everina immature. Dr. Price urged Mary to go anyway, and Mrs. Burgh was so adamant that Fanny's needs came first that in November she anonymously put up the money for Mary's trip.

When Mary landed in Lisbon in early December (after a thirteen-day boat trip), Fanny was already in labor. Four hours later, Fanny delivered a small but seemingly healthy boy. The mother, though, was "so worn out her recovery would be almost a ressurection,"[8]

Mary wrote her sisters. A week later, both Fanny and the child were dead.

"The grave has closed over a dear friend, the friend of my youth," Mary wrote of Fanny years later; "still she is present with me, and I hear her soft voice warbling as I stray over the heath."[9]

AFTER THE FUNERAL, Mary stayed on a few weeks, walking around the ruins of the earthquake that had devastated Lisbon thirty years earlier and finding little solace in Hugh Skeys's company. She was relieved, though, when he offered to send money to Fanny's parents, who were as usual in desperate straits. Just before Christmas, she set out on what turned into a harrowing, month-long journey home through turbulent winter waters: "We were several times in imminent danger—I did not expect ever to have reached land,"[10] Mary wrote George. At one point, they spotted a French ship depleted of provisions and on the verge of sinking. Its captain begged Mary's English captain to take them on board. And when the English captain refused, complaining that he had barely enough food for his own passengers, Mary inveighed against his inhumanity and, when this failed, threatened to take him to court—at which point he relented, and the French lives were saved.

When Mary at last arrived home at Newington Green, her affairs were as chaotic as Mrs. Cockburn had prophesied. Many students had not returned after the holidays. Mary's last boarder had fought with Eliza and Everina and was packing to move her sons next door—to Mrs. Cockburn's. Mary found a letter from Hugh Skeys, withdrawing his offer to help the Bloods financially. She resolved somehow to scrounge money for them, while her own debts mounted at an alarming speed. Encouraged by her friend John Hewlett, she decided to boost her income by writing a manual on female education. She gave it the long, edifying title: *Thoughts on the Education of Daughters; with Reflections on Female Conduct, in the More Important Duties of Life.*

About forty-nine pages long, Mary's first book abounds in enlightened maxims and grim depictions of the lives of women like herself. Despite Fanny Blood's lessons, Mary's grammar remains unruly. She frequently repeats her points and lets her sentences run on—as was the mode for educational primers in the era. Most of her "thoughts" are plucked from philosophers she admires.

Like Rousseau, Mary sings the praise of mothers who suckle their own children. Like Locke and Mrs. Barbauld, she warns parents to practice what they preach. Servants are vilified as ignorant and corrupt influences on impressionable children. Reason, Mary writes, must triumph over vanity, and religion over sensual pleasure, in the education of a young girl.

"Whatever tends to make a person in some measure independent of the senses, is a prop to virtue,"[11] Mary primly avers, and she insists that candor is more appealing than fashion to both God and worthy men. Opinions conceived during her contact with high society in Bath and Windsor are trotted out: an early marriage stunts a girl's improvement; playing music and dancing are admirable outlets for feelings, but contemptible when used to show off. And while Mary insists that reading is "the most rational employment, if people seek food for the understanding," she takes the view of her era that "no employment of mind is sufficient excuse for neglecting domestic duties."[12] A married woman must be a wife and mother before all else.

One of the book's more compelling sections is devoted to the love between men and women, and its urgency suggests that Mary may have secretly loved a man. "I think there is not a subject that admits so little of reasoning on as love," Mary begins. ". . . It is difficult to write on a subject when our own passions are likely to blind us. Hurried away by our feelings, we are apt to set those things down as general maxims, which only our partial experience gives rise to."[13]

But her pedantic voice returns as she chastises women like her mother who cling to ne'er-do-wells: "A delicate mind is not susceptible of a greater degree of misery . . . than what must arise from the consciousness of loving a person whom their reason does not approve." Such a passion must be "rooted out," declares Mary, who is "very far from thinking love irresistible and not to be conquered." Women who can't control their sentiments are weak, while those who claim they can be content with platonic friendships delude themselves. It is telling that she continues on this last subject so long that she winds up contradicting her earlier point:

> Not that I mean to insinuate that there is no such thing as friendship between persons of different sexes; I am convinced of the contrary. I only mean to observe, that if a woman's heart is disengaged, she should not give way to a pleasing delusion, and imagine she will be satisfied with the friendship of a man she admires, and prefers to the rest of the world. The heart is very treacherous, and if we do not guard its first emotions, we shall not afterwards be able to prevent its sighing for impossibilities. If there are any insuperable bars to an union in the common way, try to dismiss the dangerous tenderness, or it will undermine your comfort, and betray you into many errors. To attempt to raise ourselves above human beings is ridiculous; we cannot extirpate our passions, nor is it necessary that we should, though it may be wise sometimes not to stray too near a precipice, lest we fall over before we are aware.[14]

So on one page of *Thoughts,* an unworthy love must be "rooted out," while two pages farther on, "we cannot extirpate our passions."

Love is perplexing since it defies virtue and reason, cornerstones of moral life. Only faith, Mary finds, is stronger than passion. And she ends her chapter unconvincingly advocating piety, fealty to duty, and "that calm satisfaction which resignation [to God] produces."[15]

It was apparent that the author of *Thoughts on the Education of Daughters* had strong feelings, but not so strong as to dislodge her staunch ideas. Mary's thoughts on love are mostly speculative, while her life is clearly the template for a chapter dourly entitled "Unfortunate Situation of Females, Fashionably Educated, and Left Without a Fortune." Here Mary laments the few and "humiliating" opportunities open to an intelligent woman without money. She can marry a fool, become a companion or governess, or teach. Mary offers no comforting words about any of these professions, two of which she has practiced and one that she soon will pursue. "A young mind looks round for love and friendship; but love and friendship fly from poverty: expect them not if you are poor."[16]

And yet, "Nothing, I am sure, calls forth the faculties so much as the being obliged to struggle with the world,"[17] she announces with a touch of well-earned satisfaction. This is a key remark in *Thoughts on the Education of Daughters*. It speaks to all Mary has suffered—her father's gambling away his fortune, Mrs. Dawson's condescensions, Eliza's madness, Fanny's death. It embraces valiant gestures like standing up to your sister's husband or to an English captain who wants to desert a floundering foreign ship. And it applauds pipe dreams, like the Bloods' determination to return to Ireland. Mary has experienced life as a battle and concluded *ça vaut l'effort,* as the French say. Yet, whether admonishing against vanity or insisting we accept God's will, she cannot yet endorse the Dissident view that society is meliorable. There is no banishing injustice. The message of Mary Wollstonecraft's first book is that the best you can do is to improve yourself.

. . .

JOHN HEWLETT proved true to his word and hurried this book off to his publisher—who was not just any publisher, but Joseph Johnson of St. Paul's Churchyard. Johnson published some of the most important authors in England: Joseph Priestley, Mrs. Barbauld, and William Blake, to name a few. He had been bold enough to bring out an obscure book on women's legal rights in the 1770s and to publish Benjamin Franklin at the height of America's war against England's king. Johnson was a Dissident by birth and intellectually radical, though he was even-tempered. His face was stern and homely like Dr. Price's, and he shared the minister's honorable, upright ways and kind heart. The worst anyone ever said of Johnson was that he was intractable and sardonic. Most of his large acquaintanceship revered him. He would publish 2,700 works in a career spanning nearly five decades. Johnson was forty-eight and in the middle of his career when John Hewlett brought him Mary's book on education. He accepted it at once.

"You never saw a creature happier than [Mr. Hewlett] was when he returned to tell me the success of his commission," Mary reported to George Blood on the sale of her book.[18] For herself, Mary spoke of no great epiphany. She had not labored out of a need to express herself or from an ambition to see her name in print. She wrote *Thoughts* quickly and to pay the bills. But then she changed her mind and didn't pay the bills; she passed on the precious ten pounds she received from Joseph Johnson to her dead friend's parents, who used it, of course, to return to Ireland. Surely, their joy surpassed even Mr. Hewlett's. And though Ireland did not miraculously solve their problems (Mary was soon again alluding to Mr. Blood as Mrs. Blood's "torment"),[19] they would never regret the move.

And Mary would never regret giving the Bloods her first literary earnings, though it meant having no money left to pay her own growing debts, "which worry me beyond measure."[20] She left the large schoolhouse and continued to teach whomever she could round up at

Mrs. Blackburn's home nearby. Grudgingly, Ned took Everina back. Mrs. Burgh found Eliza another teaching job in Leicestershire. Now that Eliza was gone, Mary felt a perverse "glow of tenderness which I cannot describe" when she read her sister's letter: "I could have clasped you to my breast as I did in days of yore, when I was your nurse."[21]

With summer came new threats from the long list of Mary's creditors. Desperate now, Mary confided her predicament to an acquaintance named Mrs. Prior, the wife of an Eton master, who proceeded to sing Mary's praises to parents of the Eton boys. Lord Robert and Lady Caroline Kingsborough, parents of twelve and the denizens of an Irish castle, were intrigued when Mrs. Prior spoke of Mary's commitment to serious learning for females, and invited her to come home with them to teach their daughters. There would be almost no expenses, and the pay was forty pounds a year, half of which would cancel her debts, Mary—too optimistically—figured. The offer "appears so advantageous *duty* impels me to consider about it—and yet only duty would influence me if I accept it," Mary told George Blood—for had she not just expounded on the "disagreeable" lot of the governess in *Thoughts*?

Still, once she accepted the offer, Mary threw herself into learning French, which was de rigueur for upper-class pupils. "I have made a great proficiency [in French] and have a most excellent master," Mary jauntily informed George Blood at the end of August.[22] George sent Mary yards of fabric for a gown. A former assistant from her school helped her make a "great coat." And while Ned "behaved very rude to me—and has not assisted me in the smallest degree," Dr. Price was "uncommonly friendly," and Mrs. Burgh surpassed even her usual magnanimity by reimbursing all Mary's creditors so Mary would have only her to repay. "Mrs. Burgh has been as anxious about me as if I had been her daughter,"[23] Mary enthused to Eliza, and even prickly Mrs. Cockburn sent Mary off with a blue hat to dazzle the Irish.[24]

Before leaving Newington Green, Mary journeyed to the City of London to meet her publisher at St. Paul's Churchyard. She found in Johnson a short, artless, middle-aged man plagued by asthma; he saw in Mary a tallish, pleasant-looking, twenty-seven-year-old woman, shabbily dressed and with a face that betrayed all her feelings. "She was incapable of disguise," he would later write of her.[25] They spoke of authors they both admired, such as John Hewlett and Mrs. Barbauld. They spoke of education, the subject of Mary's book. There was no sexual attraction, but some important connection was forged at this first encounter, which would prove crucial for both Mary and Johnson in the years ahead. Though he'd read only her first slim volume, Johnson made the highly unusual offer to help Mary in the future when and if she followed Hewlett's suggestion and tried to make a living in the publishing world. But such low-paying work was not an option yet.

So Mary left for Ireland in October 1786. She traveled stylishly in a post chaise, escorted by Lord Kingsborough's butler and accompanied by an intriguing young Anglican clergyman named Henry Gabell, also off to tutor in an Irish castle. They amused each other debating great subjects throughout the long ride. Religion was a favorite topic. Gabell argued that God didn't care about intellectual improvement; Mary argued back: "Why have we implanted in us an irresistible desire to think—if thinking is not . . . necessary to make us wise unto salvation?"[26]

In Dublin, Mary and Henry Gabell parted, and Mary remained a few days visiting the Bloods before traveling on to the Kingsborough estate in southern Ireland, near Cork.[27] Here gloom descended. For though the scenery was magnificent and the Kingsboroughs invited her everywhere, she felt humiliatingly demeaned by her lowly role in the house. The castle was a "Bastille," she told her sisters, the work was exhausting, the children spoke "wild Irish,"[28] and what a spectacle the grown-ups made!

In the only remaining portraits of the Kingsboroughs,[29] Lord Robert wears a close-fitting vest of cerulean blue and a fur-edged silver topcoat, with a cape billowing romantically above his head. His hair is tightly curled, his thick brows are black, and his clear blue eyes look frankly at the viewer. The nose is ample, but everything else about him, from the girlish lips to the cinched waist, is delicate and *petit*. Lady Caroline Kingsborough, captured in profile, looks twice the girth of her husband, with a voluptuous bosom, long draping arms, and a full face. Her thick brown hair piled high on her head trails braids down past her shoulders. She has three beauty marks on the left side of her wide neck and a commanding air. Lady K. was "very *pretty*—and *always* pretty,"[30] Mary caustically remarked.

Mary found Lord Kingsborough vapidly jovial, while Lady Caroline was "clever" and "shrewd."[31] She doted on her dogs, but neglected her children, The house was full of company, all fatuous high society. The one intriguing visitor was George Ogle, a poet and member of Parliament, who was "between forty and fifty—a *genius* and unhappy: such a man," Mary wrote Everina, "you may suppose would catch your sister's eye."[32] And though she did not love Ogle, she enjoyed flirting with him, particularly since he was Lady Kingsborough's favorite as well. She began competing with her boss.

Still, for all Mary's pettishness, she proved an ideal governess, patiently teaching the girls music and French on top of a liberal boys' curriculum (excepting classical languages); assigning imaginative books like Sarah Trimmer's *Fabulous Histories* rather than moral tracts. Whenever she could, she avoided rote learning: she taught justice and perseverance by discussing real-life experiences and showed the importance of charity by having the girls take food to the poor. The most responsive of her three students by far was the eldest, fourteen-year-old Margaret, who shared Mary's volatile spirits, agile intellect, and strong will.[33] Soon Margaret was ignoring her frivolous mother and turning to Mary for counsel, which, coupled with Mary's flirtations with Ogle, stoked Caroline Kingsborough's resentment.

"My poor little favourite has had a violent fever—and can scarcely bear to have me a moment out of her sight," Mary wrote Eliza around Christmas.[34] Margaret's recuperation was slow, and Mary, staying by her side throughout, for the first time felt "*something like* maternal fondness." But she remained resentful of her dependent position, and, when there was little fanfare surrounding the publication of her first book in early January, she despaired of ever finding better work. "I have been thinking 'how stale, flat, and unprofitable' this world is grown to me," she informed Henry Gabell, her friend from the carriage ride, when she sent him a copy of *Thoughts*.[35]

She was even more dramatic in a letter to her publisher, Joseph Johnson: "A state of dependance must ever be irksome to me, and I have *many* vexations to encounter, which some people would term trifling—I have most of the . . . comforts of life—yet when weighed with liberty they are of little value.—In a christian sense I am resigned—and contented; but it is with pleasure that I observe my declining health, and cherish the hope that I am hastening to the Land where all these cares are forgotten."[36]

At the beginning of February, the Kingsboroughs left the castle to spend spring at Lord Robert's father's Henrietta Street town house in northeast Dublin.[37] Here Mary socialized with the Bloods and Henry Gabell, who now had a fiancée. There were excursions to plays and concerts, and there was a masquerade at which Mary dressed up in a black cape and mask and captivated all Caroline Kingsborough's friends. Since she'd arrived in Ireland, Mary had immersed herself in educational literature. At the castle, she'd enjoyed Madame de Genlis's engaging stories *Les Veillées du Chareau*. In Dublin, Mary had more time and was profoundly impressed by the first half of Rousseau's *Émile* (before the "Sophy" section, where he betrays his low opinion of women). Yet she continued to worry about Margaret, whose illness lingered. Mary's "anxiety on her account [was] very much augmented by her Mother's improper treatment—as I fear she will hurry her into a consumption."[38] The struggle over Margaret was in full force.

Then, one Sunday, Mary herself collapsed in "a violent fit of trembling."[39] Worse, she experienced new symptoms terrifyingly like Eliza's when she went mad. This could have been brought on by Mary's longing for love and, above all, money. For she could not hope to leave the increasingly irksome Kingsboroughs until she'd paid back Mrs. Burgh, and she'd either spent too much or owed more than she imagined, because her biannual salary would by no means cancel her debt.

In June, the family left Dublin to summer at the English bathing resort Bristol Hot-Wells. Here, Mary brooded over "intolerably bad" weather and began writing a new book. "I *hope* you have not forgot that I am an Author,"[40] she reminded Eliza. This time, Mary was writing as much out of personal need as financial pressure. And she was writing a novel: creating a world that *she* alone controlled. "Mary" would be not just the author but the name of the heroine and the title of this new work, which would demonize Mary Wollstonecraft's enemies and plead her superiority to most everyone she'd ever met.

The first chapters of *Mary* depict thinly fictionalized versions of Ned, Lady Kingsborough, and Mary Wollstonecraft's parents. The heroine's father, Edward, is a "tyrannical and passionate" alcoholic womanizer who despises intelligent women.[41] Her mother, Eliza, compounds Mrs. Wollstonecraft's dolor with Lady K.'s false delicacy and fussy devotion to her dogs. The favored elder brother is born "a feeble babe" and dies early.

Mary, while physically robust, is an intense, often melancholy child who cherishes lofty thoughts, tenderness, and a passion for social justice, which her parents can't comprehend. "Neglected in every respect, and left to the operations of her own mind, she considered every thing that came under her inspection, and learned to think."[42] Mary "eagerly" befriends an older girl named Ann, who is penniless but educated.[43] Ann teaches Mary refinement and "tolerable" writing. Mary loves Ann wholeheartedly. But Ann still suffers from being jilted by a wealthy suitor and cannot love Mary as much in return. "When her friend was all the world to her, [Mary] found she was not as necessary to [Ann's] happiness; and her delicate mind could not bear to obtrude her affections, or receive love as an alms, the offspring of pity. Very frequently she ran to her with delight, and not perceiving any thing of the same kind in Ann's countenance, she has shrunk back; and falling from one extreme into the other, instead of a warm greeting that was just slipping from her tongue, her expression seemed to be dictated by the most chilling insensibility."[44]

Dramatic events proliferate. To settle a land dispute, Mary's father forces her to marry his adversary's repulsive son, who, to her relief, goes directly from the wedding to study on the Continent. Still, dread of his return plagues her. "It was the will of Providence that Mary should experience almost every species of sorrow."[45] First her mother dies, then her father. When Ann develops consumption, Mary rushes her to an invalid hotel in Lisbon, hoping the warmer climate will restore her health. But Ann's body is already weakened by lovesickness, and she dies in Mary's arms.

Grieving, Mary turns to Henry, another consumptive at the hotel, who is physically ugly, but thoughtful and wise. They fall in love, and Henry follows Mary home to England. Here his health rapidly deteriorates, and like Ann he dies in her arms. In a final blow, Mary's husband returns. "Benevolence and religion"[46] help her endure life with a man she despises. But now her own body weakens and "in moments of solitary sadness, a gleam of joy would dart across her mind—She thought she was hastening to that world *where there is neither marrying,* nor giving in marriage."[47] In other words, death.

Mary Wollstonecraft told Henry Gabell that her purpose in writing *Mary* was "to illustrate an opinion of mine, that a genius will educate itself."[48] And in her introduction she forswears the usual self-effacements to announce that she, Mary Wollstonecraft, will "not be an echo," even of the great Samuel Richardson and Rousseau. She will speak her own mind in her own manner. And so she does: *Mary,* for all its patent melodrama, could be written only by Mary Wollstonecraft. And this is not just because of its abundance of autobiographical references—including a depiction of Henry that strongly suggests Henry Gabell (who, though not dying, was also romantically unavailable since he was engaged to another woman) and sketches of women at the Lisbon invalid hotel who could pass as guests in Lady Kingborough's home. Or even because of its wish fulfillments, like Mary's mother's deathbed repentance: "My child . . . My child, I have not always treated you with kindness—God forgive me! do you?"[49]

What defines *Mary* as unique is the way Wollstonecraft's contradictory personality—ardent, whiny, arrogant—informs every passage, whether her heroine is ruminating about the horrors of marriage or clamoring for the reader's love. And though Wollstonecraft's style is naïve and her prose awkward; though she disobeys cardinal rules of fiction and announces rather than displays her themes while descanting for pages on familiar topics; still *Mary* would be noteworthy beyond its biographical interest for its striking descriptions of the English poor. In an era whose readership relished Richardson's upper-class melodramas and Fanny Burney's satires of high-society life, *Mary* was the rare novel that took pains to depict not the abstract fear of losing a fortune but the concrete reality of getting through the day without sufficient food. Here, for instance, Wollstonecraft vividly evokes an indigent household:

It was crowded with inhabitants: some were scolding, others swearing, or singing indecent songs. . . . On the floor, in one corner of a very small room, lay an emaciated figure of a woman; a window over her head scarcely admitted any light, for the broken pains were stuffed with dirty rags. Near her were five children, all young, and covered with dirt; their sallow cheeks, and languid eyes, exhibited none of the charms of childhood. Some were fighting, and others crying for food; their yells were mixed with their mother's groans, and the wind which rushed through the passages.[50]

Vivid too is Wollstonecraft's point that, when supported by a benefactress, the sick mother quickly recovers to watch her infinitely improved children "sporting on the grass." Money, not virtue or piety or forbearance or even love, is what poor people require.

DURING HER MEETING with Joseph Johnson in the summer of 1786, Mary had complained about the burdens of poverty and indebtedness. Her correspondence to him from Ireland continued in the same tone. Typical is an April 1787 letter from Dublin in which she calls herself "a poor solitary individual in a strange land" and asks, "How can I be reconciled to life, when it is always a painful warfare, and when I am deprived of all the pleasures I relish?—I allude to rational conversation, and domestic affections." Though he could easily have dismissed Mary as wallowing in self-pity, Johnson sympathized and sent her money.[51] It was not a loan, he told her, but a present, and obviously not a great enough sum to pay back her creditors because she remained at her job until August 1787, when Lady K., fed up with Mary's arrogance and influence over Margaret, suddenly fired her.

It is hard to imagine that Mary was sad about losing her position, but Margaret was initially devastated, and Mary and Margaret would both speak affectionately of each other for the rest of their lives. Still, the future was before them now. In no time, Mary had packed and determined on a next course of action, which she intended to pursue joyously and with no end in sight. She would go to London and become a professional writer. "I am determined!—" she wrote Joseph Johnson. "Your sex generally laugh at female determinations; but let me tell you, I never yet resolved to do, any thing of consequence, that I did not adhere resolutely to it, till I had accomplished my purpose, improbable as it might have appeared to a more timid mind."[52]

CHAPTER THREE

At the end of the summer of 1787, Mary boarded a Bristol coach headed east toward London. She was twenty-eight years old and arrogantly unadorned—no ribbons, no scarves, no jewelry. Her dress of coarse cloth resembled a milkmaid's, an observer unkindly noted.[1] She wore fusty black worsted stockings and a mannish beaver cap with tucked-up flaps shaped like half-moons. Her light brown hair drooped to her shoulders in styleless clumps. But her features were regular, her color was high. She was clean, neat, refined, and conventionally attractive.

When she stepped down from her coach and headed for the courtyard surrounding St. Paul's Cathedral, it was an ideal moment to enter the kingdom of publishing. England was besotted with the printed word. Half the population could read. And every month, it seemed, there was a new morning newspaper and another magazine—on fashion or politics or cooking a shepherd's pie or sex. Booksellers' windows gleamed with expensive new works. A three-volume paperbound novel sold dearly at 9 shillings, while biographies in cloth were a pound at least—a prohibitive sum for most avid readers. But, at a membership fee of about 12 shillings a year, modest circulating libraries, like Frances Noble's in Covent Garden, would lend you all the latest works, and there were private book clubs and posher subscription libraries offering rarer collections and padded armchairs for the rich. While all the genres thrived, religion presided. (Three new sermons were published every week.) There was much demand as well for medical texts, philosophy, children's stories, and all varieties of adult fiction. One year, the London *Times* reported "473 novels new in the press from young ladies of fashion";[2] and books by travelers to France, America, and other exotic places were in vogue.

All the ingredients of modern publishing were present. There were typographers and paper sellers and publicists eager to tout any manuscript for pay. In London alone, over six hundred businesses devoted themselves to sending books into the world.[3] Still, the crucial figure was the publisher-bookseller, who not only sold books but edited them, cajoled authors, obtained printers and advertisers, and marketed his list throughout England and abroad—often, as in Joseph Johnson's case, with just a single shopman to help out. After work hours, a bookstore could metamorphize into a salon. The publishing brothers Charles and Edward Dilly (who published Boswell's *Life of Johnson*) hosted weekly literary dinners, as did Joseph Johnson, who took the highly unusual position of inviting intellectuals of all religions and political points of view. His dinners soothed authors exasperated by perceived or real slights, notably dilatoriness. One poet remembers striding toward 72 St. Paul's Churchyard, determined to upbraid Johnson for some delay. Then the publisher's "good-humoured face" and cordial "how-d'ye do sir, I dine at three"[4] disarmed him, and he never complained.

Each bookseller had his specialty. John Wilkie championed conservative politics, John Newbery specialized in children's books, while Johnson was best known for his Dissident pedagogy and radical titles no one else would go near. Some publishers truly were, as Dr. Samuel Johnson acclaimed them, "modern patrons of literature."[5] Others were in it for the money. Most were a little of both. They worked on top of each other in the smart low houses looping the cobblestoned Churchyard or nearby on Pater Noster Row, home to the roisterous Chapter Coffee House. Here booksellers gathered to bid for lucrative copyrights to classics by Defoe or Shakespeare, young authors came looking for publishers, and readers paid the subscription fee of a mere shilling to delve into a first-rate library while others gossiped and drank.

"I am then going to be the first of a new genus,"[6] Mary declared: a self-supporting woman writer. The Restoration playwright Aphra Behn had, of course, preceded her by a century; but Behn had written in a freer era, before King George and the Industrial Revolution consigned women to the home. Besides, authorship itself changed radically after the Restoration. In the early eighteenth century, writers became either lauded patricians who wrote to edify the public (Horace Walpole, Lady Wortley Montagu) or scorned "hacks" who slaved away for pounds. Women who wrote because they needed money were the lowliest of the low until around the middle of the century, when Dr. Samuel Johnson (no relation to Joseph) blazed into London and wrote his way to *both* wealth and acclaim. There was no contradiction, Dr. Johnson insisted, between supporting yourself and writing brilliantly. Dr. Johnson's best-selling dictionary and biographies greatly influenced the British attitude toward professional authors and paved the way for Mary's bold decision to write.[7]

Even more crucial to her was Joseph Johnson, who was born near Liverpool in 1738, the younger son of prosperous Baptist farmers. At fourteen, Johnson moved to London to apprentice as a bookseller; and nine years later he opened his first store near London Bridge, specializing in religion, agriculture, political treatises, and Dissident tracts. New friends like scientist Joseph Priestley and medical doctor George Fordyce expanded Johnson's interests, and he was soon putting out science and medical texts as well as poetry by William Cowper, his most lucrative author. Johnson also had a taste for eccentrics like the garrulous, coarse, and inspired Swiss artist Henry Fuseli, who became his best friend and a frequent housemate before Fuseli's marriage. In 1770, a fire destroyed Johnson's old offices, and he moved to the heart of the publishing world.

Johnson's house at 72 St. Paul's Churchyard was four stories high, the tallest building in the courtyard, lying between the publisher John Wilkie and a stationer's store. It was shaped like a trapezoid with a tower at the far end; a bookstore consumed the ground level, with living quarters above. The dining room was on the second floor, overlooking the west front of the cathedral. Here, Johnson held both his famous weekly dinners and daily chats. It was in the dining room that Johnson met with William Wordsworth, William Blake, William Cowper, Charlotte Smith, Mrs. Barbauld, Richard Price, Joseph Priestley, William Godwin, Thomas Paine, Henry Fuseli—and hundreds of other ardent poets, feverish partisans, innovative scientists, and brilliant artists, who were both Johnson's authors and his friends. One guest described a typical meal for eight at Johnson's: "a piece of boiled cod, a fillet of veal roasted, with vegetables, for a remove, and then a rice-pudding—a true citizen dinner."[8] Henry Fuseli gave Johnson his hauntingly erotic painting *The Nightmare* to hang in the dining room. So while the notable company consumed their meager dinner, a woman possessed by spirits writhed orgasmically above their heads.

Johnson was discreet and reticent. He never married or displayed attraction to either sex. In his portrait,[9] he looks the embodiment of rectitude—his lips pursed, his sharp eyes peering judiciously under thick dark eyebrows, his frame small, and his long thin fingers crossed over a slim waist. He wears a curled wig and black vest and coat with a ruffled white shirt with a high collar. Mary told Everina that Johnson's "sensible conversation [wears] away the impression [of] formality—or rather stiffness"[10] that he made at first.

Friends praised Johnson's aversion to self-promotion, his sincerity and good heart.[11] Long before he met Mary, Johnson was offering authors beds in his home and loans to carry them over rough patches. He paid the customary fixed sum for a manuscript, but then on his own initiative shared profits with the writer if a book did well.[12]

Johnson believed in compromise and moderation and was a clever businessman, or he would never have survived in such a highly competitive field. William Blake complained of Johnson's shrewdness. "Johnson may be very honest and very generous too, where his own interest is concerned," Blake told a friend; "but I must say that he leaves no stone unturn'd to serve that interest."[13] So his generosity was laced with self-interest, just as his righteousness was tempered by good sense. Johnson refused, for instance, to publish the second volume of Thomas Paine's *Rights of Man* for fear he'd be arrested for treason. Yet he rushed to take Paine bail money when the author himself was jailed.

On the whole, Johnson's editions were not pretty to look at. He preferred to publish cheap volumes available to a middle-class public rather than elegant pages exclusively for the rich. "I do very much dislike dear books," he declared.[14] What he cared about, deeply, was quality. Whatever Blake might imply about Johnson's financial self-interest, it was ever at the service of a larger cause. Near the end of his career, Johnson summed up his philosophy in a letter to the poet Charlotte Smith. He begins on a melancholy note, but concludes optimistically:

It is our misfortune that he who wishes to pay [an author] a liberal price and publish nothing but what is good has to combat with many who can easily procure trash for a mere trifle, put a promising title and puff[15] in the papers in a way that a respectable man cannot but which must succeed with the mass of people, until the slow operation of time shall decide in his favor.[16]

Mary arrived at Joseph Johnson's office full of conflicting emotions. For all her real self-confidence, she had no delusions about an easy future. A great struggle lay ahead. And gloomy thoughts nagged at Mary's high spirits. She continued to mourn for Fanny. She also missed Margaret Kingsborough's devotion, and she got angry when she thought of her unlucky sisters, forced to teach school: Eliza still in Leicestershire, Everina at Henley now that Ned had made her miserable in his house. The Wollstonecraft boys—nineteen-year-old James and Charles, two years younger—had only a ruined father and negligent Ned to turn to. So James kept his low-paying job as a sailor, while Charles indentured himself to learn law from his eldest brother—a bad choice, Mary believed.

Joseph Johnson gave Mary a room at 72 St. Paul's Churchyard until she could find her own housing, and a place at his table whenever she liked. She was grateful but felt perfectly entitled to such goodness.[17] "I am not born to tread in the beaten track—the peculiar bent of my nature pushes me on." And she was eager to get on with her new life. Mary brought Johnson the intriguing first chapters of a Gothic fable she called *The Cave of Fancy,* which involved a sage and an orphan girl he discovers among shipwrecked corpses in the crepuscular landscape of a place like Laugharne in Wales. These pages, dense with adjectives and details, make an elegiac contrast to Mary's fiction and expository writing. Typical is her eerie depiction of a dead body:

A huge form was stretched near [the sage], that exhibited marks of overgrown infancy; every part was relaxed; all appeared imperfect. Yet, some undulating lines on the puffed-out cheeks, displayed signs of timid, servile good nature; and the skin of the forehead had been so often drawn up by wonder, that the few hairs of the eyebrows were fixed in a sharp arch, whilst an ample chin rested in lobes of flesh on his protuberant breast.[18]

But Mary never finished *The Cave of Fancy*. She lost either interest or conviction in the genre, for she got no further than Chapter 3. (Two decades later, her husband published this fragment as part of the *Posthumous Works*.) What she did sell Johnson upon arriving in London was *Mary*, which she had finished, in "spite of my vexations" during her last days with the Kingsboroughs. Johnson promised to publish this first novel in the spring, along with a book Mary proposed to write about a governess who uses nature and everyday experience to teach sense to two pampered young girls. Johnson assured Mary she could "earn a comfortable maintenance" if she exerted herself and learned to translate as well as write books and articles. She assured him she would accomplish whatever she set out to do.

Physically, they made a curious couple—the older austere publisher, pressed into his snug white collar, and his intense, volatile young protégée in her flowing worsted dress; but in a deeper sense they were kindred spirits. Both possessed a passion for ideas and cared deeply about human suffering. Each could maintain strong convictions while keeping an open mind about what others believed. They felt responsible for the families they made or were born into; they shared an aversion to extremes. Even emotional Mary despised public scenes as much as ostentation. Both Mary and Johnson were rigid in their propriety and good manners. They were very British, for all their interest in German and Italian art and French philosophy. They complemented each other. Mary confided her distresses to Johnson, who—with his generous nature and no wife to dote on— got pleasure from calming her. And Johnson set a standard for character and intellectual excellence that Mary bettered herself to achieve.

Mary continued to worry about disconsolate Eliza and high-spirited Everina even as she rejoiced at her own good luck. No sooner did she settle affairs with Johnson than she was rushing off to Henley, where Everina taught school. Though Everina hated her "vulgar" position, she enjoyed Henley, and Mary, who loved the countryside, wrote one of her rare lighthearted letters to Johnson from this spot. "I . . . wandered . . . by the side of the Thames, and in the neighbouring beautiful fields and pleasure grounds; the prospects were of such a placid kind, I *caught* tranquility while I surveyed them—my mind was *still* though active." And whether she was walking or reading or regaling the neighborhood children with stories, Mary thought often "of my new plan of life" and felt invigorated and content.

But she was not so content that she forgot to assert her preeminence as the eldest Wollstonecraft sister, "The Princess," as George Blood had named her long before. Though Mary loved George only as a brother, she felt hurt when he began courting Everina: flooding her with letters, even blushing at the sound of her name. Now settled in Dublin, George was urging Everina and Eliza to open a school near him. Impossible, Mary declared, since "Eliza wants activity; and Everina's vivacity would by the injudicious, be termed giddiness." Mary won her point, and easily, since Everina was no more in love with George than she was and could barely bring herself to reply to his flattering letters; while envious Mary wrote George frequently, assuming the tone of a slighted friend:

You pay many fine compliments [to Everina], I have observed them,—well *pure* friendship is a rare commodity . . . let me assure you of my *simple* friendship without any alloy; it has more solidity than brightness, and therefore will not wear out or dazzle.[19]

After a week with Everina, Mary left for Market Harborough in Leicestershire to visit Eliza. Four years of teaching had exhausted, bored, and humiliated the prettiest of the Wollstonecraft girls. Eliza's large correspondence shows style, taste, a nimble wit, and deep understanding. But rather than pushing her forward in the world, Eliza's intelligence merely heightened her discontent. Mary told neither Eliza nor Everina about her new writing career, because they might disapprove, she explained to Joseph Johnson; but what she really feared was their envy, Eliza's in particular, and the inevitable expectation that she would now transform *their* lives.

So it was November before Mary sheepishly informed her family that she had been fired by the Kingsboroughs and, by the way, now worked at the writer's trade. She'd repaid her debts to Mrs. Burgh (probably with advances from Johnson) and settled in a yellow brick house near Blackfriars Bridge on quiet George Street, named Dolben Street today. From her top-floor window, Mary gazed across the Thames at Fleet Street's shops, taverns, and oddities like Mrs. Salmon's ghoulish waxworks. Up the hill stood St. Paul's Cathedral. And among a warren of beleaguered little roads heading on toward Finsbury lay the famously seamy Grub Street, where lowly indexers, fair copyists, ghostwriters, and other publishing drones converged. It was a ten-minute walk from Mary's home to Joseph Johnson's doorstep. She could take a roundabout route and pass Samuel Johnson's favorite restaurant, the Cheshire Cheese, and his grand Georgian home.

It was while visiting Joseph Johnson that Mary befriended literary women like the former child prodigy, affable Anna Laetitia Barbauld, and Sarah Trimmer, whose children's stories Mary had used to teach the Kingsborough girls. Trimmer had twelve children of her own and was one of a growing number of women writing fiction for young people. Mary studied these authors now as she conceived the book she had promised to write for Johnson to bring out in the spring. "I spent a day at Mrs. Trimmer's and found her a truly respectable woman," Mary informed Everina. Mrs. Trimmer was philosophically as pious and old-fashioned as the famously gruff charity-school advocate Hannah More. But while More preached, Trimmer beguiled her readers and, like Rousseau, immersed her lessons in concrete details.

Trimmer's *History of the Robins,* for instance, closely follows the intersecting lives of young Harriet and Frederick Benson and a family of red-breasted robins who settle in the Bensons' walled-in land. Mr. Benson has made his property a paradise for fledglings that, like his own growing children, learn to find food, amuse themselves, and study—in their case the art of flight. Caring for the birds teaches Harriet and Frederick Benson self-discipline and kindness, while the robins discover they must be brave and cautious even in Mr. Benson's yard. Trimmer's moral is that character determines fate for all living creatures: the good triumph, the arrogant are wounded, and those who think only of pleasure are easily trapped by the shrewd.

Another children's book writer who employed animals as characters is a woman who signed her work "a Lady." Along with Trimmer, "a Lady" contributed stories to *Easy Lessons,* a collection that Mary surely knew. Typical of "a Lady's" writings is a tale called "The Bird's Nest." Here a mother walking out with her two children comes upon a "naughty boy" who has stolen a nest of young birds. The human children readily identify with the offended animals, but their mother urges them to sympathize with the boy as well. He was "naughty," she suggests, because he is idle: he is idle because his family is poor. She resolves to pay for the young thief to join the other children marching through the village in their "neat brown clothes" to charity school. His morals will naturally ameliorate when his time is gainfully employed.

Like Mrs. Trimmer, "a Lady" assumes that virtue is rewarded. Her final story in *Easy Lessons* shows a gratified mother addressing her cheerful boy and girl: "Good children must be happy. . . . Grown up

people have their cares and sorrows and even those who are most virtuous must sometime be unhappy! but *children* have only to be *good*,
and for them all is pleasure and joy."[20]

"A Lady" and Mrs. Trimmer were on Mary's mind in the fall of
1787 as she began her own *Original Stories* for children. She mimics
their methods, but can no more believe that virtue brings happiness
than that earth is the place for joy.

Her stories revolve around two motherless girls whose wealthy
father entrusts them to the care of their benevolent relative Mrs.
Mason. The eldest daughter, Mary, is fourteen, clever, and headstrong.
Her twelve-year-old sister, Caroline, is beautiful and self-involved.
Up until now, both girls have been raised capriciously by uneducated
servants. Mrs. Mason will strive to tease them from their faults.

The volume is composed of twenty-four didactic stories. The first
begins as Mary, Caroline, and Mrs. Mason stroll down a pleasant
path on a clear spring day. The "half-shut flowers" and tingly air buoy
Mrs. Mason's spirits, but the children ignore their surroundings to
race about destroying bugs. When Mrs. Mason jumps to avoid crush-
ing some snails in her path, young Mary scoffs. And Mrs. Mason
gently reprimands her:

> God created the world and every inhabitant of it. . . . He made
> the snails you despise, and caterpillars, and spiders; and when he
> made them, did not leave them to perish, but placed them where
> the food that is most proper to nourish them is easily found. . . .
> And when such a great and wise Being has taken care to provide
> every thing necessary for the meanest creature, would you dare
> kill it merely because it appears to you ugly?[21]

Mrs. Mason's argument appeals to the children's piety and reason,
and when they discover a wounded lark in a nearby field, Mary and
Caroline feel pain for it and rush to help. Their hearts as well as their

minds have been instructed. And so it continues, as Mrs. Mason discourages Mary's sarcasm and Caroline's vanity. Punishments, like lessons, evolve naturally from the girls' experiences. In one tale, Caroline gets sick because she grabs more than her share of fruit off the dinner table. In another, Mary vents her temper at a servant, then must humbly beg pardon or do everything without help. The children trample their bird to death while fighting over who most deserves to feed it. "It is easy to conquer another; but noble to subdue one's self,"[22] Mrs. Mason observes. The more the children love her, the easier Mrs. Mason's task becomes, for to please her they struggle to be good.

The girls learn about a wider world than their own from visits with Mrs. Mason's large acquaintanceship. There is the deceitful Lady with the fine carriage and horses who's devoured by self-hatred; and the cousin this deceiver has swindled of her fortune, who remains dignified, though poor. There is jolly, half-blind, and limping "honest Jack," whom Mrs. Mason rescued from a sea wreck and resettled with his family, and a vain sloven named Mrs. Dowdy, who dresses only when company appears. Most vividly, there is a tuneful old harpist, harassed by a staggering list of life's injustices, whom Mrs. Mason encounters when her carriage overturns near his airless hut in Wales. As with "good Jack," she determines to improve the harpist's condition, and he repays her by appearing in her fields each year at harvest-time, playing merry tunes for the gleaners when their day's work is done.

Mrs. Mason further instructs her pupils with melancholy tales about fabulous characters like "crazy Robin," whom she knew when she was growing up. Then, Robin was industrious and hopeful. He married her father's dairymaid. And, joining their savings while borrowing a "trifle," Robin and his wife procured "a little farm in a neighboring county." Robin worked hard. Still, his debts grew as his family expanded. The kind landlord never pressed his overworked tenant for rent. But when the landlord died, his greedy son seized all Robin's livestock. Then the man who'd lent him the "trifle" threw Robin in debtor's jail, while Robin's wife, lying in with their last baby, was made to get up and tend house.

Exhausted, she died along with two of her children from putrid fever. The remaining offspring begged by day and slept in their father's prison cell. "Poverty and dirt soon robbed their cheeks of the roses which the country air made bloom with a peculiar freshness; so that they soon caught a jail fever,—and died."[23] And still Robin's trials were not finished. When he escaped from jail and returned to his old village, his loyal dog trotted by his side. Robin lavished all his meals and tenderness on this last remnant of family. But one day the fun-loving dog chased a "young gentleman's" horse, and the rider shot him. Now thoroughly bereft, Robin died at his side.

Like Robin, Mrs. Mason has suffered, she tells the children, but she is neither mad nor embittered, and she describes the source of her inner peace:

I have been very unfortunate, my young friends; but my griefs are now of a placid kind. Heavy misfortunes have obscured the sun I gazed at when first I entered life; early attachments have been broken; the death of friends I loved has so clouded my days, that neither the beams of prosperity, nor even those of benevolence, can dissipate the gloom; but I am not lost in a thick fog. . . . I am weaned from the world, but not disgusted; for I can still do good, and in futurity a sun will rise to chear my heart. Beyond the night of death, I hail the dawn of an eternal day![24]

Mrs. Mason's unwavering belief in God speaks to the central idea of *Original Stories*, which, as it turns out, is not so much about developing children's native abilities as about teaching them to suffer well. Far more than Sarah Trimmer, Mary stresses the importance of resignation. Her most virtuous characters are persecuted and impoverished. Wistfulness pervades even the music of the birds and the harpist, for how easily can they be silenced by the tricks of fate. Goodness itself is a perpetual battle, as Mary and Caroline discover. But God is always righteous and always comforting.

The character of young Mary in *Original Stories* is based on Margaret Kingsborough. Mrs. Mason takes her name from the Wollstonecrafts' teaching assistant in Newington Green and her character from the author herself or rather from an idealized Mary, free of rancor and feverish attachment to the world. More encompassing than *Education* and far more clear-eyed than *Mary*, *Original Stories* is the darkest and most impassioned of Wollstonecraft's early books. Its ideas are deeply considered and gloomy, reflecting Mary's philosophy during her twenty-ninth year. As with *Education*, the social optimism of the Enlightenment is conspicuously absent. Temporal justice is unimaginable. Only charitable individuals like Mrs. Mason can make a difference, and a small one at that.

"I have *done* with the delusion of fancy—I only live to be useful—benevolence must fill every void in my heart,"[25] Mary wrote Everina in the fall of 1787, taking the resigned tone of her manuscript. But she assumes a regal air replying to Johnson's criticism of her tirade against lazy parents in *Original*'s preface: "Though your remarks are generally judicious—I cannot *now* concur with you. . . . A general rule *only* extends to the majority—and, believe me, the few judicious parents who may peruse my book, will not feel themselves hurt."[26]

So the preface was published as she wrote it. For Johnson gave his authors the final say. And he hired William Blake to create the striking illustrations—including a lithograph of emaciated "crazy Robin," clenched with grief from shoulders to toes.

William Blake was an acquaintance, but not a "*standing* dish,"[27] as Mary called regular visitors to 72 St. Paul's Churchyard. Among the "standing dishes" Mary especially liked were mathematician John

Bonnycastle and the medical doctor George Fordyce, who had a passion for literature and gadded about in eccentric clothes.[28]

Another eccentric "standing dish" was Johnson's Swiss friend Henry Fuseli, an ordained minister, who'd rejected the Church and run off to England to paint. He was on the verge of fame when Mary met him. He adored Rousseau, idolized Homer and Shakespeare, and supplied fervent opinions on any subject at all. He spoke multiple languages and did not suffer fools or small talk.[29] Johnson introduced him to company as "a most ingenious foreigner, whom I think you will like; but, if you wish to enjoy his conversation you will not attempt to stop the torrent of his words by contradicting him."[30] Fuseli was an impish-looking man with large round eyes and prominent cheekbones. Like the Kingsboroughs' friend George Ogle, he was moody, sensitive, and in his mid-forties: just the sort to attract Mary. The philosopher William Godwin called Fuseli "the most frankly and ingenuously conceited man I ever knew. . . . He hated a dull fellow, as men of wit and talent naturally do, and he hated a brilliant man because he could not bear a brother near the throne."[31]

Like Rousseau, Fuseli romanticized the savage state; but he was not concerned with the world at large. "Self-preservation is the first duty of the eighteenth century," Fuseli announced.[32] And he advised: "Never try to guide a young man in the path of improvement: the more obstacles and discouragement are thrown in his way, the better."[33] Genius was inborn and all-important in Fuseli's eyes. Fuseli believed that Dürer, for instance, could never have hoped to paint as well as Rembrandt, because Rembrandt had genius and he did not. It went without saying that Fuseli considered himself a genius. Luridly proportioned women and emotional scenes from Shakespeare were favorite subjects. His style was audacious. Paintings like *Lady Macbeth Seizing the Daggers*—with its chiaroscuro, its graphically splattered blood, grotesque breasts, and floating hand—captivated as many as it repulsed.

As uninhibited as Joseph Johnson was reticent, Fuseli drew porno-
graphic sketches and flaunted the fact that he slept with whores. He
was bisexual. There were rumors that he'd loved the Swiss phrenolo-
gist Johann Lavater as well as Lavater's niece Anna, to whom he
wrote sad, passionate poems.[34] Fuseli was engaged to marry his
model Sophia Rawlins in June when he first met Mary, who was fas-
cinated by his paintings and penetrating insights on art. Some say she
fell in love with the man at first sight, but this is not likely, given her
guardedness and Fuseli's obvious faults.

Besides, during her first year in London she was deeply involved
with her work and family. While finishing *Original Stories*, she studied
languages late into the night so she could translate Johnson's foreign
acquisitions. And while she gave up on an Italian manuscript, plead-
ing, "I cannot bear to do anything I cannot do well,"[35] she eagerly
took on the Swiss author Jacques Necker's new *De l'Importance des
Opinions Religeuses*, written in French. As well as an author, Jacques
Necker was a controversial political figure, recently fired from his
post as French finance minister by Louis XVI. Necker's book "pleases
me,"[36] Mary wrote Everina in late March 1788, and she asked her sister to send "all the news you can get" about Necker's character and
reputation in France.

For Everina was now living in Paris. Knowing that proficiency in
French greatly enhanced a working woman's options, Mary had
come up with the money to send her to stay a few months with a
Mademoiselle Henry on the rue de Tournon between the Luxem-
bourg Gardens and the Church of St-Sulpice. She was in the heart
of the Faubourg St-Germain, where new mansions were sprouting
up and intellectuals gathered. The talk was all about France's im-
pending financial crisis and the cruelty of the rich. Probably, Joseph
Johnson helped Mary pay for Everina's trip to France on the eve of
its revolution. He makes clear that he likes her in a teasing adden-
dum scribbled at the bottom of one of Mary's notes: "[Mary] told

me I might add a postscript and you see what room she has left me, not to make love surely! only to express my good wishes, for your happiness/JJ."[37]

But Everina was not happy. She got sick as soon as she arrived in Paris and filled two long letters to Mary with "accounts of disasters and difficulties," exasperating her sister, who dismissed them as whiny complaints. "So much the better" if Everina suffered a bit, Mary confided to George Blood, echoing Henry Fuseli: "it is proper that some people should be roused."[38] By May, Everina was "more tranquil," though not, as Mary had hoped, enraptured by Paris. And Eliza was still miserable, teaching in Leicestershire. Mary wanted to help but was adamant that Eliza should not join her. "I have determined on one thing, *never* to have my Sisters to live with me," she wrote George Blood, explaining, guiltily, "my solitary manner of living would not suit them, nor *could* I pursue my studies if forced to conform."[39] On a cheerier note, Mary's favorite brother, Charles, visited often, asked for nothing, and was "improved in every respect."[40]

In April, both of Mary's books were published. Though *Mary* attracted little notice, *Original Stories* was soon translated into German and found a second printing both in Ireland and at home.[41] So Mary had the pleasure of imagining her woe-filled tales carried off to foreign countries, or she could see them bound up with Blake's lithographs in the windows of London stores. She was right to be proud of this latest effort. While writing as quickly as usual, she had at last succeeded in sustaining a measured tone and an engaging narrative. This was the first book Mary wrote on George Street, under Joseph Johnson's auspices. Her second large endeavor was to translate the Necker book while simultaneously embarking on a project she would pursue for the rest of her life.

That project was writing articles for the *Analytical Review*, a monthly magazine tackling new religious, political, scientific, and literary works. Its editors were Joseph Johnson and Thomas Christie, an idealistic young Scotsman determined to make his mark in the world. Christie came from two generations of Scottish merchants. He had trained in a bank and considered becoming a doctor before his first trip to London in 1784, when he had gotten caught up in the book world. He was twenty-three at the time, a handsome man with much charm and intelligence. Authors and publishers befriended him. Soon he was writing for John Nichols's popular *Gentleman's Magazine.* Three years later, he convinced Johnson to collaborate with him on their own review.

Christie was a Unitarian, as committed to the Dissident cause as Johnson, though more interested in standing out from the crowd. Their reviews should be far less opinionated, more analytical, and more focused on foreign works than those of their competitors, who thrived on polemics, Christie suggested. But the more practical Johnson called for a compromise between Christie's analytical approach and the contentiousness readers expected. Though their plan was not the best they could conceive, the editors admitted in their first issue, it was "the best that can be put in practice" at the present time.[42]

The *Analytical Review* came out monthly and lasted eleven years. Never a commercial triumph, it made an impact on London intellectuals and sold well in Christie's Scotland too. Its contributors, mostly "standing dishes," included Mary's old friend John Hewlett, the poet William Cowper, Fuseli, and Mary, of course. At the *Analytical Review,* Mary came of age as a writer, contributing several reviews to every issue and also working as assistant editor when Johnson and Christie needed help. Her voice was bold at the outset.[43] The first sentence of her first review reads: "*The Happy Recovery* is an heterogeneous mass of folly, affectation, and improbability." She is writing in the June 1788 issue and has so little regard for her subject—a self-described "Sentimental Novel. By a Lady"—that she veers immediately into a diatribe against novels and their celebration of romantic love.[44] In a July review, she pauses to acknowledge

Charlotte Smith's talent but complains that her new book, *Emmeline*, is psychologically "preposterous" and its narrative twists are absurd.[45] In the August issue, Mary reviews a travel book called *Sketches of Society and Manners in Portugal* with guarded enthusiasm, and she lavishes praises on Samuel Johnson's emotional *Sermon* for his dead wife.[46]

"If you do not like the manner in which I reviewed Dr. J——'s [sermon] on his wife, be it known unto you—I *will* not do it any other way—" Mary had informed Johnson, anticipating disapproval of her effusive tone. "I felt some pleasure in paying a just tribute of respect to the memory of a man—who, spite of his faults, I have an affection for— I say *have*, for I believe he is somewhere—*where* my soul has been gadding perhaps;—but *you* do not live on conjectures."

Johnson believed strongly in religious freedom, but religious faith, which was so crucial to Mary, eluded him. What sustained Johnson through life's hardships was reason, while for Mary reason alone did not suffice. "I am afraid reason is not a good bracer—" Mary told Johnson, "for I have been reasoning a long time with my untoward spirits—and yet my hand trembles."[47]

But Mary's spirits were not perpetually "untoward": quite the contrary. Most days brought a new challenge. She was reviewing a volume of Rousseau's selected writings or a translation of Goethe's *Werther*. ("To pity Werther we must read the original," she writes; "in it we find an energy and beauty of language, a uniformity in the extravagances of passion that arrests our attention, and gives such reality to his misery, that we are affected by his sorrows, even while we lament the wanderings of his distempered mind.") She reread Shakespeare and Milton and pored over news of current events. She conversed to her heart's content with people she admired. "Blessed be that Power who gave me an active mind!" Mary wrote George Blood, "if it does not smooth it enables me to jump over the rough places in life."[48] And she now had more than religious thoughts to comfort her. "During her stay in George Street, [Mary] spent many afternoons and more of her evenings with me," Johnson wrote, ". . . whatever was the state of her mind it appeared when she entered, and the turn of her conversation might easily be grief, when harrassed, which was very often the case, she was relieved by unbosoming herself generaly returned home calm, frequently in spirits."[49]

Sometimes, Mary took advantage and made emotional demands too great for even Johnson to bear. Then he withdrew, and she was remorseful. "You made me very low-spirited last night, by your manner of talking—" she began one contrite note. "You are my only friend—the only person I am *intimate* with.— I never had a father, or a brother—you have been both to me, ever since I knew you—yet I have sometimes been very petulant.— I have been thinking of those instances of ill-humour and quickness, and they appeared like crimes."[50]

Other times, Mary assumed a saucy tone with Johnson. "You perceive this is not a gloomy day,"[51] she jokes in the middle of a note, enthusing about her new life. And she sounds like a proud student when she teases: "My dear sir, I send you a chapter [of the Necker] which I am pleased with, now I see it in one point of view—and, as I have made free with the author, I hope you will not have often to say—what does this mean?"[52]

After she'd finished her version of Necker, Mary learned German so she could translate Christian Gotthilf Salzmann's *Moralisches Elementarbuch* (*Elements of Morality*), which advanced her own educational views. (Fittingly, Salzmann would later translate *A Vindication of the Rights of Woman* into German.) And she began a campaign to undermine nefarious Ned by transferring young Charles to another law firm and demanding to take over their father's financial affairs. These affairs were in such chaos, thanks to the senior Edward's increasing helplessness, that Ned readily passed the burden to Mary, who by the fall of 1788 was collecting rents on her father's Spitalfield property and with "no little trouble"[53] assuring him and his wife enough money to live. Mary also managed to move Eliza to a school in Putney, nearer to London.

"I succeed beyond my most sanguine hopes, and really believe I shall clear above two hundred pounds this year," Mary exulted to George Blood. Less propitious for George was the news that Mary could now afford to keep his beloved Everina in France for a longer time. And the time expanded to include the fall of 1788 and the spring and summer of the following year. What a pity that not a word Everina wrote then has survived to the present day! For she was witness to the event of the century and the turning point in Mary Wollstonecraft's life.

PART TWO

Revolution

CHAPTER FOUR

*W*hile Everina Wollstonecraft was learning the French language at Mademoiselle Henry's on the rue de Tournon, a clamor for change was spreading throughout France. A decade earlier, the French had leapt into America's struggle for independence from England. Now the United States was a democracy, but France plodded on under absolute rule. What's more, one French finance minister after another failed to stabilize the economy. French industry lagged way behind British. Louis XVI's subjects began expressing discontent.

First, the usually docile *parlement,* or French court, refused to endorse Louis's demands for a tax rise. Then, when Louis retaliated by closing the courts and banishing magistrates, citizens of all classes denounced the king. Throughout 1788, hundreds of angry pamphlets proliferated. At Pau, crowds beat down the locked doors of the courthouse; at Grenoble, they pelted the king's troops from their roofs. A cry went out for the king to convene the nobles, the clergy, and the "people," who, respectively, comprised the three houses of the Estates-General, the French legislature, which had last come to-gether in 1614.

On August 8, 1788, the king finally capitulated and set a May 1 date for the crucial meeting. Mary read this news in the British press, which had backed the insurgents from the start. "The character of the *Frenchman* seems never before properly probed or understood," the London *Times* exulted. "They have been considered by most writers as volatile and unfixed in their determinations; their conduct in this contest with the King will give a very different idea. It has been such as would adorn the most illustrious British patriot—it has been tem-perate though firm and decisive."

The average Englishman affected a superior air toward French people, who had no Magna Carta, no House of Lords or Commons, whose Estates-General appeared only at regal bidding, and whose courts had until the past year slavishly toadied to the king. Further-more, because the French had emptied their coffers supporting the American Revolution, by 1788 they were on the verge of financial ruin. Louis's first impulse was to stifle protest and raise taxes. But the unexpected riots, compounded by summer hailstorms devastating the harvest and the Treasury's inability to raise loans, made govern-ing by fiat impossible. So the king set out to win back the favor of his people. His calling of the Estates-General was widely applauded as a wise first move.

Every Englishman had an opinion on events across the Channel. Of course, radicals like Thomas Paine and enlightened Dissidents like Price and Priestley immediately supported the patriots. But many Anglicans who despised Rousseau and Voltaire were also awed by the pluck of the French. Even traditionalist Edmund Burke declared it "impossible not to admire" the "spirit" of the French people.[1]

And Mary on principle admired righteous anger, though she wrote little about France during the fall of 1788. The previous spring, she had informed Everina:

I am studying French, and wish I had an opportunity of conversing indeed, if I have ever any money to spare to gratify myself, I
will certainly visit France, it has long been a desire floating in my
brain, that even hope has not given *consistency* to; and yet it does
not evaporate.[2]

So Mary would be gratified rather than overjoyed to behold the
French soil and culture. Furthermore, she was suspicious of this idea
that "the people" were good. "The voice of the people is only the
voice of truth, when some man of abilities has had time to get fast
hold of the GREAT NOSE of the monster,"[3] she wrote Joseph Johnson at the end of 1788.

Mary had monsters of her own to grapple with that winter. She
fretted about "drawbacks on my spirits and purse."[4] For as well as
missing Fanny and Margaret Kingsborough (with whom she con-
trived to carry on a secret correspondence), she now was coping with
her brother James, never a favorite, who had come home from sea
and—like Charles, Eliza, and Everina—turned up at George Street
looking for help. James said he wanted a promotion in the British
Navy, and Mary agreed to finance his studies for the qualifying exams, though she doubted he would stick to his plan. Charles, meanwhile, was getting into trouble at his new law firm, and Eliza was
teaching in Putney, where she liked the headmistress, Mrs. Bregantz,
but despised the work.

Mary's own latest work, her translation of Necker's *De l'Importance
des Opinions Religieuses*, had come out, and she critiqued it in the January 1789 issue of the *Analytical Review*. Reviewing one's original work
or translation was common practice in the eighteenth century. What
distinguished Mary was that she did not seize the opportunity to pub-
licize her book. Her remarks are evenhanded. While she praises
Necker's piety, she finds his organization sloppy, his epithets "too nu-
merous," and certain of his concepts flawed. Tellingly, Mary rejects

Necker's thesis that the human soul is evolving toward "that magnificent period, when it will be thought worthy of knowing more intimately the Author of Nature." Human progress is unlikely enough, in Mary's opinion. The idea that men and women could be "worthy of knowing" God appalls her. As for her own tinkering with the text, Mary points out "some liberties occasionally taken, and we think very properly, by the translator," explaining that Necker can be a bore.[5]

"I am become a critic,"[6] Mary announced to Joseph Johnson. Every month, she had the opportunity to air her opinions in print. In the February issue of the *Analytical Review*, she is trouncing a familiar target, lady novelists, with their "unnatural characters, improbable incidents, sad tales of woe rehearsed in an affected, half-prose, half-poetical style, exquisite double-refined sensibility, dazzling beauty, and *elegant* drapery."[7] In April, reviewing Samuel Hayes's *Verses on His Majesty's Recovery*, she pities the recent insanity of King George III. "Every feeling heart now rejoices that a tender father, an affectionate husband, is restored to his family and to his country, who have no longer to watch with anxious solicitude the progress of the heaviest of all human calamities."[8] Which, of course, was madness, a curse that had stricken Eliza and maybe their brother Henry too.

Mary's perfectly sane brother Charles had just fled London and hurried off to join George Blood in Dublin. Charles had been fired from his law job, and it was his own fault, he was irresponsible, even underhanded, Mary strongly implies in her April 16 letter to George. She implores George to "try to fix [Charles] in a situation or heaven knows into what vices he may sink!" Mary feels "agitated" and "unwell" from what she perceives as Charles's betrayal. Her hand trembles. She had depended on Charles for "a little remnant of comfort." Now he has joined a long list of her "difficulties" and "vexations," such as the exhausting challenge of translating Salzmann's *Elements of*

Morality from the German and the drudgery of collecting rents for her father and supporting James.[9]

Over the next five months, there is no record of Mary writing to *anyone*, which is curious since so much was happening in the world. At Versailles, King Louis XVI at last convoked the three houses of the Estates-General. But rather than binding France together, the king's lavish ceremonies alienated the people's Third Estate, which broke off from the nobles and clergy and formed a national assembly of its own. Sympathizers from all classes quickly joined them. An effusion of pamphlets and journals hailed the dawn of liberty in France. On July 14, the citizens of Paris rousted the king's guards and seized the Bastille prison, grasping the power to define justice.

News spread quickly. On July 16, 1789, the thirty-three-year-old London journalist William Godwin wrote excitedly in his column for the *New Annual Register:* "Advice is received from Paris, of a great revolution in France, the capture of the Bastille, and the execution of the governor of that fortress, and other obnoxious persons, by the populace."[10] But thirty-year-old Mary made no such pronouncements in the *Analytical Review.* Rather, she lauded Mrs. Trimmer's Roman history for children, mocked Mrs. Piozzi's "childish, feminine" approach to travel writing, and inveighed against the "antic tricks" of Italian divas. Even when reviewing a book on French morals or a novel suggestively entitled *The Bastille,* she avoided allusions to the present excitement.

Nor did she speak of France when on September 15 she wrote chidingly to George Blood, who still had not replied to her April letter. "You know how anxious I am to hear a just and particular account of Charles, to be informed what company he keeps and in what manner he spends his time &c., and you will not afford me that satisfaction," she sulks. It is clear Mary is less angry than hurt at George's silence. As an imperious adolescent, Mary had swept Fanny's brother under her wing. He'd called her The Princess and indulged her every whim.

Now George was balking. He took two months to reply to her letter, and then he was curt and defensive, blaming his dilatoriness on business (he was working long hours for a wine merchant) and "pecuniary difficulties."

"Had you in a frank manly manner sent me a true account of your situation—Heaven knows, I would have put myself to any inconvenience rather than have added to your vexations," Mary half-pled, half-rebuffed him. But "Your unaccountable neglect of a friend who placed the most unreserved confidence in your affection and goodness of heart—all this appears inexplicable."[11] Yet it was not, it seems, inexplicable to George, who refused to reveal anything about Charles's activities. Nor had Charles himself written; so perhaps both men were fed up with Mary's harsh judgments and relentless needs. Or perhaps George still smarted from Mary's indifference to his love for Everina. Certainly, he'd decided they could not continue on their former footing.

And though Mary saved face, claiming, "It would be vain for me to attempt to think of you as I formerly did" and "I loved you because I gave you credit for more substantial virtues then I now think you possess," it was George who reimagined their relationship. They would write cordially from time to time, and twenty-seven years later, George would sing Mary's praises to her eldest child. But these 1789 letters marked an end to their familial intimacy. And it was a painful end for Mary, not just, as she claimed, because of the "reflected affection" she felt for Fanny's brother, but because she loved George himself. Besides, who else could she scold and boss?

Certainly not Charles, who was now flagrantly ignoring her wishes. He would soon leave Ireland and descend on his dissolute father and long-suffering stepmother in Wales. The men would drink and quarrel and squander all the rent money Mary struggled to collect for them. It would be two years before Mary saw Charles again.

But in the fall of 1789, Mary was distracted from thoughts of

Charles and George by an intriguing debate in the public sphere. It began on November 4, when Richard Price addressed the Revolution Society, a group of Dissidents and freethinkers celebrating the anniversary of William of Orange's peaceful succession to the British throne. King William had put a stop to James II's persecution of the Dissident religions. So, "As Protestant Dissidents . . . we have particular reason to rejoice on this : . . . Anniversary of our deliverance,"[12] Price reminded his audience. His sermon, he promised, would explain "the duty we owe to our country and the nature, foundation, and proper expressions of that love to it which we ought to cultivate."[13]

But the mumbling preacher had more than unctuous patriotism to recommend, as it turned out. Soon he was nagging at the British Constitution. Why, he challenged, should Dissidents still be denied places in universities and government jobs? A bill to repeal the prejudicial Test and Corporation Acts recently had been rejected by a mere twenty votes by the House of Commons. And Price urged the repealers to persevere, but also to look beyond Parliament. Great Britain was an "imperfect state," Price announced with growing fervor.[14] The divine rights of George III were downright absurd:

> Civil governors are properly the servants of the public; and a King is no more than the first servant of the public, created by it, maintained by it and responsible to it; and all the homage paid to him is due to him on no other account than his relation to the public. His sacredness is the sacredness of the community. His authority is the authority of the community; and the term MAJESTY which it is useful to apply to him is by no means *his own* majesty, but the MAJESTY OF THE PEOPLE.

Besides, King George the recovered madman was no worthier than other people. On the contrary: "in respect of personal qualities [the

85

king is] not equal to, or even far below many among ourselves."[15]
These surprising remarks had a suspiciously French ring to them. As
Mary noted in her review of Dr. Price's sermon in December 1789,
when Joseph Johnson brought it out in book form, "a late event in a
neighboring kingdom . . . apparently floats uppermost in the Doctor's
mind, and appears to be such a favourite subject of contemplation
that it tinctures all his reflections."[16]

The passage she quotes shows Price at his most fervent:

What an eventful period is this! I am thankful that I have lived to
it; and I could almost say, *Lord, now lettest thou thy servant depart in
peace, for mine eyes have seen thy salvation.*[17] I have lived to see a dif-
fusion of knowledge, which has undermined superstition and error—I have lived to see the rights of men better understood than
ever; and nations panting for liberty, which seemed to have lost
the idea of it. . . . And now, me thinks, I see the ardour for liberty
catching and spreading; a general amendment beginning in human affairs; the dominion of kings changed for the dominion of
laws, and the dominion of priests giving way to the dominion of
reason and conscience.

Be encouraged, all ye friends of freedom, and writers in its de-
fence! The times are auspicious. Your labours have not been in
vain. Behold kingdoms, admonished by you, starting from sleep,
breaking their fetters, and claiming justice from their oppressors!
Behold, the light you have struck out, after setting America free,
reflected in France, and there kindled into a blaze that lays
despotism in ashes, and warms and illuminates Europe.[18]

Mary's review of Price's sermon is her first written allusion to the
French Revolution. But it is not an endorsement by any means. Her
language bristles with irony. The French Revolution is reduced to "a

late event" in her description. The French revolt is *Price's* "favourite subject of contemplation," not, she implies, *hers*. And while Mary praises Price's "ardent virtue" and dutiful patriotism, she coyly avoids judging his eulogy to France.

And this was at a time when Price's sermon was polarizing Great Britain. Conservatives denounced the Dissident minister, while radicals applauded his endorsement of the French.

The London *Times* still supported the Revolution, every day reporting some new momentous incident across the Channel. A Declaration of the Rights of Man had been inscribed by France's new National Assembly in the summer of 1789. In October, mobs descended on the royal family at Versailles and forced them to move back to the Tuileries Palace (across the Pont Royal from Everina in St-Germain). For English radicals like Thomas Christie, who rushed to witness the changes in Paris, a century of enlightened thought seemed to be bursting off the page. And revolution was all the talk wherever London intellectuals gathered. At Joseph Johnson's dinners and outings to concerts or the theater, Mary's pessimism about temporal happiness was challenged by prophecies of a Golden Age.

By January 1790 (when she reviewed *Gallic Liberty: A Poem* in the *Analytical Review*), Mary was calling the French uprisings "a memorable occasion."[19] Her spirits were high. No matter that she was thirty; she was as curious and full of life as anyone she knew. And for all her complaints, she knew she was lucky to be a writer rather than a governess or teacher. No longer did she pine for joyous work. Her pleasures came "from the employments that are within my reach," Mary told Joseph Johnson:

I feel at this moment particularly grateful to you—without your humane and *delicate* assistance, how many obstacles should I not have had to encounter—too often should I have been out of patience with my fellow-creatures, whom I wish to love!— Allow me to love you, my dear sir, and call friend a being I respect.[20]

And she signs off with a French "Adieu!"

Violence horrified Mary, but she convinced herself that reports of bloodshed in France were exaggerated, or, if not, then bloodshed was necessary to the improvement of mankind. Increasingly, Mary was moved by the triumphs of the poor and the powerless. Creatures as lowly as "crazy Robin" and "honest Jack" in her *Original Stories* were rising up to demand a fairer world. And little by little, Mary let down her guard and reached out to them. "The destruction of the Bastille was an event that affected every heart—even hearts not accustomed to the melting mood," she observed in the *Analytical Review*. And she and the artist Henry Fuseli began translating revolutionary pamphlets from the French.

The French Revolution intensified Mary's relationship with this complicated individual. When Mary and Fuseli met, both were pessimists and "excellent hater[s]." They now also shared a passion for radical change. And though Fuseli had married his young model Sophia Rawlins, he lingered for hours chatting with Mary in Joseph Johnson's dining room or swigging wine from a teacup in her makeshift George Street home. Here he met witty Eliza, whom he teased about her love of luxury, and sensible Everina, who came home from Paris in the spring and joined Eliza at Mrs. Bregantz's school in Putney.

During that spring of 1790, Mary declared that Fuseli was an "original genius" with "uncommon diligence."[21] Many agreed. Paintings commissioned by Alderman John Boydell's Shakespeare Gallery had at last brought Fuseli money and some fame as well. The London *Times* raved about his *Tempest* scene,[22] and the Royal Academy elected him president. His work showed beside Joshua Reynolds's and John

Opie's. At forty-nine, he was a success, while Mary, eighteen years younger, was beginning to make her mark in London's intellectual community. They spoke as equals, only Mary wanted more than conversation. She yearned for a passionate connection to another human being.

Fifteen years had passed since Mary had fallen head over heels for Fanny Blood. Now she saw in Fuseli a man "possessed of those noble qualities, that grandeur of soul, that quickness of comprehension, and lively sympathy" that matched her own.[23] Of course, just as Fanny had come burdened with deficiencies and obligations, Fuseli was unpredictable, bisexual, and married to boot. Although *Thoughts on the Education of Daughters* had warned women against platonic love affairs,[24] Mary proudly declared her feelings for Fuseli a "rational passion." "I always catch something from the rich torrent of his conversation, worth treasuring up in my memory, to exercise my understanding."[25] The fact that Fuseli was married precluded their making love, but not intellectual attraction. Mary hoped, she said, "to unite herself to his mind."[26]

Throughout this early phase of her love for Fuseli, Mary conceived no new books but did continue churning out articles for the *Analytical Review*. One of the most revealing is a review of a new romance called *Julia*, written by the English poet and novelist Helen Maria Williams, who was now living in France. Tellingly, Mary singles out Williams's "sentiment" and "artless energy of feeling" for praise, noting that the best novels excite emotions, not rational thought.[27]

At the time Mary reviewed *Julia*, her convictions had been deeply affected by love and the French Revolution. While in *Original Stories* passion was an evil to be quashed by reason, now passion was capable of effecting both private and social good. And, unlike so many philosophers before and after her, Mary refused to dissemble to defend her former ideals. She espoused what life taught her and scorned theories built purely on abstract thought.

. . .

WHILE MARY'S ideas were evolving, her daily life remained much the same as it had been since she came to London three years before. She wrote, she read, she absorbed new languages and went to gallery shows and concerts and the theater. She scurried around collecting rents for her father and bemoaned Charles's laziness and her sisters' ineptitudes while retaining a fervent desire to do good. When, in the spring of 1790, she unwittingly betrayed a friend's confidence, Mary histrionically informed Joseph Johnson:

> Perhaps you can scarcely conceive the misery I at this moment endure—that I, whose power of doing good is so limited, should do harm, galls my very soul. . . .—My stomach has been so suddenly and violently affected, I am unable to lean over the desk.[28]

Beyond her failing to do good, Mary was sickened by her frustrating relationship with Fuseli. She comforted herself that while Fuseli lived "I shall never want an indulgent warm friend," but that friend had a wife.[29] And Mary found more to rattle her when, at the end of August 1790, she arrived in the Warminster countryside to visit another married friend, Henry Gabell, whom she'd met when they were both struggling young tutors bound for Ireland four years before. Gabell, now master of a school in Warminster, had a wife named Ann, and the visit began inauspiciously when Mary decided Ann was like a Doric pillar: having "porportion without beauty— symmetry without grace."[30] Although Mary had to admit the Doric pillar loved Henry, Ann's demonstrativeness drove Mary to long even for Eliza and Everina, who were "*very* clever, and *most* agreeable," not to mention without men.[31] Metaphysically, Mary decided, the Gabells were her inferiors because they could be happy in this awful world.[32] And while Mary enjoyed her healing walks through tranquil Warminster, she was grateful, in mid-September, to leave the

Gabells to their misguided pleasures and return to noisy London, where everyone was aghast about events in France.

Two months before, 350,000 euphoric French citizens of all ranks had danced in the rain through the Champs de Mars, celebrating the first anniversary of the capture of the Bastille. But now, in the fall, dissension was growing. The National Assembly, already having stripped the Catholic Church of its property and income, was eliminating Catholicism's privileged status by granting equal rights to Protestants and even Jews. All clergy were forced to pledge exclusive loyalty to the Revolution. And when thirty bishops asked to consult the pope before pledging, they were promptly dismissed, which troubled pious Anglicans in London as well as Catholics throughout Europe. British conservatives recalled how Dr. Price had denounced state religions in his speech to the Revolution Society a year earlier. Once again, the minister's words became a lightning rod for debate.

At the beginning of November 1790 the eloquent Whig MP Edmund Burke published *Reflections on the Revolution in France,* a long, deeply considered defense of traditional values. The previous February, Burke had broken with his friend Charles James Fox and the rest of the pro-French contingent in Parliament. *Reflections* praises British common sense and attacks Dr. Price as a Francophilic visionary. King George does not, as Price implies, "owe his crown to the choice of the people,"[33] Burke argues. On the contrary, by law the English people owe their fealty to the king, as they do to the Church of England.[34] France's strategy of plundering its Church to boost the Treasury is shortsighted; alienating the Army from the king augurs civil unrest; and if France fails, as seems likely, to form a strong judiciary, the Assembly "will extinguish the last sparks of liberty in France."[35] Burke condemns the "plots, massacres, and assassinations"[36] that have already marked the Revolution and predicts even worse in the months ahead.

"To give freedom is . . . easy," he warns, ". . . it only requires to let go the rein. But to form a *free government*—that is, to temper together these opposite elements of liberty and restraint in one consistent work—requires much thought,"[37] which the passionate French cannot muster, he suspects.

Thus, England, in Burke's view, has nothing to learn from France and much to cherish in its own heritage:

> From the Magna Carta to the Declaration of Right, it has been the uniform policy of our constitution to claim and assert our liberties, as an *entailed inheritance* derived to us from our forefathers, and to be transmitted to our posterity. . . . A spirit of innovation is generally the result of a selfish temper and confined views.[38]

Reflections predicts with uncanny accuracy the course of the French Revolution. And it has endured these past two centuries as a fluent defense of the status quo. But *Reflections* was also a sensation in its own time. Thirty thousand copies sold. Sections appeared in the London *Times*, which also printed a letter hailing it as "equal, if not superior in merit to any thing that has been published since the Revolution."[39]

Meanwhile, defenders of the French rushed to excoriate Burke's disdain for progress. Over a hundred angry books and pamphlets were published in the following year. Thomas Paine's *Rights of Man* became the most famous. But the first reply to Burke was printed by Joseph Johnson less than a month after *Reflections* arrived in the bookstores: it was Mary Wollstonecraft's *Vindication of the Rights of Men*.

Mary's first book since *Original Stories*, *Rights of Men* is brief and spontaneous. While Burke polished his arguments, Mary wrote as she thought. And why not? she demands. Burke's fluency is ingratiating, his arguments are sentimental, and his caution absurd. She despises his alms-giving approach to poverty. Charity, which she'd warmly advocated in *Original Stories*, is now inadequate: the poor need opportunity, not gifts. And her God no longer demands humility. "Fear of God makes me reverence myself,"[40] Mary exclaims.

Burke's "servile"[41] reverence for the past and primogeniture disgusts her. She mocks his desire to dethrone King George III when he was mad: "Impressed as *you are* with respect for royalty, I am astonished that you did not tremble at [confronting a king]." At this point, Mary unexpectedly moves into a long, feeling rumination on insanity. Below are some of her most vivid thoughts:

> The ruling angel leaving its seat, wild anarchy ensues. . . . The eccentricities are boldly relieved when judgment no longer officiously arranges the sentiments, by bringing them to the test of principles. . . . Every thing [is] out of nature in that strange chaos of levity and ferocity, and all sorts of follies [are] jumbled together. . . . The most opposite passions necessarily succeed, and sometimes mix with each other in the mind; alternate contempt and indignation; alternate laughter and tears; alternate scorn and horror. This is a true picture of that chaotic state of mind, called madness; when reason is gone, we know not where, the wild elements clash and all is horror and confusion.[42]

Mary's two pages of intense musings on madness make an intriguing detour from her otherwise heated text. They may have evolved out of feelings elicited by Fuseli, or memories of Eliza deranged by her husband, or maybe from events in France itself. Yes, maybe the "strange chaos" of madness and the unboundedness of liberty became confused in Mary's imagination. And though she never explicitly draws this connection, Mary does imply reservations about the cause she touts. "The passions are necessary auxiliaries of reason," she observes in one of her book's most moving passages:

a present impulse pushes us forward, and when we discover that the game did not deserve the chace, we find that we have gone over much ground and not only gained many new ideas, but a habit of thinking. The exercise of our faculties is the great end, though not the goal we had in view when we started with such eagerness.[43]

So Mary's fervor for human improvement is tempered by some skepticism about the particular "game" at hand. Like Burke, she mistrusts mobs and abhors violence. Dr. Price's visions of progress without sacrifice may be "Utopian reveries," she admits in *Rights of Men*. Still, the effort justifies the cause.[44]

Mary wrote the first pages of *Rights of Men* in a flash, and Johnson rushed them to the press as she handed them in. Then, in the middle of November, she was "seized," she said,

with a temporary fit of torpor and indolence, and began to repent of her undertaking. In this state of mind, she called one evening, as she was in the practise of doing, upon her publisher, for the purpose of relieving herself by an hour or two's conversation. Here, the habitual ingenuousness of her nature, led her to describe what had just past in her thoughts. Mr. Johnson immediately, in a kind and friendly way, intreated her not to put any constraint upon her inclination, and to give herself no uneasiness about the prints already printed, which he would cheerfully throw aside, if it would contribute to her happiness. Mary had wanted incentive. She had expected reproach, rather than to be encouraged in what she well knew was unreasonable. Her friend's so readily falling in with her ill-humour, and seeming to expect that she would lay aside her undertaking, piqued her pride. She immediately went home; and proceeded to the end of her work, with no other interruptions but what were absolutely indispensible.[45]

How well Joseph Johnson understood Mary's nature. And how she depended on him to cajole and brace her when she was out of sorts. So it came as an alarming shock when Mary stopped by to visit Johnson one Tuesday evening late in the fall of 1790, and he told her he had symptoms of a stroke and was calmly preparing to die. Mary stayed up most of the night worrying about her great friend, and was still lying in bed the next morning when a frantic note from her sisters arrived. She raced to join them in Putney, but then deemed their troubles "trivial" beside Johnson's and berated them for calling her away. Writing Eliza after she returned to London from Putney, Mary offers a cursory apology for her angry outburst: "My mind was off its poize," she acknowledges, "I grew unreasonable and out of humour and behaved in a manner to you, I blush to recollect." But Mary was obviously hurt by whatever vicious exchanges followed, for her letter goes on to attack Eliza and Everina at their vulnerable points. First, Mary alludes to a long visit Eliza paid her at George Street. When at last the younger sister left, "I gave way to the hope that respecting you I should have a little peace. . . . Indeed this hope had a good effect on my mind—I mentioned in one of my letters that I was in better health." So having Eliza out of her life was a boon to Mary, but in case her sisters should for a moment consider *her* expendable, "the two last years of my life might have passed tranquilly," Mary reminds them, had her relatives not "embittered" her existence with financial requests.[46]

The great goal of all the Wollstonecraft women was to overcome dependence. But so far Mary alone had succeeded in supporting herself. Being human, Eliza and Everina could not help envying her, though Mary in the past had appeased their resentment with assurances that she would do all she could to empower them. Now she was high-handedly taunting them with their failures. They were humiliated. And they struck back with the only weapon they had to hurt her—their reserve.

"My sisters . . . certainly do not adore me," Mary complained at the end of 1790; nor did they especially wish her well at this crucial point in her career. But others did—for instance, Joseph Johnson (who did not die, but recovered to bring out the first volume of *Rights of Men* at the end of November), Fuseli, and hundreds of readers she'd never met. The *Rights of Men* became both a critical and a commercial triumph. On the verge of death, Dr. Price wrote Mary that he was "particularly happy in having such an advocate,"[47] and Johnson sent the book back for a second printing at the beginning of the new year. This time Mary's name, cautiously withheld from the first edition, stood proudly on the title page. She was building a following. And no longer was she just a writer for women and children. Mary was prepared to address the world.

CHAPTER FIVE

*A*fter *A Vindication of the Rights of Men*, Mary was no longer simply Johnson's protégée, but a philosopher and minor celebrity in her own right. And she thoroughly enjoyed being fussed over—as when the famous portraitist John Opie clamored to paint her picture. Joseph Johnson's friend, the Liverpool arts patron William Roscoe, insisted that she sit for *his* painter as well.

She left George Street behind and moved to a larger, nicer house on Store Street near Russell Square, two blocks from the British Museum. She was spreading her wings, gaining real confidence to buttress her superior airs. "Tranquility does not fly from my quiet study, and the pictures, which fancy traces on the walls, have often the most glowing colours," she wrote George Blood.[1] Now she was an hour's walk from Joseph Johnson's doorstep, and she no longer stared up at St. Paul's spire or down at the Thames. But her street was tree-lined and cheerful, she could stroll through lush Bloomsbury parks nearby and receive the increasing number of callers who thought it worth their while to come visit her.

Gone was the angry penuriousness that had reduced Mary to brash beaver caps and serving wine in teacups. She bought fashionable new furniture and suddenly took an interest in clothes. Mary "is grown quite handsome," Charles, back in London, informed Eliza. "Being conscious that she is on the wrong side of thirty she now endeavors to set off those charms she once despised to the best advantage."[2]

Success did not stop Mary from worrying about Charles's "boiling blood"[3] and idleness. "He is a thoughtless youth, with common abilities, a tolerable person, some warmth of heart, and a turn for humour,"[4] Mary informed William Roscoe. James, who had passed his qualifying exams but failed to receive his Navy advancement, was now captaining a merchant vessel. Everina firmly refused a marriage proposal from George Blood and went to Ireland as a governess. Eliza took a similar post in Wales.

In a beneficent mood (and maybe curious to see what mothering was like), Mary invited the seven-year-old orphaned niece of Hugh Skeys's second wife to come live with her. The girl's name was Ann, and she was Irish and high-spirited, maybe another Margaret Kingsborough, Mary suspected at first. But then, while Ann was "affectionate and artless," she was "very troublesome." Her perpetual cheerfulness "sometimes oppresses me," Mary guiltily complained.[5] And while others remarked that Ann wonderfully "improved" under Mary's guidance, Mary was skeptical. Then too Ann proved to be less artless than she had seemed. "A few days ago I discovered that [Ann] had been stealing sugar out of my closet constantly, and the artful way she managed it, not to mention the lies, really vexes me," Mary wrote Everina.[6]

Besides, Ann must have gotten in the way when Fuseli came to visit or when Mary sat down in October 1791 to begin writing her next book, which she alludes to in an October 6 letter to William Roscoe: "I do not imagine that [the portrait you have commissioned] will be a very striking likeness, but, if you do not find me in it, I will send you

a more faithful sketch—a book that I am now writing, in which *I* myself . . . shall certainly appear."[7]

THE BOOK was Mary's great work, *A Vindication of the Rights of
Woman*, which would survive her own woes and the hopes of her gen-
eration to speak eloquently to both genders in all times. Her whole
life had prepared her for this mission. Her abusing father, her indolent mother who blatantly favored Ned, her sister Eliza, who sacri-
ficed everything to leave an unhappy marriage, and the laws and
mores that reduced all the girls in the family to demeaning work were
on Mary's mind as she began the first frankly feminist manifesto in
the history of human rights. It was a cry for justice, demanding nothing less than a radical reconception of family roles. Family is the state
in microcosm, Mary announces: power must be redistributed in both
the nursery and the courts.

Though she was the first explicitly to demand equality for women,
Mary drew from a tradition of bluestockings, who sought access to
knowledge for themselves as privileged individuals, and from essayists, like Mary Astell and Catharine Macaulay, who could not conceive of emancipation but did want expanded rights for their sex. A
century before *Vindication*, Astell, a charity-school teacher, wrote *A
Serious Proposal to the Ladies*, declaring that women are "as capable of
Learning as Men are"[8] and exhorting young girls to throw away their
mirrors and cultivate their minds. Deeply religious, she scorned the
bawdy mood of the Restoration but also despised unthinking piety.
For Astell as for Mary, virtue demands understanding and an active
mind.

Yes, women are for the most part inferior, Astell acknowledges, but
if they cannot compete with men intellectually, if they are slaves to
"Tyrant Custom"[9] and "think it an unpardonable mistake" to defy the

fashion of their friends, the fault, she insists, should "be ascribed to the mistakes of our Education, which like an Error in the first Concoction, spreads its influence through all our Lives."[10]

And if a "mistaken" education, focused on the senses, has demeaned the typical female, an emphasis on intellectual rigor will revitalize her soul. Since men ridicule studious females, Astell proposes a retreat, "rather academical than monastic,"[11] where women can immerse themselves in study free from pressures to attract mates. "It is not my intention that you shou'd seclude yourselves from the world [forever]. . . . But it is Unreasonable and Barbarous to drive you into't, e're you are capable of doing Good in it, or at least of keeping Evil from your selves."[12]

Mary Wollstonecraft apparently never read Mary Astell, though Astell's ideas attracted considerable attention (Daniel Defoe was an admirer) during the seventeenth century, when women artists like Aphra Behn were writing dramas and farmers' and shopkeepers' wives played an important economic role in family life. But, by the mid-eighteenth century, the Industrial Revolution and the redistribution of farmland marginalized women in the workplace, while domestic virtues, touted in Addison and Steele's influential magazines the *Spectator* and the *Tatler,* became an obsession for the British middle class. Under the three Hanoverian Georges, propriety was the watchword, and women were expected to answer to higher moral standards than men. When popular young George III ascended the throne in 1760, he issued a proclamation "for the encouragement of piety and virtue, and for preventing and punishing vice, profaneness, and immorality."[13] Until the end of the century, no one publicly challenged his view of women as cheerfully housebound wives and mothers. Abstract learning, both sexes agreed, was futile for females, while studying music, dance, painting, dress, religion, and submission to the will of a man was more to the point.

But then came Catharine Macaulay, whom Mary Wollstonecraft

called "the woman of the greatest abilities, undoubtedly, that this country has ever produced."[14] Born in 1731 and rigorously trained by her father, she wrote an eight-volume history of England (1763–1783)[15] before publishing in 1790 *Letters on Education*, endorsing serious education for girls.

Like Astell's *Proposal*, *Letters on Education*[16] appeals to a small, enlightened section of the middle- and upper-class population, and deplores the "false system of beauty and delicacy" that "depraves" ignorant members of her sex. "The admiration of the other sex is held out to women as the highest honour they can obtain; whilst this is considered as their *summum bonum*, and the beauty of their persons the chief *desideratus* of men, vanity, and its companion Envy, must taint . . . every native acquired excellence."[17]

And Macaulay agrees with Astell that the antidote to vanity is knowledge. But where Astell believed in isolating women, Macaulay insists that girls and boys learn better under the same roof. "Let your children be brought up together; let their sports and studies be the same, let them enjoy, in the constant presence of those who are set over them, all the freedom which innocence renders harmless."[18] The plan is bold but unsatisfying, for Macaulay never explains how it will come to pass.

Reviewing Macaulay's *Letters* in the November 1790 issue of the *Analytical Review*, Mary Wollstonecraft declared herself "perfectly coinciding in opinion with this sagacious writer."[19] And *Vindication* freely acknowledges its profound debt to *Letters*.

Yet, *Vindication* was also fresh and new, in part because it appeared in the glory days of the French Revolution, but also because it was written in a swaggering, heroic voice. Mary Astell urged women to retreat to female colleges because men were incorrigible. Catharine Macaulay thought up a reasonable system for educating both sexes, but failed to say how it could be implemented in an unfair world. It was for Mary Wollstonecraft to put the rights of women in the context of social optimism: "Rousseau exerts himself to prove that all *was* right originally; a crowd of authors that all *is* now right; and I, that all will *be* right." Where Astell and Macaulay were succinct and even-handed, Wollstonecraft was long-winded and enraged.

The point of *Vindication* is that women become silly creatures because the goal of their education is to lure a man. Girls are not born to love dolls or submission, Mary argues. It is no more "natural" for them to simper than to reason: you have to be taught, as you have to be taught to prefer dressing up to romping. The minds of women are no different from the minds of men. This was the defining theme of *Vindication*, flouting a favorite eighteenth-century fancy that mind and body are somehow mystically connected;[20] that having a uterus affects whether you can learn Latin and Greek; and that thinking can make a woman infertile by sapping her creativity! Yes, woman had a soul, the philosophers granted, maybe a soul as worthy in its own way as the wiser soul of man. But Rousseau saw nothing odd in declaring that "a perfect man and a perfect woman should be no more alike in mind than in face."[21] Men and women might be equal, but they were certainly not the same. And to this Mary thunders, Nonsense! Men and women differ in their bodies only. What's more, a system based on one sex's dependence is demeaning to everyone. A slave cannot be virtuous; virtue requires the power to choose.

Mary dedicated her book to the well-born French statesman Talleyrand, who had just denounced all hereditary privilege and rank in France. Man should thrive by his talents only, Talleyrand argued in his sixth principle of the groundbreaking *Declaration of the Rights of Man and Citizen*. So why not women also? Mary asks. "I plead for my sex, not for myself," she notes with the reverse of humility. *She* would succeed in any world. But woe to the revolution that neglects half the human race, for if the ordinary woman "be not prepared by education to become the companion of man, she will stop the progress of knowledge and virtue"; the Enlightenment will fail.

The French were celebrating their Revolution as new and cataclysmic. Whereas the Americans had merely won their private independence from England, France would liberate all men from history itself. (It is not coincidental that before 1789, the definition of revolution was a "turning back"; afterward, it became a siege on tradition.)[22] And so Mary feels about her own cause. From the dawn of time, man has used his physical superiority to dominate history:

> Probably the prevailing opinion that woman was created for man, may have taken its rise from Moses' poetical story; yet as very few, it is presumed, who have bestowed any serious thought on the subject ever supposed that Eve was, literally speaking, one of Adam's ribs, the deduction must be allowed to fall to the ground, or only to be so far admitted as it proves that man, from the remotest antiquity, found it convenient to exert his strength to subjugate his companion, and his invention to show that she ought to have her neck bent under the yoke, because the whole creation was created for his convenience and pleasure.[23]

Vindication founds its arguments equally on Reason and God's virtue. The two are compatible, since Reason is good and God is wise and exacting. Like a Dissident minister, *Vindication*'s God sees through the hypocrisy of the history books and the arrogance of Rousseau's paean to adorable housewives in the Sophy section of *Émile*. God despises the measly homes that barely keep alive those women debased or duped into selling their bodies. What prostitutes need are not asylums, but decent jobs. "It is justice, not charity, that is wanting in the world,"[24] Mary declares, turning full circle from the emphasis on resignation and personal transcendence in her early works.

Mary's 449-page volume (a sequel is promised) was written in haste and passion with a weak structure and sprawling theme. The eighteenth-century repetitiveness can be maddening, but the sentences soar. Her first chapters attack inertia. "Indolent sailors" and "idle superficial young men" as well as women spread the "baneful lurking gangrene" of tyranny. "As a sex, women are habitually indolent,"[25] and it is this indolence rather than some imagined flaw in their nature that makes them oppress their lovers and corrupt their homes.

Dissipation begins early in life. So while Mary warmly urges mothers to suckle and bond with their babies, she cautions against obsequious obedience to parents by the growing girl. "The absurd duty . . . of obeying a parent only on account of his being a parent, shackles the mind, and prepares it for . . . slavish submission," she declares, doubtless remembering her own childhood. But family attachments take a toll on parents as well. "'He that hath wife and children,' says Lord Bacon, 'hath given hostage to fortune; for they are impediments to great enterprises, either of virtue or mischief. Certainly the best works, and of greatest merit for the public, have proceeded from the unmarried or childless men.' I say the same of women,"[26] she avers. In a chapter on "modesty," Mary inveighs against girls who "disfigure" themselves wearing hooped skirts and grandiose hairstyles to attract husbands. "They only dress to gratify men of gallantry; for the lover is always best pleased with the simple garb that fits close to the shape. There is an impertinence in ornaments that rebuffs affection, because love always clings round the idea of home."[27]

There is a chapter full of often hilarious quotes from "Writers Who Have Rendered Women Objects of Pity, Bordering on Contempt," which prominently features Rousseau with his Sophy and the well-meaning Dr. John Gregory,[28] who in *A Father's Legacy to His Daughters* implores his motherless girls to hide their clever minds. "It is this system of dissimulation, throughout [Dr. Gregory's] volume, that I despise," writes Mary. "Women are always to *seem* to be this and that—yet virtue might apostrophize them, in the words of Hamlet— Seems! I know not seems! Have that within passeth show!"[29]

Most strikingly, *Vindication* goes far beyond Catharine Macaulay's vague speculations about educating brothers and sisters under the same roof to call for coeducational government-sponsored schools. That even rich children could profit by studying out of the home was a shocking concept in eighteenth-century England. Mary defends it, writing:

> The good effect resulting from attention to private education will ever be very confined, and the parent who really puts his own hand to the plough, will always, in some degree, be disappointed, till education becomes a grand national concern. A man cannot retire into the desert with his child, and if he did he could not bring himself back to childhood, and become the proper friend and playfellow of an infant or youth. . . . In order to open their faculties they should be excited to think for themselves; and this can only be done by mixing a number of children together, and making them jointly pursue the same objects.[30]

And she exclaims:

> Let an enlightened nation then . . . [allow women] to share the advantages of education and government with man, see whether they will become better, as they grow wiser and become free.[31]

According to her scheme, between the ages of five and nine "rich and poor" children of both sexes would attend national day schools, studying reading, writing, math, botany, philosophy, religion, mechanics, astronomy, and the history of nature and man.[32] Not every child has an intellectual future, however, Mary cautions. After the age of nine, only boys and girls of wealth or ability would pursue academic courses; there would be trade schools for the rest. But all would profit from their diversified grade schools. Coeducation is crucial, Mary argues, for "Men and women were made for each other, though not to become one being, and if [men] will not improve women, they will deprave them."[33]

Mary wrote a lot about love. Five years before *Vindication*, in *Thoughts on the Education of Daughters* (1787), the twenty-seven-year-old Mary had disparaged romance and condemned women to a passive role in sex. ("It has ever occurred to me," she wrote, "that it was sufficient for a woman to receive caresses, and not bestow them.")[34] Except in the passage warning women against platonic attachments, *Thoughts* ignores sexual feelings. There was as yet no place for desire in Wollstonecraft's ideology. There was only need. And what society needed was myriad husbands and wives, bound by friendship, raising enlightened families for an enlightened world.

Now, when she began writing *Vindication*, Mary was greatly troubled by her more than friendly feelings for Fuseli. Troubled and indignant, but also—it comes through in her prose—thrilled. Love was exhilarating. That was the surprise. Yet, Mary still refuses to validate romantic passion, comparing it unfavorably to "the most sublime of all affections," friendship, and insisting that the two cannot coexist. A husband can't be simultaneously his wife's friend and her lover. Mary would clearly be happier if falling in love never happened. After all, it depressed her and made her dependent in ways even patriarchy could not. She paints a scary picture of love's role in the social scheme of things, where it "will reign, like some other stalking mischiefs, by its own authority, without deigning to reason."[35] But though love is an enemy to reason, Mary admits that "to endeavour to reason love out of the world would be to out-Quixote Cervantes, and equally offend against common sense."[36]

The reference to Quixote is telling. In *Vindication*, a new realm is heard from: the imagination, the mind's power to transform both reason and love. And no matter that things "romantic" and "quixotic" are almost invariably derided in *Vindication*, imagination has slipped into Mary's vocabulary; soon she will join the early Romantics and champion the fanciful mind.

MARY WROTE *Vindication* in less than six weeks, and Johnson published it immediately, in early January 1792. As with *Rights of Men*, the minute Mary finished a page, it was rushed to the printer—which precluded a final revision. Mary was annoyed by the many errors and vowed in the future to take more time.

Her book was both extolled and ridiculed, but it was not ignored. The newspaper reviews were full of praise, though the misogynist writer Horace Walpole called Mary a "hyena in petticoats."[37] And the moralist Hannah More refused even to read *Vindication* (which she unconsciously honored by presuming everyone else *had*).[38] The philosopher William Godwin, then just finishing his own major work, *An Enquiry Concerning Political Justice*, found *Vindication* "eminently deficient in method and arrangement";[39] while the fledgling writer Mary Hays was so enraptured she broke off writing her own *Appeal to the Men of Great Britain in Behalf of Women* and began courting Mary as a mentor and friend.

Eliza Wollstonecraft saw *Vindication* as yet another spur to Mary's vanity. "I never think of *our sister* but in the light of a friend who has been dead many years," Eliza bitterly informed Everina, ". . . I sigh to think we shall never meet, as such, again—though perhaps in a better world Love of Fame cannot corrupt the soul."[40]

Mary's Dissident friend Anna Barbauld had an ambivalent reaction. *Vindication* alludes to Barbauld as a learned essayist but cringes at her sentimental poem equating painted flowers and the female sex. Barbauld answered *Vindication* with yet another poem, this one entitled *The Rights of Woman* and intended, it seems, to rebut Wollstonecraft's theories, though it in fact joins Mary in mocking cunning females who use their beauty to rule men. Where the two women separate is on the issue of love and power. In her final stanza, Barbauld exhorts women:

> Then, then abandon each ambitious thought,
> Conquest or rule thy heart shall feebly move,
> In nature's school, by her soft maxims taught,
> That separate rights are lost in mutual love.[41]

For Mrs. Barbauld, love between two people frees both from the need for power, whereas for Mary love is a sham until issues of power have been resolved. The point is tricky—and timeless—and must have challenged many of Mary's admirers as well as those who scoffed at her cause.

AMERICANS applauded *Vindication*. In Massachusetts, John Adams's sister-in-law Elizabeth demanded a copy from Abigail[42] while she was in London; the Connecticut-born Joel Barlow counted himself one of Mary's greatest fans. Also an author of political texts, Joel shared Mary's conviction that power was central to human happiness. He liked to view himself as an idealist, but also clearly loved adventure and strife. To Mary, he and his wife, Ruth, seemed the embodiment of domestic happiness—which annoyed her no end when she first met them in London, in 1791, as they were joining Joseph Johnson's circle.

They were a handsome couple, Joel in particular, with his prominent cheekbones and zealous air. Educated at Yale, he'd written a lot of acclaimed (gushing) patriotic poetry and been, briefly, a minister, a publisher, a lawyer, an essayist, and a businessman in the United States. He'd left for Europe in 1788, when he was thirty-four, as part of an ill-fated scheme to sell French people land in America. Three years later, when that endeavor failed, Joel crossed the Channel to England, where Ruth joined him, reluctantly. For she'd wanted Joel to sail home to her; and even now he promised they'd soon return together to New Haven.

Meanwhile, the Barlows settled on Litchfield Street near Charing Cross Road. Quickly, they befriended such prominent British radicals as Joseph Johnson, Thomas Paine, William Godwin, Thomas Hardy, and Mary herself. Joel was planning a literary attack on all the old regimes in Europe. "I have such a flood of indignation and such a store of argument accumulated in my guts on this subject that I can hold in no longer,"[43] Joel wrote his brother-in-law. The result was *Advice to the Privileged Orders*, a rousing defense of the Revolution, which enraged the British—now scandalized by the increasing violence in Paris—and ingratiated him with the French.

Joel began frequently traveling to Paris, while Ruth stayed behind with her new friends. Many mornings, Mary invited the American woman to breakfast with her in her apartment on Store Street. "Mrs. B. has a very benevolent, affectionate heart, and a tolerable understanding, a little warped it is true by romance," Mary wrote Everina six months after *Vindication* appeared, "but she is not the less friendly on that account."[44] What made Ruth romantic in Mary's eyes was the way she rushed to show off Joel's letters, which were full of effusions such as "My dearest life and soul, I long to see you."

"I was almost disgusted with the *tender* passages which afforded [Ruth] so much satisfaction," Mary reported, "because they were turned so prettily that they looked more like the cold ingenuity of the head than the warm overflowings of the heart." But of course, Mary, more miserable every day because she couldn't possess Fuseli, was far from an impartial judge of lovers at that point. Later she would revise her opinion of the Barlows.

In the spring of 1792, Joel was assuring Ruth that some month soon they'd book passage to America. He offered to take Mary's brother

Charles along—to find Charles farmwork and then a farm of his own, when he could afford it. Charles liked the plan, and Mary, who had described America as "the land of liberty, independence, and equality,"[45] encouraged him to go.

"Mr. B. has some thoughts of keeping [Charles] in his own family," Mary wrote Everina, "but he waits till he sees more of him before he avows his intention. . . . The other day he clapped C., in his dry way, on the knee and said—'that as his wife and he could never contrive to make any boys they must try what they could do with one ready brought up to their hands.' "[46]

The American scheme could include Everina and Eliza, if they wanted. Ruth Barlow "is continually saying how well you might be settled in America," Mary informed them. Life and marriage were so much simpler in the New World than in Paris or London. The Wollstonecraft sisters would be "respected by the first families," which intrigued Eliza in particular, though her plan at the moment was to find a position in France.

Unfortunately for Charles, Joel Barlow too was preoccupied with France and its revolution. "Mr. Barlow . . . is a worthy man, but devoured by ambition," Mary wrote Everina. "His thoughts are turned toward France and till the present commotions are over, I am much mistaken if he do not find some excuse every month to make to *himself* for staying in Europe." Joel was "lingering amidst alarms instead of returning to the peaceable shades of America because, may I moralize? rest is the rack of active minds, and life loses its zest when we find that there is nothing worth wishing for, nothing to detain the thoughts in the present scene, but what quickly grows stale, rendering the soul torpid or uneasy."[47]

Torpor and uneasiness well describe Mary's own state of mind in the summer of 1792. Writing *Vindication* had buoyed her spirits. Still, "Had I allowed myself more time I could have written a better book."[48] She promised to lavish greater care on a second volume. But there's no sign that Mary ever began volume two of *Vindication*. Nor did she start any other major projects in the coming year, though she embeds a memorable observation on history in one of her reviews in the *Analytical Review*: "It is almost impossible . . . to consider [the French Revolution] as an *abstract question* during the present day for it is immediately connected with the political sentiments of the times, and is but too apt to take its colouring from the prejudices of the human mind. It will afford a noble subject for the pen of some future historian, and for the contemplation of an enlightened posterity."[49]

EVENTS IN FRANCE continued to spark Mary's interest, but Fuseli obsessed her. "I love the man and admire the artist," she daringly informed William Roscoe.[50] And she grew more daring with Fuseli himself, telling him that his absences destroyed her concentration, that she deserved more than random chats. She wanted to ritualize their encounters. She wanted a name for what they were.

Many facets of Mary's nature can be seen in the two portraits painted during the time she was in love with Fuseli. In the one, commissioned by William Roscoe, she appears imposingly with powdered curls, a starched, crimped white bodice neatly arched from her chest to the bottom of her sucked-in cheeks, her beautiful long fingers unnaturally thin and crooked, as in a Van Dyck drawing. Her mouth is pinched in a look of determination: she is the formidable public figure. In the other portrait, by her friend John Opie, Mary's hair is still powdered, she wears the same white bodice and maybe even the same dress, but the effect is altogether softer and more undulating. A scarf twists abstractly through her flowing waves, her fingers are nicely rounded, her face is youthfully plump, decidedly pretty. She's holding a book, and Opie has softly illuminated a set of pens at the edge of the table toward which she leans. Her liquid eyes stare thoughtfully up from the page.

Mary was pleased to inform Everina, at the end of June: "For some time past Mr. & Mrs. Fuseli, Mr. Johnson and myself have talked of a summer excursion to Paris; it is now determined on and we think of going in about six weeks. I shall be introduced to many people," she could not resist boasting, "my book has been translated and praised in some popular prints; and Fuseli, of course, is well known."[51] But the famous party got only as far as Dover before turning back because someone other than Mary panicked at reports of violence across the Channel. The reports were accurate—in early August, Louis XVI was torn from the Tuileries Palace, stripped of his kingship, and imprisoned with the rest of the royal family in the gloomy Temple fortress. During the first week in September, 1,400 French prisoners, including priests and ex-ministers, were murdered in their prison cells. English moderates now wholeheartedly embraced Edmund Burke's judgment: the Revolution was spiraling out of control.

Back in London, Mary gave up all pretense of work and bombarded Fuseli with imploring letters, which he began stuffing in his pockets, where he left them unread for days. He mocked her protestations that all she wanted was a platonic union. "If I thought my passion criminal, I would conquer it, or die in the attempt," she insisted, objecting to his taunts that she wanted sex with him. "For immodesty, in my eyes, is ugliness; my soul turns with disgust from pleasure tricked out in charms which shun the light of heaven."[52] Still, Mary's passion was obvious even to Joseph Johnson. And the matter came to a head when the author of *Vindication*, exasperated by Fuseli's evasions, took her case to Sophia, his wife. Sophia was welcome to her husband's body, Mary informed the flabbergasted former model. But "I find that I cannot live without the satisfaction of seeing and conversing with [your husband] daily."[53] So they had to live in the same house. Sophia responded by ordering Fuseli to cease all contact with this astonishing creature. Fuseli agreed.

But Mary's ardor persisted. Throughout the early fall of 1792, she languished, grew sick, even delirious. She revealed her distracted state to Joseph Johnson, writing how in a dream "I imagined [Fuseli] was thrown into great distress by his folly; and I, unable to assist him, was in an agony. . . . We must each of us wear a fool's cap; but mine, alas! has lost its bells, and is grown so heavy, I find it intolerably troublesome.—Good-night! I have been pursuing a number of strange thoughts since I began to write, and have actually both wept and laughed immoderately— Surely I am a fool—Mary W."[54]

The weeping and laughing were reminiscent of Eliza Bishop's breakdown, and the idea that Fuseli was in agony was delusional indeed. Fuseli got on with his paintings and his friendships, ignoring Mary's heartbreak. Even Joseph Johnson's sympathy wavered. He didn't visit, "though you perceived that I was ill," Mary chastised her trusted friend, who'd written a note that, she complained, "hurt me." Doubtless, Johnson had counseled Mary to give up her useless and embarrassing love.[55]

And she did recover somewhat, for by October 1792, Mary was able to make arrangements for Charles to precede the procrastinating Joel Barlow to a farm in America and for young Ann, now decidedly a nuisance, to move back to her Irish kin. Mary found a possible situation for Eliza with a French family and planned a six-week trip to Paris for herself. Joseph Johnson would pay her costs and publish whatever she saw fit to say about the Revolution. Chiefly, he hoped she'd recover her peace of mind.

In a November 12 letter to William Roscoe, Mary officially gave up Fuseli:

I intend no longer to struggle with a rational desire, so have determined to set out for Paris in the course of a fortnight or three weeks; and I shall not now halt at Dover, I promise you; for as I go alone neck or nothing is the word.

And while the British government scaldingly denounced the French Revolution, Mary begged Roscoe "not to mix with the shallow herd who throw an odium on immutable principles, because some of the mere instrument of the revolution were too sharp.— Children of any growth will do mischief when they meddle with edged tools. It is to be lamented that *as yet* the billows of public opinion are only to be moved forward by the strong wind, the squally gusts of passion; but if nations be educated by their governments it is vain to expect much reason till the system of education becomes more reasonable."[56] She for one would continue to promote that glorious endeavor. She would journey to the scene of the battle and join the fight for a better world.

CHAPTER SIX

*H*er first morning in Paris, Mary woke up at 22 Rue Meslée[1] in a spacious apartment with black wrought-iron terraces and
swinging French windows. The Rue Meslée was in the Marais district.
Less than a mile from Mary's door stood Place des Vosges, the oldest
square in Paris, with its thirty-six majestic stone and brick houses,
their slate roofs sloped like the thatched roofs of English cottages. In
Paris, as opposed to London, Mary would soon discover, the nicest
buildings did not have flattened roofs.

And today those gracious homes and the peaceful square remain
almost as they were in December of 1792, as do parts of the stone
ground floor of Mary's apartment; though the upper stories have
been reconstructed. The residences—then called *hôtels*—on her street
are now interspersed with bars and fabric shops and designer-clothes
outlets. Then as now, the Rue Meslée ran straight and narrow, widening into the Rue du Temple. Not far down that boulevard, Citizen
Capet, the former Louis XVI, sat awaiting trial for treason in the dour
gray Temple with its storybook conical towers. The Knights Templar
asserted their independence from the *ancien régime* and its edicts and

taxes by building this medieval fortress. But Louis had been chased here. He was a prisoner of the new order, or the general will, of France, depending on how you saw it. His upcoming appearance before the National Convention was all the talk of Paris that Christmas week.

And Mary was eager to join in the discussion, only she was tongue-tied. What French she knew came from translating books; she blanched at the "flying sounds" of the spoken language[2] and all the whizzing ideas. "In France . . . new opinions fly from mouth to mouth, with an electrical velocity, unknown in England," she would write a year later in her book on the French Revolution.[3]

By then, she would know more about the French *mentalité*. Now, though, Mary Wollstonecraft was very much the Englishwoman abroad. She'd caught a "violent" cold on the long journey from London and was coughing madly when at last she drew up to the Rue Meslée *hôtel* of her sisters' friend Aline Filliettaz. Aline was the daughter of Mrs. Bregantz, mistress of the Putney boarding school where Eliza and Everina had taught. Aline had recently married a Frenchman and invited Mary to stay in their Paris home, but then some event called the couple out of town the week Mary arrived. Aline instructed her servants to indulge their guest, and the servants smiled and bustled about and seemed eager to accommodate her. So Mary was perplexed, she wrote Everina, that one "quick" maid in particular frequently ignored her simplest requests, and when Mary questioned her, the girl talked so abstrusely, yet self-confidently, that Mary wound up pretending to be pleased.[4] Her intention, she told Everina, was to spare the servant embarrassment, but it's clear the usually unflappable Mary was flustered by this wily, exuberant *jeune fille*.

"I apply so closely to the language, and labour so continually to understand what I hear that I never go to bed without a head ache," she wrote Everina the day before Christmas. She'd also exerted herself trying to make sense of the new landscape, where she saw so much less brick, so many fewer parks and benches than in London; the houses were crowded together and higher than London houses, with more terraces and shuttered windows, which were really snugly linked doors. What beautiful buildings, thought Mary: "Proportion and harmony gratify the sight."[5] And yet it was a walled city. There was stone piled seventeen feet high separating the capital from the nearest suburb. And it was all very well to know the wall had been built to stop tax evaders from smuggling produce *into* Paris. But witness the king—it could prevent your going out just as well.

The "striking contrast" between "urbanity and deceit," rich and poor, saddened her. Despite a flurry of construction in the wealthy faubourgs, the poor, trapped in the center of Paris, were crushed together in stunted run-down buildings on tortuous filthy streets. Parisians were superficial and complacent, "buoyed up by animal spirits," and not the likeliest people on earth to appreciate liberty,[6] Mary felt. The social classes did not mix. Yet, Mary watched them mingle at the teeming Palais Royale, a huge funfair seated between the dignified Tuileries and the scurrilous Pont Neuf—a haven for thieves and hawkers. A creation of the king's cousin the Duc d'Orléans, the Palais Royale was the embodiment of democracy, Mary thought. It was like a miniature Paris, with arcades and promenades, lace stores, elegant cafés, and circus acts as well as orators on chairs prophesying a golden age of liberty, prostitutes seducing lurking patriots, and shopkeepers offering every one of the myriad French pamphlets and newspapers that expressed all conceivable slants on the events of the day. Mary came home from the Palais Royale "warmed with the love of freedom."[7] It could make her forget the enclosing wall and the frequent lash of the tocsin bell, announcing trouble for someone.

Church bells were out of grace with the Convention, which despised the higher clergy as appendages of the monarchy and had begun wondering if religion weren't an enemy of enlightened thought.

Theater, on the other hand, flourished. Love of a good show—the more outlandishly emotional the better—was in the national blood, Mary disapprovingly noted.[8]

French men and women went out together far more than the British. The French language was sinuous and sexual; people of all classes had a physical ease Mary admired. And they dressed with bravado. The rebellious workingmen, or "sans-culottes," strutted about in striped long trousers and red wool cockade "liberty" hats, which some professionals donned as well, though most kept to their stolid ruffled shirts and breeches. And all the while the French fashion industry was dreaming up gowns for balls throughout the Continent. Exquisite mannequins stared out from the ground-floor windows of clothing shops, oblivious to breadlines and constitutions. Needless to say, Mary, scorner of all contrivance, was not beguiled.

And Mary, who loved walking, was appalled by Paris's narrow, winding, dirty streets where you were harassed by splattering, trampling carriages since there were none of London's civilized sidewalks for pedestrians to stroll along. A hundred pedestrians a year were run over by carriages; more were doused by filthy water hurled from windows above the street. This was one of the many barbaric French customs Mary daily discovered; yet, she was caught up by the French vitality. She'd socialized with some Frenchmen at the home of the British expatriate author Helen Maria Williams, whose novel *Julia* Mary had guardedly praised in the *Analytical Review*. Mary now told Everina that she planned to see a lot of Miss Williams because she was kind, though her manners were affected: "Authorship," Mary wryly reflected, "is a heavy weight for female shoulders."[9] Everina and Eliza must have gotten a bitter laugh out of that.

For since the success of *Vindication*, already in its second French printing, authoress Mary Wollstonecraft had become increasingly vain in her sisters' eyes. These two intelligent women still suffered the indignity of governessing, while Mary was paid to expostulate on the great issues of her time. These days, Eliza especially could not mention Mary's name without some rueful or biting comment slipping out. And Mary's pride was the more vexing as there was nothing to be proud of in *Eliza's* life, despite her wit and beauty. In 1792, as Mary took off in a blaze for Paris, Eliza was looking after a young boy in a cold thirteenth-century castle in Pembrokeshire, Wales. Like Mary, Eliza was buoyed by natural beauty: the mossy, overgrown castle gardens in late fall enthralled her. But she despised her crude, narrow-minded employers and all she had seen of the rustic Welsh.

So Eliza was determined to escape to Paris: to gaze at the shopwindows as well as to witness the Revolution, for she loved gaiety. Besides, in France, she imagined meeting "beings that I could love" and, most poignantly, freedom. "Liberty!—" she wrote Everina, "and its attendant Égalité! sounds so pleasing to a poor dependent's ear."[10] Eliza lacked faith that she might affect her destiny, but did, grudgingly, believe that Mary would. And while Mary was pleased with her success, she had not forgotten her siblings. "Every family might also be called a state," she announced in *Vindication*. And by going to France, Mary hoped to change not just the world, but her family's fortune.

Mary made finding a position for Eliza a priority during her early days in Paris. Her first letter home was addressed to Eliza. Her second letter, to Everina, promised, "I shall not leave Paris till I have settled [Eliza] here."[11] This was, of course, not entirely altruistic. Mary thoroughly enjoyed the authority she'd snatched from her no-good older brother. In the state of Wollstonecraft, she'd banished worship of the eldest son.

"Mary is not one who ponders, when she ought to act," Eliza noted approvingly.[12] Mary was an effective person who enjoyed wielding power, but she also enjoyed doing good. With her influence and money when she had it, she looked out not just for her sisters but for James and Charles and her father, who was now—according to

Eliza—"*constantly convulsed* by ill humour, and every unamiable feeling that can be expressed."[13] Mary Wollstonecraft's books are filled with depressed characters cheered by helping others, not to mention bossing them around a bit. And while she disparaged the skewed balance of power in the current British family, she never questioned that it was better to operate as a family than as a free agent, any more than she questioned the necessity of government. She was not an anarchist. The idea of the citizens of France rising up together to demand their liberty appealed to her sense of community, as well as her sense of justice. She wanted to believe in a Golden Age when all checks and balances would be internal, when what was good for the citizen was good for the state, just as what was good for her was good for Eliza.

So like most loyal French citizens, she embraced Rousseau's utopian aspirations. They would be tested as she watched one of the great family dramas of all time, the trial of Louis XVI. Louis was accused of betraying France—of attempting to flee the country and, worse, conspiring with the Austrians to defeat the French in the war the Convention was now waging "to spread revolution" throughout Europe. Louis was also accused of such travesties as gaping at "orgies" where the patriotic tricolored ribbons were trampled and the nation gleefully blasphemed.[14] However bemusing this last accusation, Louis was certainly guilty of fleeing as far as Varennes and conspiring with the Austrians. And yet the real issue was not the king's culpability but whether it was a crime to be king. On this point, as with all moral issues, Rousseau's *Social Contract* was studied for answers.

As everyone knew, this essay called for liberty, equality, and rule by the general will. But what constituted the general will, and how should it get what it wanted? Through murdering nobles and priests? Through planting liberty trees? Through sober debate? It was hard to discern from Rousseau's book. *The Social Contract* was full of freighted words like "the homeland" and "public safety" and syllogisms that invited misreadings. At one point, it seems to advocate the death penalty, heatedly asserting: "Every malefactor who attacks the social right becomes through his transgressions a . . . traitor to the homeland. . . . Thus one of the two must perish." But a couple of paragraphs down, Rousseau is musing: "There is no wicked man who could not be made good for something. One has the right to put to death, even as an example, only someone who cannot be preserved without danger."[15] And *The Social Contract* also has its share of surprisingly unambiguous statements—such as that there are people for whom the best ruler is a king.[16]

Mary Wollstonecraft revered Rousseau, but was lucid about his shortcomings. In *Vindication*, she had mocked *Émile*'s "angel in the house" wife, Sophy, who is educated exclusively for the pleasure of her man. "The *divine right* of husbands like the divine right of kings, may, it is to be hoped, in this enlightened age, be contested without danger."[17]

Yet, Mary sensed danger now, the day after Christmas, waiting for the divine rights of Louis XVI to be contested by the French. Louis was to confront his accusers at the Manège, a former royal riding school at the north end of the Tuileries, where the current Convention (elected September 11) met. Of its 749 deputies, nearly half were lawyers—including the moralistic extremist Maximilien Robespierre and his eloquent, pockmarked, blatantly corrupt friend Georges-Jacques Danton. A third of the delegates had served in earlier Conventions.[18] But there were newcomers too, like the British Thomas Paine, whose famous attack on Burke in *The Rights of Man* had earned him honorary citizenship in France and a treason charge in England. Indeed, as he prepared to vote on the fate of the king, Paine himself, Eliza Bishop reported to Everina, was being burned in effigy in Pembrokeshire; and there was talk of "immortalizing" the almost equally notorious "[Mary] Wollstonecraft in the like manner."[19]

Thomas Paine sat in the middle of the Manège with the moderate

Girondists, most of whom wanted the king out of the picture but not guillotined. Above them were the more extreme "Mountain," or Jacobin, deputies—including Robespierre and Danton—who insisted the sovereign republic demanded Louis's head. Personal antagonisms were building among these legislators, below whom sat the "Plain," or undecided, deputies: it was they who would swing the vote in the end.

Early on the morning of December 26, the king began his journey from the Temple prison to the Manège. About nine o'clock, he "passed by my window," Mary begins her memorable description of the scene in a letter to Joseph Johnson,

> moving silently along (excepting now and then a few strokes on the drum, which rendered the stillness more awful) through empty streets, surrounded by the national guards, who, clustering round the carriage, seemed to deserve their name. The inhabitants flocked to their windows, but the casements were all shut, not a voice was heard, nor did I see anything like an insulting gesture.— For the first time since I entered France, I bowed to the majesty of the people and respected the propriety of behaviour so perfectly in unison with my own feelings. I can scarcely tell you why, but an association of ideas made the tears flow insensibly from my eyes, when I saw Louis sitting, with more dignity than I expected from his character, in a hackney coach going to meet death, where so many of his race have triumphed. My fancy instantly brought Louis XIV before me, entering the capital with all his pomp, after one of the victories most flattering to his pride, only to see the sunshine of prosperity overshadowed by the sublime gloom of misery.[20]

This "gloom of misery" speaks to the beleaguered state of Paris under the rule of a self-serving monarch. But the gloom is "sublime," suggesting an unexpected nostalgia on Mary's part. Her emotions surprise her. Standing alone at the window of the Filliettaz apartment, she is moved to tears by the physical presence of Louis XVI and thoughts of fickle history. Already, she imagines the king condemned to die.

In fact, the first day of Louis XVI's trial went reasonably well for him. His youngest lawyer, Romain de Seze, argued that the king's only conceivable crime was being king, and if being king was a crime, the people were responsible since it was they who had crowned him at Reims seventeen years before. Now the king's power was gone. "*Vous avez certainement toute la puissance nationale,*" de Seze flattered the delegates, "*mais la puissance que vous n'avez pas, c'est celle de n'être pas justes.*" ("You certainly have all the national power; the only power you don't have is the power to be unjust.") Louis was misguided but well meaning, de Seze continued. He had the same goal as the Convention—a more just France. And even supposing that Louis had strategized with the Austrians: that had been on his wicked ministers' bad advice.

"*Le peuple a voulu la liberté et Louis lui a donnée*" ("The people wanted liberty, and Louis gave it to them"), de Seze arrogantly announced in an off-guard moment, infuriating the delegates, who took a three-hour break after his speech finished and then began their debate.[21] Predictably, the Jacobins found the king guilty and wanted him guillotined, while the Girondists shrewdly invoked—who else?—Rousseau and clamored for a national plebescite, so they could deflect responsibility onto the "general will."

Both the Jacobins and the Girondists, Mary could see, loathed the monarchy. But they were divided by very different superstitions and myths. If you reversed Mary's metaphor and saw the state as a family, then the Jacobins wanted to ritually slay the father and seize his power,[22] while the Girondists wanted the power without the crime.

The night after this first day of the trial, Mary was haunted by "lively images," she told Joseph Johnson:

Nay, do not smile, but pity me; for, once or twice, lifting my eyes from the paper, I have seen eyes glare through a glass-door opposite my chair, and bloody hands shook at me. Not the distant sound of a footstep can I hear. My apartments are remote from those of the servants, the only persons who sleep with me in an immense hotel, one folding door opening after another.— I wish I had even kept the cat with me!— I want to see something alive; death in so many frightful shapes has taken hold of my fancy.— I am going to bed—and for the first time in my life, I cannot put out the candle.[23]

The helplessness of the king and Mary's being all by herself in a strange house and country inspired this torrent of horror-tale pictures. For all her staunch ideas, she feared for Louis, and also for France, where, more and more, fear and violence prevailed over reason. Authorities now opened private mail. So Mary cautiously wrote Eliza, a month after she arrived in Paris, that she had no "reason to alter the opinion which I formed of the French from reading their history and memoirs."[24] But her actions suggest the opposite. For Mary, being in France was as different from reading about France as the real Revolution was from her portrait of it in *The Rights of Men.* Gone were the bold certainties Mary had formerly touted. She was confused but also invigorated by the contradictions she beheld every day. Mary wrote a letter to Henry Fuseli asking him to correspond with her, but did not pine at home when he failed to reply. She was an attractive woman in her early thirties. She began going out on her own.

. . .

IT WAS AN EXCITING time to be a woman in Paris. Unlike the British, most Frenchwomen did *not* retire after dinner. Nor were they expected to repine all day in the nursery while their husbands read Latin and Greek. Far more than in London, adultery was condoned for unhappy wives as well as husbands, and women were encouraged to seek solace in talk.

Since the turn of the sixteenth century, female aristocrats had hosted salons where men and women conversed freely on all topics, including politics and religion, which the English bluestockings spurned. Of course, formal study eluded women in France as well as England, but courtship in France was spiced by intellectual discourse, so men went out of their way to teach women ideas. Visiting France in the late 1780s, the British writer Arthur Young was surprised to see "persons of the highest rank pay an attention to science and literature."[25] In London, nobles socialized exclusively with nobles. In Paris, intellectuals held their own at a wide range of salons—including Madame de Staël's swank Thursday night dinners, which created the aura of "the temple of Apollo,"[26] according to one guest.

Madame de Staël's dinners took place on the Rue du Bac at the Swedish embassy, for she was the flagrantly unfaithful wife of the Swedish ambassador to France. Daughter of the Swiss economist Jacques Necker (whose *Opinions Religeuses* Mary had translated), she'd conversed knowledgeably since childhood and at thirty-two published a first philosophical essay on Rousseau that had begun her vaunted career. In the fall of 1792, de Staël was a heavyset thirty-eight-year-old woman with masculine features. But she flirted like a young girl and exuded confidence in her power to seduce men. Artists, playwrights, and politicians flocked to her salon. She'd had an affair with Talleyrand (to whom Mary had addressed *Vindication*), and she was carrying the child of her current aristocratic lover, the Comte de Narbonne, the fall Mary arrived in France. Though ambitious for herself, Madame de Staël scoffed at prominence for women in general. "It is right to exclude women from public affairs. Nothing is more opposed to their natural vocation than a relationship of rivalry with men."[27]

Across the Seine, in a lavish salon near the Louvre, the Marquise de Condorcet advanced more progressive ideas. Her husband, the Marquis de Condorcet, had gone further even than *Vindication* and declared that women deserved to vote. "Isn't it because he is a sensitive being, capable of reason and morality, that man has his rights? Women should have absolutely the same rights, and yet never, in any so-called free constitution, have women exercised the rights of citizens."[28]

Still, as Condorcet well knew, women's rights had expanded considerably in France since the start of the Revolution. According to the decree of April 8, 1791, daughters could inherit property, and four months before Mary arrived in Paris, the French legalized divorce, granting women custody of their children in most cases, while both parents were required to pay support. Now Condorcet had been commissioned by the Convention to devise a plan to educate the masses. What he had in mind involved free mingling of the sexes as described in *Vindication* and practiced at his wife's salon.

The wife of Minister of the Interior Jean-Marie Roland, on the other hand, forbade women even to appear at her salon because she believed females were innately inferior; though like Madame de Staël, Manon Roland had a high opinion of herself. Unlike de Staël, she scorned flirts and ostentation. She was an artisan's daughter with an abiding mistrust of wealth. (It is possible, though unlikely, that Mary and Manon Roland met through their mutual friend Helen Maria Williams.)[29] Visiting Versailles as a child, Manon had been sent to sleep in servants' quarters; she never forgot her humiliation and resentment of the high-living queen. Priding herself on the virtues *Vindication* championed, Manon Roland refused to leave the husband she merely respected for the man she adored (François Buzot). The Revolution and her husband's career were inseparable in her eyes. When in December 1792 the Convention falsely accused Roland of corruption, it was Manon who composed the elegant speeches he delivered in his defense. She also wrote hundreds of letters to newspapers arguing the Girondist cause—always anonymously. For a woman's ideas were demeaned by her public signature, Manon felt, just as her womanhood was diminished by worldly ambitions. Twice a week, she hosted dinners for Roland's colleagues where she remained vigilantly silent and like Joseph Johnson served only simple food. She was a poor engraver's daughter, a true republican.

And her Rue de la Harpe salon, a few blocks from the Sorbonne, far more than Madame de Staël's or the Marquise de Condorcet's, reflected the spirit of the new revolutionary clubs that since 1788 had been sprouting up in Paris: the Society of the Thirty, committed to "war" on privilege;[30] Robespierre's radical Jacobins Club; and the even more radical Cordeliers. The first mixed-sex club, Confédération des Amis de la Vérité, opened in 1790. Its aims were to banish primogeniture, reconceive academia, free slaves, and grant women equal rights. Important Girondists like Condorcet and Jean-Marie Roland gathered Friday nights in the Palais Royal to hear the club's weekly speeches.

One Friday, a Dutch baroness named Etta Palm d'Aelders spoke movingly about the horrors of domestic violence. Her cause was the improvement of everyday life. Little is known of Etta Palm's own life, except that in 1774 she emigrated from Holland to Paris, where she lived on a comfortable income and later was accused of spying for the Dutch. (The truth of this accusation has never been ascertained.) In 1791, Etta Palm received an audience with the Convention at which she defended citizenship for women. Later she presided over a small woman's club dedicated to charitable work.

Charity held little appeal for another powerful spokeswoman, Olympe de Gouges, who founded the Club des Tricoteuses to promote her exalted schemes. Born Marie Gouze to a butcher's wife in Languedoc, she insisted her real father was a poet and an aristocrat, and at eighteen she left a tedious marriage to travel to Paris, where love affairs with prominent men brought her knowledge and wealth. In her thirties, she began writing plays and radical tracts—or rather dictating them, because she was illiterate. Some laughed at her awkward phrases; others—like influential Mirabeau—lauded her radically feminist views.[31] "Ignorance, forgetfulness or misunderstanding of the rights of woman are the only causes of public misfortune and the corruption of governments," she declared.[32]

Equally audacious in her own way was dramatic Théroigne de Mericourt, who sported Grecian robes and a red riding costume, set off by a feather and festooned with pistols at the waist. An unsuccessful singer, she studied politics, sitting quietly at the Convention all day, and she founded the Club des Amis de la Loi, urging the opposite of Madame de Staël. "Why," she demanded, "should [women] not compete with men. . . . We too wish to gain a civic crown and gain the right to die for liberty, a liberty perhaps dearer to us since our sufferings under despotism have been greater."[33]

Allying herself with the poor, de Mericourt joined the militant women of Paris who marched on Versailles the October after the fall of the Bastille. Their complaint was a bread shortage following a good harvest. They suspected Louis *wanted* Paris to starve. So 6,000 well-armed females walked six hours through the rain to chase down the terrified king and queen and drive them back to the capital. More than any of the clubs or salons, they achieved their goal.[34]

Ultimately, Mary Wollstonecraft would condemn the October

march for its violence. Now, though, she kept an open mind about all political tactics, though the many friends she made were almost exclusively moderate Girondists, including the delegates Isnard and Servan, the expatriate Swedish Count von Schlabrendorf, and the British "Young" Johnson, who idolized Thomas Paine. Swiss Mrs. Schweizer, who'd once flirted with Fuseli, was Mary's "favorite," she told Eliza;[35] Mr. Schweizer loved hearing Mary lament the great man's faults.[36]

Girondist expatriates tended to gather at White's Hotel, where Mary found Thomas Christie, who'd left the *Analytical Review* for the moment and was representing the English Thurball Forbes & Company, which supplied flour to the French. It was through Christie's firm that Joseph Johnson sent Mary money to support herself, and Christie frequently invited Mary to his dinners, where she established a close friendship with Rebecca, his new wife.

Rebecca Christie was good company but had no literary qualifications, while the bluestocking Helen Maria Williams had been among the first English writers to witness and analyze the Revolution in France. Three years younger than Mary, Williams was plump, with long ringlets, an emotional, flirtatious air, and lots of published books. Williams was best known for her sentimental political verses and two volumes of letters from France; the prose was by turns gushing and incisive. On the king's acceptance of the 1792 Constitution, Williams effuses: "living in France at present appears to me somewhat like living in a region of romance."[37] But she was shrewd about French pretensions and sexual mores. Williams herself was living openly with the married English businessman John Hurford Stone, which might have shocked Mary a few years before. "Miss Williams has behaved very civilly to me and I shall visit her frequently because I *rather* like her. . . . Her manners are affected, yet the *simple* goodness of her heart continually breaks through the varnish, so that one would be more inclined, at least I should, to love than admire her," Mary wrote Everina.[38]

ON JANUARY 15, 1793, the Convention by a large margin voted King Louis XVI guilty of betraying his country. The Girondists lost their appeal for a national plebiscite by 141 votes. What remained was to decide on Louis's punishment. At 8 P.M., the delegates began parading to the dais to cast their open votes. All through the night, the voting continued. The result was close, but a majority favored unconditional death.

It was now that Thomas Paine came up with his idea of exiling Louis to America, which was generally ignored, though the Mountain would later hold it against him. More popular was the motion for a *sursis,* or the suspension of the king's death sentence until some happy day when the war was over and/or the new Constitution ratified. This was a hard call, in Condorcet's judgment. (He would ultimately vote *"Je n'ai pas de voix,"* "I have no voice.")[39] If Louis were executed immediately, he predicted, France would be accused of "inhumanity" and "cannibalism." These allegations could be proved false, however, if France subsequently abolished capital punishment, instituted merciful and just laws, and enlightened the world.[40]

Mary had recently been appointed to assist Condorcet's Commission on Education. She, Catharine Macaulay, and Condorcet were the foremost educational theorists during the late eighteenth century, and history would link them—though their daily lives were far apart. On January 20, while Condorcet was at the Convention deciding whether or not to postpone the execution of the king, Mary sat in her room at the Filliettazes', writing a letter to her sister Eliza, who was governessing at Upton Castle in Wales.

"I have put off writing to you day after day, because I waited till I cd write in a satisfactory manner, but I have met with several disappointments with respect to you, yet, do not despair, nay, I repeat the promise, which I made to Everina, I will not leave P. till you are settled, so let the hope, or rather the moral certainty, keep you warm this cold weather [no period]." This run-on opening sentence betrays Mary's agitation on the day that would decide not just the king's fate but the likelihood of war between France and England and thus her own safety in a foreign land. Only once does she openly refer to "the unsettled state of public affairs," but she embeds a clue about the prevailing censorship in a seemingly innocuous sentence concerning their brother James: "were he once a [lieutenant] he would have an annuity for life I can only now write about family affairs."[41] The king's trial was, of course, a "family affair" she could not write about, though she seems to be contemplating it when she urges Eliza to forget some hurtful incident and remember only pleasure "to keep you from almost hating your fellow [creatures]."[42] *As I almost hate the French*, she must have longed to add, but she turned to the cheerier topic of her hosts' return.

It is an odd coincidence that, unaware of Mary's letter, Eliza on the very same day wrote Everina: "I am weary of expecting a letter from France. . . . Indeed I am now in that kind of painful suspense that is hardly to be described—[wishing] for a letter, yet afraid it will . . . crush the something like hope that now keeps me alive—though [it is] often damped by the cry of *war* and the horrid Butcheries that are hourly committed in Paris[.] I fear not their knives and would rather dwell in the midst of alarms than reign in this horrible place."[43]

And surely Eliza would have preferred danger to her stultifying safety in a position as distant from Mary's as Mary's was from Condorcet's. Better to be stabbed in dirty Paris than waste away in beautiful Wales, she thought. She may have gone to the pleasant little Romanesque Upton chapel, snuggled in the winter garden, and thought of her mean or feckless brothers and her dear sister Everina, heading off now to yet another dependent position in Dublin, and their dead mother, and the father living an hour from Upton Castle in a "comfortless dwelling"[44] in pretty Laugharne, where he was probably haranguing his beleaguered second wife or maybe just staring at the old castle by the sea.

Meanwhile, at the Convention in Paris, three fervid weeks of debate were drawing to a close. By seventy votes, the appeal for a suspended sentence was quashed. A delegation was sent to take the news to the royal family at the Temple prison. Louis would perish not in some arcadian future when reason and justice had triumphed, but the next morning at 10 A.M.

CHAPTER SEVEN

No one in Paris ventured far from home the foggy morning of January 21. You could hear the barrier gates snap closed and see guards flooding the narrow streets looking for outbreaks for or against the condemned monarch. Windows were ordered shuttered. At the Temple, Louis woke at dawn, heard mass, was confessed, and at eight o'clock requested that his hair be shorn to avoid humiliation at the scaffold. But the request was refused, and he went out with all his hair and, in the company of his confessor, boarded a coach for the two-hour ride through Paris, a city he had never liked. To pass the time, he read David's Psalms and the prayers of the dying, while he could still occasionally spot through the window posters proclaiming that he was a good man.

At 10 A.M., he arrived at the Place de la Révolution.[1] Thousands of eyes peered as Louis removed his own suit and collar and stood at the foot of the scaffold in a simple white flannel gown. It was the issue of the hair that set him off: he would be barbered before the crowd, like every common criminal, Louis was informed. He seemed about to break down when the priest took him aside and reminded him of Christ's suffering.

Calmer then, Louis mounted the scaffold with dignity, "his face very red," the weekly *Révolutions de Paris* reported. Drums were beating. For a moment Louis gazed about him, then asked for silence so he could speak. Some in the crowd protested. "Do your work!" they exhorted the executioners. But in this the king prevailed, and, while his body was being strapped, Louis clearly articulated that he died innocent, that he pardoned his enemies and hoped that no more blood would be exacted from the people of France.

At ten after ten, the huge blade of the guillotine descended. The thirty-nine-year-old monarch became a body separated from a head. Over the past half-decade, so much had been projected upon this unremarkable creature. He'd been the good father, congregating the Estates-General; the hypocrite, conspiring with the Austrians and the priests; the reluctant constitutional monarch; the traitor, the epitome of all that was rotten in the state of France. And now he was the ghoulish head the deft executioner brandished for the delectation of the crowd, who were shouting, *"Vive la république!"* as if all their problems were over.

People rushed for souvenirs: a piece of the white robe, a thread of hair. One man mounted the scaffold and plunged his entire arm in Louis's blood, which he sprinkled down on his comrades, informing them that a king's blood brought luck. There were embraces, speeches, prophecies about the future, and, as Louis's remains were transported in a cart to the cemetery, a seeming normalcy returned. "The milkwoman sold her milk, the soldiers carried their vegetables and with their usual gaity sang couplets about a guillotined king."[2]

To read the contemporary French reports, it all sounds like business as usual. Only businessmen all over the world were up in arms about Louis's death. The death of one monarch threatened all monarchies. So while the milkwomen were selling their milk in Paris, the English stock exchange closed, the London *Times* filled with notices of parties canceled in Louis's honor, and English troops gathered,[3] knowing that George III—who canceled all his plans and went into mourning—would imminently declare war.

British journalists declared a war of words on everything French—except Louis, whom they eulogized so extravagantly it infuriated Eliza Bishop, who was relieved to read the Whig leader Charles James Fox's opposition speech defending the Revolution. Still, Eliza was unsure where she herself stood. What do you think of the death of the French king? she asked Everina and admitted, "I own I was shocked, but not deluged in tears. In short I . . . hoped they had some motive for such an act of cruelty that our newspapers did not explain."[4]

It was early February before Mary even dared to allude to Louis's execution in a letter to her American friend Ruth Barlow: "I will not now advert to public news excepting to tell you that the new constitution will soon make its appearance, and that Paris has remained perfectly tranquil ever since the death of the King. All the affection I have for the French is for the whole nation, and it seems to be a little honey spread over all the bread I eat in their land."[5] She then trotted out some of her favorite complaints—that the weather was bad, the Paris streets were unfit to walk on, and the vitality of the French people was exhausting for any Anglo-Saxon with sense.

More lashing were Mary's comments in the first and only "letter" she wrote for what was intended to become an epistolary volume:

Before I came to France, I cherished, you know, an opinion, that strong virtues might exist with the polished manners produced by the progress of civilisation; and I even anticipated the epoch, when, in the course of improvement, men would labour to become virtuous, without being goaded on by misery. But now, the perspective of the golden age, fading before the attentive eye of observation, almost alludes my sight; and losing thus in part my theory of a more perfect state, start not, my friend, if I bring forward an opinion, which at the first glance seems to be levelled against the existence of God! I am not become an Atheist, I assure you, by residing in Paris; yet I begin to fear that vice, or, if you will, evil, is the grand mobile of action, and that, when the passions are justly poized, we become harmless, and in the same proportion useless.[6]

She goes on to add that even "the desire . . . of being useful to others is continually damped by experience," and that the leaders at the Convention are only monarchs with different names.

Writing to Everina, Eliza hypothesizes that Mary's bleakness has been triggered by events in her personal life: "I am convinced M. has met with some great disappointment lately—her letters are not in the same strain as when she was in London."[7] In other words, maybe Mary was projecting her loneliness and unrequited love for Fuseli onto events in the larger world. But, more probably, Mary—with her commitment to history—invested public life with private passion and cared on a deeply personal level about the death of Louis XVI. As the French say, she was *désolée.* She was also angry, which brought out her cynical side. But Mary Wollstonecraft could not have been quite as despairing as she seemed, for why then did she not leave Paris and go home to London, with its civilized pavements and vaunted common sense?

"Yesterday a Gentleman offered me a place in his carriage to return to England and I knew not how to say no," Mary wrote Ruth Barlow, "yet I think it would be foolish to return when I have been at so much trouble to master [the French language], when I am just turning the corner, and I am besides, writing a plan of education [for Condorcet's committee at the Convention]."[8] The impulse for self-improvement and her hope of changing the world kept Mary in Paris, she tells Ruth Barlow, though she also notes that a man "to whom I frequently replied, oui, oui, when my thoughts were far away, told me that I was acquiring in France a bad custom, for that I might chance to say oui, when I did not intend it PAR HABI- TUDE." And she surprised Eliza by declaring, "those who wish to live for themselves . . . ought to live in Paris for they have the pleas- antest way of whiling away time. . . ."[9]

DURING THE SPRING of 1793, Joel Barlow was one of those living for himself in Paris. He had spent most of the fall and winter trying to get elected to the French Convention from the Savoy district. So he was out of town when Mary arrived at the Rue Meslée in mid- December, when the king was beheaded, and on January 31, when England declared war on France. He was still in the Savoy when the new French Constitution was unveiled on February 15, 1793, and two days later, when he was officially named a citizen of France. Joel lost the election in the Savoy and returned to Paris in late February, as the rift between the Girondists and the Jacobins was widening. On March 6, he met up with Mary, who handed him a letter from Ruth she'd been carrying since December, and during the following weeks, at White's Hotel or the Christies' parties, Joel confided in Mary his various plans to get his wife through wartime waters so she could join him in France. After France declared war on Spain on March 7, Barlow joined a group pushing for the French to wrest back their former colony Louisiana from the Spaniards. The power- ful Girondist delegate and editor J.-P. Brissot supported this enter- prise, as did a young man named Gilbert Imlay, soon to be the love of Mary's life.

. . .

WHAT LITTLE WE know of Gilbert Imlay is that he was American, born about three years before Mary,[10] and raised in Monmouth County, New Jersey, in a town bearing his family name: Imlaystown. Patrick Imlay, Gilbert's great-grandfather, was the first Imlay to settle in Monmouth. He was a wealthy Protestant from the Aberdeenshire Highlands of Scotland. The name Imlay is a variation on the Gaelic clan name Ianla. Gilbert, also a common Scottish surname, means "bright pledge."

Then as now, Imlaystown was a crescent of pretty houses leading to a creek with a mill and a hillock. Beyond lay miles of flat, arable farmland, including the grand plantation Patrick Imlay bought in his middle years. His will ceded a hundred acres to Gilbert's father, who raised his two boys and a daughter there—eight miles from prospering Allentown, New Jersey, and about forty miles from the coast. To the north was New York, where Gilbert's cousin William would open an import store and become a socialite, and south was Philadelphia, where his uncle John would make a fortune shipping goods. So while the child Gilbert was immersed in his father's world of plantings and harvests, he must also have dreamed of travel and money and boats.

In 1776, Gilbert's older brother Robert and his cousins Isaac and David rushed to join the American Revolution, while cousin William, off in New York importing foreign merchandise, was suspected of sympathizing with the British and thrown into jail. Monmouth contained more Royalists than any other county in New Jersey, and it's possible Imlay himself equivocated about the Revolution, because he did not enlist until January 11, 1777, at which point he joined Colonel David Forman's regiment as first lieutenant. By then, he was patriotic enough to sign on for the duration of the war. And yet, he obviously sympathized with cousin William and all the others punished for their British loyalties. For he petitioned the New Jersey governor to release eleven Monmouth citizens, arrested for treason, whom he'd convinced to join the rebel cause.[11]

Imlay's April 1777 petition, neatly preserved among the New Jersey war records, provides a glimpse of Mary Wollstonecraft's great love at twenty. How plucky he seems, and righteous and loyal both to the theory of American independence and to those wayward boys from Monmouth. There's a hint of bumptiousness in his marching off to redeem the errant. And he appears to have been a successful negotiator, for six weeks after his petition, on May 22, 1777, seven of the eleven prisoners were pardoned and delivered to Imlay's company. (The four others had changed their minds and refused to fight.)

Imlay was wounded and "omitted" from his regiment in July 1778, shortly after the long Battle of Monmouth.[12] He never reinlisted, nor was he promoted from first lieutenant, though now and for the rest of his life he called himself Captain—whether out of insecurity or ambition is uncertain—his first deviousness as far as we know. At the end of the Revolution, Imlay, now in his late twenties, joined the thousands heading west to Kentucky. He was handsome and impetuous, with a keen eye for soil and climate and, even without the "Captain," a respected name. Daniel Boone lent Imlay 2,000 pounds to purchase his first tract of Kentucky farmland, in 1783.[13] For the next two years he continued borrowing and buying, and in April 1785, was appointed deputy surveyor, an honorable position. Less honorably, he was accumulating large debts.[14]

In the fall of 1785, Imlay, borrowing again, became partner in an ironworks project. The idea was that industry could coexist with agriculture and Indian wars, and the plan was audacious, but the partners couldn't pull it off. Imlay gave up almost immediately and headed down Daniel Boone's Wilderness Road, back to Virginia. His last official action in America was to repay part of an old debt on December 3, 1786.[15] Four years afterward, he was still being chased by a creditor named Isaac Hite, who called him "Deft Imlay"[16] and felt sure he'd left the country and gone abroad.

Either Hite was right or Imlay was in hiding, for the American courts posted notices and ran advertisements trying to track him down for years, to no avail. Between the winter of 1786 and the summer of 1792, while his married brother Robert became a successful merchant with his firm Imlay & Potts in Philadelphia, Gilbert vanished from record. And when he reemerged, it was as an author. He had written a book called *A Topographical Description of the Western Territory of North America,* published in the summer of 1792 in London, where apparently he'd been settled for some time.

Imlay's first book is a series of letters addressed from a Kentucky settler to a friend in England. It mingles nature writing with philosophical ruminations, rather like Helen Maria Williams's travel books on France. And like a travel book, it is full of discoveries. Here, for instance, Imlay enthuses about a strip of land called Limestone:

> You ascend a considerable distance from the shore of the Ohio, and when you would suppose you had arrived at the summit of a mountain, you find yourself upon an extensive level. Here an eternal verdure reigns, and the brilliant sun of lat. 39 degrees, piercing through the azure heavens, produces, in this prolific soil, an early maturity which is truly astonishing. . . ."[17]

Imlay's writing is propelled by emotion, his grammar is frequently tortured, but a fine intelligence shows through. And the book does much more than gush about vistas. It offers an extensive list of native crops and minerals, discourses knowledgeably on the soil and the fauna, and points out minute variations in climate from one district to the next. Imlay recommends certain authors who've written on related topics and contradicts others, such as Thomas Jefferson, who in Imlay's opinion overstates the balminess of the Virginia winter.

More intriguingly, Imlay attacks Jefferson's racial prejudice: "We [Americans] have disgraced the fair face of humanity, and trampled upon the sacred privileges of man,"[18] by permitting African slavery. For Imlay, it is obvious that no race is better than another, we are all "essentially the same in shape and intellect."[19] This holds also for the American Indians, whose present impoverished condition Imlay blames on marauding Europeans bent on plying them with liquor. And he speaks up for a woman's right to own and inherit property.[20] (A 1797 revision of the book goes further to insist women should not have to answer to laws they cannot write.)[21]

The Imlay of *A Topographical Description* sounds as bold and enlightened as the Imlay who made loyal patriots of the imprisoned New Jersey draft dodgers—and hardly at all like Imlay the fleeing debtor. Though that face of Imlay does show briefly in a passage defending "poor and unfortunate debtors" as victims of the economy and even their creditors, who "ought to be made cautious in their security"; otherwise they deserve to lose their loans.[22]

While in England, Imlay met none of Johnson's "standing dishes," but he did befriend a Manchester radical named Thomas Cooper, who early in the spring of 1793 recommended him to Brissot and Joel Barlow for their Louisiana scheme.[23] Imlay arrived in Paris in March 1793 and immediately got to work.

He also began socializing with Barlow and all the English Girondists. The Girondists had been increasingly marginalized at the Convention since the death of Louis XVI. Their General Dumouriez suffered humiliating defeats trying to "liberate" Belgium and the Rhineland, while peasants in the eastern, Vendée district were defying the Convention at home. Meanwhile, the Treasury ran out of money. The Jacobins blamed a conspiracy, insinuating the Girondists were behind it.[24]

So in the spring of 1793, there was an anxious mood at White's Hotel and at Rebecca Christie's parties. It was at one such party, in early April, that Mary Wollstonecraft and Gilbert Imlay met. She didn't like him, she would later say, giving no explanation. She would say she had gone out of her way to avoid this American captain, with his strong physical presence.

But she could not have resisted Imlay *too* strenuously. He was charming, after all, and a friend of Barlow's. He and Mary shared political convictions. Both, for instance, applauded the current Girondist imperative to oust Robespierre's bloodthirsty ally Marat from the Convention. They were sickened by his unjust accusations, by his fervor to send innocents to the guillotine. They still believed a Golden Age was coming. And right now there was spring; it was Mary's first April in Paris. She was feeling proud and elastic. She was trying out the French language and the French ease.

One of the first things Gilbert told Mary was a lie. He told her he'd grown up in the western territories.[25] He told her truthfully how he loved the American frontier, and soon had her imagining living there with him—like the American captain and the young British girl in the novel Imlay was now finishing. That novel, *The Emigrants*, was about falling in love and starting a new life in a new country. Maybe Imlay felt homesick, writing about the Appalachian Mountains. Maybe he saw married men like Joel Barlow and Thomas Christie and, in his mid-thirties, thought it was time he settled down himself. Or maybe he had no such thoughts as he and Mary exchanged meaningful looks at parties, over dinner tables, at hurried gatherings where everyone was gasping about new atrocities in the streets and in the National Convention. The Paris mobs were calling for the expulsion of the Girondist delegates, and Mary was falling in love. One of Mary's friends noticed that Imlay paid her "more than common attention."[26] By April 19 (so much for first impressions), Joel Barlow was writing Ruth in London that he suspected an affair.[27]

Gilbert confided in Mary about a "cunning" woman who'd hurt him, and she told him all about Fuseli and her former life. One night, she went to Gilbert Imlay's apartment in St-Germain-des-Prés and made love with him. This was not an insignificant event, *Vindication* to the contrary.

Sex, Mary said, was rapture. And it would affect all her future theories. But in the spring of 1793, she was content just to indulge her feelings, the "rosy glow"[28] of her body, her heart "trembling into peace."[29] Imlay's eyes "glisten[ed] with sympathy"; his lips were "softer than soft." He and she both had the "hue of love" about them,[30] and Mary developed a larkish humor, teasing her lover that if he wasn't attentive she would take on other men—like the deformed, ardent, reckless (and safely dead) Mirabeau, whom she felt sure she could whip into shape. At a party one night, a woman bragged to Mary: *"Pour moi, je n'ai pas de tempérament"* ("I am not troubled by passion"). And Mary boasted right back: *"Tant pis pour vous,"* for she reveled in her sexuality. Discussing her views with her new bachelor friend Count von Schlabrendorf, Mary declared that chastity meant fidelity, not abstinence. And while sensual life was crucial, marriage was unnecessary, she continued to proclaim.[31]

THE MEMOIRS OF MARY WOLLSTONECRAFT expatiates on Mary's happiness with Gilbert Imlay:

> [Mary's] whole character seemed to change with a change in fortune. Her sorrows, the depression of her spirits, were forgotten, and she assumed all the simplicity and the vivacity of a youthful mind. She was like a serpent upon a rock, that casts its slough, and appears again with the brilliancy, the sleekness, and the elastic activity of its happiest age. She was playful, full of confidence, kindness and sympathy. Her eyes assumed new lustre, and her cheeks new colour and smoothness. Her voice became cheerful;

her temper overflowing with universal kindness; and that smile of bewitching tenderness from day to day illuminated her countenance. . . . [32]

Mary's passion also gave her a new view of her past life. Her childhood had been not just meaningless suffering, but a struggle for "pleasure, for which I had the most lively taste."[33] She had not been created to suffer. Love could—*would*—face down even the most dire external events.

Mary forgot her reserve and leapt at pleasure, in April and May and June, as the trees exfoliated and the days lengthened. The "noble square" of the Tuileries,[34] the narrow, winding streets of St-Germain, the gleaming white houses of the Marais spread before her. Walking was a joy again. Everywhere were "clustering flowers, with luxuriant pomp"; it was a "fairy scene."[35] Couples were sauntering. She and Imlay sauntered, they talked, they made love in hotel rooms. On cold nights, they read books in front of the fire. Mary's mordant, dissecting letters gave way to bantering notes to Gilbert, and she signed them not "Mary Wollstonecraft" or "M.W.," as she'd always done before, but simply "MARY."

She was also now Mary when she wrote her "poor" sisters—Everina plodding along in Ireland, Eliza wildly unhappy in "this friendless dungeon,"[36] Upton Castle, where everyone, she sighed to Everina, was a Royalist and not a soul spoke French.[37] Eliza herself remained devoted to the French language and Revolution and continued to believe all her problems would finish when she crossed the Channel to France, which would be foolhardy with England and France at war, of course. So Mary dangled an alternative: "I am not apt to give false hopes; yet I will venture to *promise* that brighter days are in store for you. I cannot explain myself excepting just to tell you that I have a plan in my head." Her plan was that Eliza and Everina should accompany herself and Gilbert to America. For now, Mary regretted Eliza's suffering, but could not help noting that *she* was in marvelous health and spirits and, what's more, "writing a great book."[38]

That book was a history of the French Revolution, a mighty subject. But she felt equal to it. She began collecting books on French history and perplexingly divergent accounts of the Revolution's early days.

Meanwhile, all around her, the Revolution's hard-won freedoms were vanishing. On March 12, 1793, J.-P. Brissot was forbidden to write for *Le Patriote Français*, his own newspaper. In April, when the Jacobins appropriated control of the powerful new Committee of Public Safety, the Girondists retaliated, indicting Marat. But the Paris mobs declared Marat a "friend of the people" and deflected his arrest, sealing a crucial victory for the extremists, who were grasping control among women as well. Madame Condorcet's and Madame Roland's salons were long out of favor. Members of the Société des Républicaines-Révolutionnaires, lead by former chocolate maker Pauline Léon, now terrorized the streets in red woolen liberty hats and pantaloons; on May 15 they stripped, flogged, and literally drove moderate Théroigne de Mericourt mad. On May 31, Madame Roland was arrested. And on June 2, the Jacobins, supported by the Committee of Public Safety, most men's and women's clubs, and an estimated eighty thousand sans-culottes,[39] definitively triumphed. The Girondist deputies were placed under house arrest. The Terror began.

And, needless to say, Brissot's Louisiana scheme collapsed. As Mary began her *Historical and Moral View of the Origins and Progress of the French Revolution,* Imlay finished *The Emigrants,* a sentimental epistolary novel with a competent narrative and effusive style. There's much extolling of the heroine's manners and the hero's valor; villains conveniently die, the good people marry, and the long-suffering uncle comes into a fortune at last. Like Ann Radcliffe's Gothic romances, *The Emigrants* has an exotic setting—America—but its plot and characters are routine. Mary the literary critic would have dismissed it in a few paragraphs. Still, it drops some intriguing hints about Imlay's views.

On the close-to-home subject of debts, for instance, he clearly disapproves when the heroine Caroline's father runs off to the frontier to escape his creditors. Caroline's brother George, on the other hand, sincerely repents for his extravagance, giving the impression that debtors can reform. On the feminist front, *The Emigrants* blames laws forbidding wives to divorce for the unhappiness of three good women at the center of the story, and the hero, Captain Arl-ton, dismisses weddings as "idle ceremony."[40] But American Arl-ton and his British love, Caroline, do marry: *The Emigrants* is not that radical, after all. Nor, despite many claims to the contrary, is there any indication that so much as a line of it was written by Mary Wollstonecraft, though a disagreement between Captain Arl-ton and the equally worthy Sir T. Mor-ly toward the end of the novel reflects a subtle philosophical difference between Gilbert and Mary.[41]

The subject is human perfectibility, a dubious prospect, Sir T. Mor-ly argues, in Imlay's voice. Constitutions should be written for people as they are at the moment. "When we talk of our privileges we should mention them as belonging to a man in a state of society . . . with his passions, and not as a perfect being."[42]

"Philosophers of the present day, by aiming at too much, will produce evils equivalent to those they have laboured to remove," Sir T. Mor-ly/Imlay cautions;[43] while his friend, the younger Captain Arl-ton, believes wholeheartedly that the world will improve. Or, as Mary would plead in *An Historical and Moral View of the Origins and Progress of the French Revolution*:

Several acts of ferocious folly have justly brought much obloquy on the grand revolution, which has taken place in France;

yet, I feel confident of being able to prove, that the people are essentially good, and that knowledge is rapidly advancing to that degree of perfectibility, when the proud distinctions of sophisticating fools will be eclipsed by the mild rays of philosophy.[44]

The piousness of a younger Mary can be heard in her new book's righteous language, but the hopefulness is new. The *French Revolution* makes no mention of a compensatory afterlife. Mary Wollstonecraft is now looking for rewards on earth and in the foreseeable future, when "men will insensibly render each other happier, as they grow wiser."

Captain Arl-ton's/Mary's optimism was more popular than Sir Mor-ly's/Imlay's enlightened skepticism among the British expatriates in Paris. It acknowledged Rousseau and Locke and also William Godwin, who had, the past January, created a sensation in London with his philosophical tome on progress, *An Enquiry Concerning Political Justice*. Perfectibility, *Political Justice* blithely declared, was "one of the most unequivocal characteristics of the human species."[45] We are moving toward a world in which reason will govern passion, Godwin felt confident. And Imlay too hoped an enlightened government would produce a more reasonable society, but he doubted human nature would change.

Neither Imlay nor Wollstonecraft had much good to say about the French at present. Mary, in her book's opening chapters, satirizes their propensity to theatrics and dubs them "an injured people, in whose hatred, or admiration, the mellowed shades of reflection are seldom seen";[46] while a character in *The Emigrants* briefly visits Paris, seemingly just for the chance to lament the superficiality of everyone there. Yet, if the French were so unworthy, why did Mary and Gilbert linger among them all through the summer of 1793, as the tocsin rang and the guillotine fell, as Revolutionary power grew ever more centralized and the war made it increasingly reckless for a British citizen to remain in France?

Later, Mary said she had planned to follow Madame de Staël across the border to Switzerland. But she had some trouble obtaining a passport, and then Imlay came along, so she stayed in France to be with him. This explanation is not entirely convincing. For why couldn't the two of them have left together? Perhaps because Imlay and Joel Barlow were starting an import–export business crossing through wartime waters. Imlay told Mary he hoped to make a thousand pounds so he could buy them a farm in America. And Mary liked the idea of America and also of not leaving France so soon. The suffering of people with high ideals, like Madame Roland, grieved but also riveted Mary. "I certainly am glad that I came to France, because I never could have had else a just opinion of the most extraordinary event that has ever been recorded," Mary wrote.[47]

Still, after the arrest of the Girondists, Paris was no longer safe for foreigners with "enemy" passports, and if she continued living with the British-born Aline Filliettaz and her husband, she would imperil them as well. So early in the summer of 1793, Mary moved to the secluded house of an elderly gardener in the Paris suburb of Neuilly. Here no officials harangued her about her British citizenship; no parties of anxious expatriates traded tales of their latest woes. The gardener doted on her—fighting her for the "privilege" of making her bed or foraging for a particularly scrumptious grape for her dinner.[48] Life in Neuilly was charmed, Mary felt in her amorous, diligent mood. She had an invigorating love, gardens and trees for neighbors, and stirring events nearby. This was what the British Romantic poets would advocate for the creative spirit—and what the French bourgeoisie sought annually when they fled Paris in the summer months. Mary flourished in her garden hideaway. She read books and wrote her own and walked and waited for Imlay, who, as often as he could, scampered through the barrier gate from Paris to reward her with his face full of eager love—his "barrier" face, she called it.

In a hurried note in June, Mary rearranged a rendezvous with Imlay:

My dear love, after making my arrangements for our snug dinner to-day, I have been taken by storm, and obliged to promise
to dine, at an early hour, with the Miss ——s, the *only* day they
intend to pass here. I shall however leave the key in the door,
and hope to find you at my fire-side when I return, about eight
o'clock.[49]

So loving Imlay did not diminish Mary's loyalty to friends like the Miss ——s in Paris and faraway Joseph Johnson, whom she had not heard from in months. "Should any accident happen to my dear and worthy friend Johnson during my absence I should never forgive my-self for leaving him," she told Everina.[50] And though she finally un-derstood all the fuss about sexual pleasure, she had no desire to become "one being" with any man.[51] She would have her own friends, her own work, and yet . . . And yet—and this was tricky—she did want a domestic life with Gilbert Imlay, and even the right to lean on him if she pleased. "You have, by your tenderness and worth, twisted yourself more artfully round my heart, than I supposed poss-ible," she wrote him.

Let me indulge the thought, that I have thrown out some tendrils
to cling to the elm by which I wish to be supported.—This is
talking a new language for me![52]

Mary began talking this new language during her months in Neuilly, and it drew her closer to domestic women like Madame Schweizer and Ruth Barlow, who had at last arrived in Paris and was living with her adoring Joel on the Rue Jacob in St-Germain. "A word or two, which dropt from you, when I last *saw* you, for circumstances scarcely allowed me to speak to you, have run in my head ever since—" Mary wrote Ruth that summer. "Why cannot we meet and breakfast together, *quite alone*, as in days of yore?"[53] And so they stole moments to gossip and exchange intimacies. Mary made no more snide remarks about Joel Barlow's effusiveness. She was eager to believe that all American men remained infatuated with their women, that—except for the marriage vows—her relationship with Gilbert would be like Ruth's with Joel. Mary's condescension toward Ruth the homebody completely vanished. She valued her friend's American know-how when it came to their men's baffling import–export scheme. And she believed it a great achievement that Ruth lived happily with a difficult man.[54]

On July 13, a young Girondist named Charlotte Corday stabbed the extremist Marat in his bath, intensifying the Jacobin paranoia that conspiracies lurked everywhere. On July 28, Olympe de Gouges was arrested for putting up anti-Jacobin pamphlets, which she continued writing and smuggling from jail. Increasingly, Robespierre fulminated against untrustworthy foreigners, especially the British. So when Mary, walking by the Place de la Révolution, cried out at the fresh blood streaming on the pavement, she put herself in danger, a passerby warned her; and she reluctantly held her tongue.[55]

Another day, researching for her book, Mary walked eleven miles to the deserted Versailles Palace.[56] Climbing the regal staircase, she was suddenly struck by the sort of imaginary terrors that had depressed her that long-ago December night after the king had gone to trial. Now she saw the royal family as hunted creatures and sumptuous Versailles as their haunted home. The "gigantic" portraits of kings stretching up the walls "seem to be sinking into the embraces of death," she thought. ". . . The very air is chill, seeming to clog the breath; and the wasting dampness of destruction appears to be steal-ing into the vast pile, on every side." She passed through apartment after lifeless apartment, then looked for relief in the garden, but even there all was "fearfully still." The images of kings kept appearing in her mind's eye. France had rooted out monarchy; but still she wept

> —scarcely conscious that I weep, O France! over the vestiges of thy former oppression; which, separating man from man with a fence of iron, sophisticated all, and made many completely wretched; I tremble, lest I should meet some unfortunate being, fleeing from the despotism of licentious freedom, hearing the snap of the *guillotine* at his heels; merely because he was once noble, or has afforded an asylum to those, whose only crime is their name—.[57]

What a striking conceit, "licentious freedom"—binding the Ja-cobins, who so prided themselves on their rectitude, to the philander-ing, inebriated, overdressed, and gluttonous former rulers of Versailles. For centuries, monarchs had exploited the vulnerable French people; now the Jacobins were visiting the sins of those mon-archs on their hapless kin, even if the kin were ardent republicans. Like the monarchy, the Terror debauched on power.

And the Terror was in full swing by August, when Thomas and Re-becca Christie were arrested (though they were soon released and es-caped to Switzerland). Clearly, Mary could no longer remain in France as a British citizen. Since she'd be safe as the wife of an Amer-ican, the obvious solution was for her to marry Imlay. But she was committed to *not* marrying, and he may have been no more eager to marry than she; we'll never be sure, as his half of their correspon-dence is missing. What we do know is that Imlay registered Mary as his wife at the American embassy. This may have been a mere heroic gesture—like his getting the New Jersey traitors out of jail and into the American Army. Or it may have been an act of possession, of conscience, of love.

For her part, Mary was delighted that without making any humiliating vows she had managed to become an American citizen in the eyes of the French government. She could go and live where she wanted. And what she wanted was to live in Paris with Imlay. Or "almost" to live with him, she writes past midnight on a Monday in August. Mary calls herself "your own dear girl," and laments causing Gilbert "pain" recently because she had been moody and quick to imagine a slight and fearful of depression, though (here she puts the burden on him) "whilst you love me, I cannot again fall into [that] miserable state."[58]

She is eager to look at the bright side, concluding the letter with one of her most endearing passages: "But good-night!— God bless you! Sterne says, that is equal to a kiss—yet I would rather give you the kiss into the bargain, glowing with gratitude to Heaven, and affection to you. I like the word affection, because it signifies something habitual; and we are soon to meet, to try whether we have mind enough to keep our hearts warm."[59]

For Mary, this was a challenge—as risky and consequential as the Revolution itself.

CHAPTER EIGHT

At the end of August 1793, Mary left peaceful Neuilly for Imlay's apartment in the Faubourg St-Germain. Driving by the Convention, she may have glimpsed the flamboyant leaders of the new *enragés'* party (Jean Varlet and Jacques Roux) standing on portable tribunes screaming views more radical even than the Jacobins'. Or perhaps she saw Jacques-René Hébert, leader of the Paris Commune, who despised the *enragés* personally, but shared their extremist views. Once, St-Germain had been a grassy suburb. Now streets like the Rue de l'Université and the Rue Jacob boasted mansions as elegant as any in the Marais—with smart stone walls, floor-high windows, and a profusion of pillars and reliefs. The medieval abbey of St-Germain-des-Prés had been sacked and burned by anticlerics,[1] and the streets were filled with foreigners fearing for their lives. Still, Mary was happy to be here, for the foreigners were her friends, the winding, tree-lined streets were pretty, and she was for the first time in her life preparing to live with a man she loved.

"You would smile to hear how many plans of employment I have in my head, now that I am confident my heart has found a place in your bosom," she told Imlay.[2] In her book, she was describing an early hero of the Republic, Comte de Mirabeau, the black sheep of wealthy Provençals. Banishing all checks on personal freedom had become his mission when he was elected as a delegate to the first National Assembly, where he denounced inherited wealth, demanded equal rights for Jews and Protestants, and declared the national debt should be paid by the rich. What Mary admired most about Mirabeau was his courage to stand up to mass opinion (he angered most of his colleagues, calling for a constitutional monarchy like England's), but she also admired the masses, who overthrew the Bastille. "Let not the coldly wise exult, that their heads were not led astray by their hearts" on that memorable July 14, wrote Mary;[3] and she ends her chapter envisioning a "change of government, gradually taking place to meliorate the fate of man."[4]

Her optimism is striking in the fall of 1793, when the Terror was mounting, when the Jacobins were dragging her Swedish friend Gustav Graf (Count) von Schlabrendorf to the dread Conciergerie prison, where Marie Antoinette was also awaiting trial. The Girondists were either in prison or under house arrest, and a half-mile from Mary's door, on the Rue Mouffetard, the poor were as poor as they'd been before the Bastille fell. All France, in fact, was plagued by hunger, military losses, and wild political discord. The new *maximum* food prices, meant to alleviate economic crisis, were only pitting indigent shopkeepers against indigent shoppers, while from Caen to Marseilles, rebels of all classes defied the new puppet governments the Paris Convention foisted on their towns. The final blow to French pride came in August, when the British fleet captured the French port of Toulon.

The Jacobins retaliated, on September 10, by officially rejecting the Convention's "principles of union and fraternity" and announcing that all foreigners "born within the territory of Powers with which the French Republic is at war" would be jailed. This marked the end of the Revolution to convert the world and gave notice to Mary, Helen Maria Williams and her lover, John Hurford Stone, Thomas Paine's young friend I. B. Johnson, and technically even Paine himself (though he was a French citizen) that they could be arrested simply because they were British-born. No precaution was too extreme, declared Robespierre, for "the country is in the greatest danger, our enemies have formed a plan for assassinating the *holy Mountain*, the Jacobins, and all the patriots. . . . Watch today, tomorrow, and the day after tomorrow—the plot is ready to burst."[5]

Eliza and Everina worried about their absent sister. "Heaven only knows when she will [be allowed to] return," lamented Eliza to Everina, though she quickly added, "and I still regret I had not gone with her."[6] For the Terror had not inclined Eliza to count her blessings. More than ever, she despised her conservative employers with their smug anti-Revolutionary opinions. "Nature never meant me for a philosopher," moaned Eliza, "though it has been my fate to spend half my life away from every friend, and all society and conversation whatever— Buried among fanaticism without speaking ten words a day."[7]

It was, of course, not Wales alone that derided French idealism. The Revolution was devouring its children, exactly as Edmund Burke had prophesied. This secretly pleased the typical Englishman, who'd never been taken in by the *politesse* or subtle thoughts of all those glib speakers of the impossible French language who were forever threatening Britain's shores. It's hard to miss the pleasure in this September 13, 1793, London *Times* lyric:

SITUATION OF FRANCE

The Arts and Sciences from hence are flown,
And every Province now turn'd upside down.
That gay Politeness, which had mark'd her race
Is fled, and Murder has usurp'd the place.

To live by plunder is their settled plan.
And this they call the natural Rights of Man.

Amid its advertisements for lotteries and "bilious pills," the *Times* also ran notices from expatriated French aristocrats desperate for any honest work.[8] "WANTS EMPLOYER, a FRENCH EMIGRANT, a GENTLEMAN of RANK, and, previous to his leaving France, of large Fortune, who is prevented joining the Army by the Necessity of providing Support for his Wife and Children," read one such ad. All the English papers were predicting France's imminent downfall. Still, Eliza agreed with Mary that the Revolution would triumph in the end. And she imagined herself happily ensconced in Paris no later than the following spring.[9]

This was not altogether a delusion, for it was still possible that the Revolution would change course. At the beginning of October, France—having conscripted all males between eighteen and twenty-five—defeated rebels in Marseilles and Lyon and, on the foreign front, halted Britain's advance to the north. The influential Jacobins Georges-Jacques Danton and Camille Desmoulins founded a group nicknamed the Indulgents, arguing that the Terror should be abolished, for it had run its course. And because Danton was Robespierre's close ally, the Convention listened, though the violence went on.

Mary, Imlay, and the Barlows were safe for the moment, since the men's trading with enemy countries, though illegal, was useful to France, which was short on provisions.[10] Still, Imlay's long business absences—and so soon after she'd moved into his apartment in Paris—pained Mary. "On Friday then I shall expect you to dine with me—" she wrote Imlay one Wednesday in late August, "and if you come a little before dinner, it is so long since I have seen you, you will not be scolded. . . . "[11] Sometime in September, Imlay left Paris altogether and moved 126 miles northeast to the port of Le Havre to oversee his ships. The move was temporary, he told Mary, but what, she wondered, had become of their domestic quest?[12]

Domesticity was especially on Mary's mind in the fall of 1793 since she'd missed periods, felt "inclined to faint,"[13] and was sure she was pregnant—which was fine with her. In fact, it was thrilling. Conceiving a child at the height of the Revolution was almost as satisfying in its very different way as loving a man. Not everyone could get pregnant at thirty-four, she prided herself. She wanted Imlay to be proud of their "gentl[y] twitch[ing]" fetus. And he claimed to be proud and happy. He claimed he felt responsible for supporting the new family: this was one reason he was so preoccupied with business now.

He left on a bleak day—"comfortless weather," Mary thought it, and her first letter seethes with discontent:

> When I am absent from those I love my imagination is as lively, as if my senses had never been gratified by their presence—I was going to say caresses—and why should I not? I have found out that I have more mind than you in one respect; because I can, without any violent effort of reason, find food for love in the same object, much longer than you can.[14]

Mary seems to be accusing Gilbert of an infidelity, and she proceeds in the same vein:

> With ninety-nine men out of a hundred, a very sufficient dash of folly is necesary to render a woman *piquante*, a soft word for desirable; and beyond these casual ebullitions of sympathy, few look for enjoyment by fostering a passion in their hearts. One reason in short, why I wish my whole sex to become wiser, is, that the foolish ones may not, by their pretty folly, rob those whose sensibility keeps down their vanity, of the few roses that afford them some solace in the thorny road of life.[15]

The "casual ebullitions of sympathy" . . . the "thorny road of life" . . . Mary could be writing to her childhood friend Jane Arden, or to Henry Fuseli in 1792. The proud "we" of her earlier letters has given way to "I." "I have found out," she writes. "I wish." And she speaks of her sex and his sex. They are still lovers, but they are no longer a team. "I do not know how I fell into these reflections," she continues, "excepting one thought produced it—that these continual separations were necessary to warm your affection.— Of late, we are always separating.—Crack!—crack!—and away you go."

There is satisfaction in outright accusing a man who's set off on a nasty day without you. And yet if Mary *really* believed what she said, she would destroy her own happiness, because her happiness depended on Gilbert's loving only her and being good. So she experiments with a less dire—and, who's to say?—maybe truer interpretation: "A glow of tenderness at my heart whispers that you are one of the best creatures in the world," she writes, and finishes her letter asking Imlay to "bear with me a *little* longer. When we are settled in the country together, more duties will open before me, and my heart, which now . . . is agitated by every emotion that awakens the remembrance of old griefs, will learn to rest on yours, with that dignity your character, not to talk of my own, demands."[16]

Mary had plenty to occupy her in Gilbert's absence. She exercised to keep her health up; she worked on her book. "So you may reckon on its being finished soon, though not before you come home, unless you are detained longer than I allow myself to believe you will," she wrote Imlay.[17] She visited her friend Count von Schlabrendorf in jail, though it was risky for British-born Mary to enter any prison, much less the rat-riddled Conciergerie, known as the gateway to the guillotine. Still, she went often and "enthralled me more and more," von Schlabrendorf later confessed. She was "the noblest, purest and most intelligent woman I have ever met. . . . There was enchantment in her glance, her voice, and her movement."[18] She was also brimming with information from the outside world: the queen had been beheaded; the old Christian calendar had been replaced by a ten-day week; anticlerics were turning Notre Dame into a so-called Temple of Reason. Helen Maria Williams and John Hurford Stone had been arrested, and the Marquis de Condorcet, hiding in the shuttered Sorbonne, where he continued to write about human improvement, had been condemned to death.

And Mary's pregnancy had its embarrassing moments. One day, she ran into two women who ogled her belly. "I told [them] . . . simply that I was with child: and let them stare! and ———, and ———, nay, all the world, may know it for aught I care!— Yet I wish to avoid ———'s coarse jokes."[19] Such mortifications notwithstanding, Mary's tenderness and concern for the baby grew so intense that she was terrified one day when suddenly its twitches stopped as she lifted a log for the fire. She remained "in an agony, till I felt" them return.

"Do you think the creature goes regularly to sleep?" she wondered. "I am ready to ask as many questions as Voltaire's Man of Forty Crowns."[20] And she carried on animated talks with the "little twitcher," whom she could imagine safely born and snuggled with his or her parents, "whilst I mend my stocking," and Gilbert read out loud.[21]

Other times, she saw Imlay as a sly and avaricious enemy of domesticity, who longed to be "laughing away" with some fellows in London.[22] Not hearing from him as often or as ardently as she wanted, Mary became physically sick. "A few more of these caprices of sensibility would destroy me," she wrote after two days passed without a letter from Imlay.[23] Soon she was blaming all her problems on his business, which rather than uniting them on a farm in America was keeping him happily employed in Le Havre, while she waited around.[24] "I hate commerce! . . . You will tell me, that exertions are necessary: I am weary of them! The face of things . . . vexes me."[25]

Public life also vexed her. Long gone was French feminism. Rather than calling for equal rights, women now brawled in the street over the issue of whether it was or was not feminine to sport the national cockade. Since prevailing views changed from arrondissement to arrondissement, a *citoyenne* could be whipped for wearing a cockade in one market and for not wearing it down the road. Then, on October 30, the Convention settled the question, closing women's clubs and banning women's participation in all political action. Female aggression, hailed four years earlier when women had chased the king from his Versailles palace, was now an affront to male pride. Though women would be "*tolérés*" ("tolerated") as "*spectatrices silencieuses et modestes*" ("silent and modest spectators") in political societies, they could not so much as leave their houses to retrieve political news. "Let them wait to receive it from the mouths of their fathers, or their children, or their brothers or their husbands," one weekly gloated, adding, "True patriotism consists in fulfilling one's duties, and not in giving rights to everyone, whatever their sex and age, and not in carrying a bonnet and a spade, pants and pistols. Leave that to the men, who will protect you and make you happy."[26] Fighting women disappeared from the national iconography and were replaced by chaste young girls, embodying Liberty in the Festivals of Reason that (opposing church ceremonies) were flourishing throughout France.

Olympe de Gouges did not live to comment on the new image of republican womanhood. Nor did she repent her contempt for the majority view. Yes, it was perfectly true, she had condemned the Jacobins, she told her inquisitors at the Convention. "My sentiments have not changed and I still regard them and always will regard them as ambitious and self-seeking men."[27] She cried and shouted her polemics all the way to the scaffold, where she collapsed in fright.[28]

On October 31, the Girondists—singing the "Marseillaise"—followed de Gouge to the Place de la République. "The anguish [Mary] felt at hearing of the death of Brissot, Vergniaud, and the twenty deputies, [was] one of the most intolerable sensations she had ever experienced," said a friend.[29] Madame Roland cried, "O Liberty! What crimes are committed in thy name!" just before she succumbed to the guillotine. Tom Paine went to prison, despite his French citizenship. And it was only through an oversight, Helen Maria Williams believed, that she was actually removed from the Abbaye prison and transferred to an English convent and then to house arrest.[30]

AFTER MONTHS of silence from home, Mary at last received a "very long and very affectionate" letter from Joseph Johnson; "but the account he gives me of his own affairs, though he obviously makes the best of them," was depressing, as was a "melancholy letter" from Eliza, though it was a relief to learn Charles was safely in America and doing well. "I think you would hail him as a brother," Mary writes Imlay,

> with one of your tender looks . . . that he would meet with a glow half made up of bashfulness, and a desire to please the—where shall I find a word to express the relationship which subsists between us?—Shall I ask the little twitcher?—But I have dropt half the sentence that was to tell you how much he would be inclined to love the man loved by his sister. I have been fancying myself sitting between you, ever since I began to write, and my heart has leaped at the thought![31]

Mary's heart was leaping one minute and plunging the next. On a Sunday morning in December, she writes Imlay with no little sarcasm: "You seem to have taken up your abode at [Le Havre]. Pray sir! when do you think of coming home? or to write very considerately, when will business permit you? I shall expect (as the country people say in England) that you will make a *power* of money to indemnify me for your absence."[32]

But after she receives a comforting letter on Tuesday, he is once again "My best love," and she is chiding him to be more openly affectionate: "Do not bid [your sensibility] begone for I love to see it striving to master your features; besides, these kinds of sympathies are the life of affection: and why, in cultivating our understandings, should we try to dry up these springs of pleasure, which gush out to give a freshness to days browned with care."[33]

Mary's next day is certainly browned with care, for on Wednesday, January 1, she is telling Imlay, "A man is a tyrant!" And:

> Considering the care and anxiety a woman must have about a child before it comes into the world, it seems to me, by a *natural right*, to belong to her. When men get immersed in the world, they seem to lose all sensations, excepting those necessary to continue or produce life!— Are these the privileges of reason? Amongst the feathered race, whilst the hen keeps the young warm, her mate stays by to cheer her; but it is sufficient for a man to condescend to get a child, in order to claim it![34]

Reading only Mary's half of the correspondence, it is possible to pity overextended Imlay, though his promises to be quickly back in Paris certainly lead Mary on. She felt misunderstood and undervalued. "My own happiness wholly depends on you,"[35] Mary forlornly and manipulatively wrote her lover on January 7. And when, on the following day, she received a warm letter, inviting her to join him in Le Havre, she accepted on the spot. "What a picture you have sketched of our fire-side! my love," she wrote, casting off her ire, "my fancy was instantly at work, and I found my head on your shoulder, whilst my eyes were fixed on the little creatures that were clinging about your knees. I did not absolutely determine there should be six—if you have not set your heart on this round number."[36]

Helen Maria Williams pleaded with Mary to burn her manuscript in progress on the French Revolution, whose anti-Jacobinism would assure her of jail at the very least, if it was opened at any of the checkpoints on the road to Le Havre. But Mary refused and carried her dangerous words boldly past the teeming guards as she headed west.

LE HAVRE, where the Seine bleeds into the English Channel, was a prosperous port town recently expanded for peaceful import of cotton, coffee, and tobacco from the Americas, as well as for waging war. The day Mary arrived, battle and cargo ships floated side by side in the winter harbor. New houses lined the old port where Mary and Gilbert Imlay settled into "lodgings pleasantly situated."[37] Their *quartier* was named for the Romanesque Church of Notre Dame, with its salamander gargoyles. Nearby stood a mansion of gray wood and yellowed stone panels strikingly offset in the irregular Normandy style.[38] The weather then as now was moody, the rains tumultuous, but this did not trouble Mary with her Yorkshire past.

The summer before Mary arrived, Le Havre had renamed itself Havre-Marat. For it was as Jacobin as Paris, with the difference that here politics was tempered by a passion for selling goods. Breaking the British blockade mattered more than sleuthing for British conspiracies. Expatriates were left more or less to themselves. So Mary's landlord, John Wheatcroft, an English soap merchant, was free to trade as he wished while Thomas Paine languished in a Paris jail. Virtue, Robespierre's consuming interest, was less imperative in Le Havre, and the surveillance was looser. Writing Everina from her new home, Mary for the first time explicitly bemoans the Terror: "I . . . have met with some uncommon instances of friendship, which my heart will ever grately store up, and call to mind when the remembrance is keen of the anguish it has endured for its fellow creatures, at large—for the unfortunate beings cut off around me. . . . "[39]

The mounting violence in France tempted Mary to revert to cynicism. And yet she was happy during a winter and a spring and a summer by the sea with Gilbert Imlay. It was a new life altogether, without friends of her own or much intellectual discourse. In January, Mary promised not to "ruffle" Gilbert's good temper "for a long, long time—I am afraid to say never,"[40] and he rewarded her restraint with love—or at least he allowed her to love *him* unconstrainedly. The cheekiness returned to her letters. She resumed speaking of "we" and "us." "You perceive that I am acquiring the matrimonial phraseology without having clogged my soul by promising obedience &c &c—" Mary teased Ruth Barlow. She was "more seriously at *work* than I have ever been";[41] still, she had time to worry over Imlay's boats delayed at sea and the "whipping" French embargoes.[42] Gone was her scorn for making money. Blockading could be positively heroic, Mary implies in a letter to Ruth:

> I indulge the expectation of success, in which you are included, with great pleasure—and I do hope that [Joel] will not suffer his sore mind to be hurt, sufficiently to damp his exertions, by any impediments or disappointments, which may, at first cloud his views or darken his prospect— Teasing hinderance of one kind or other continually occur to *us* here. . . . Still we do not despair— Let but the first ground be secured—and in the course of the summer we may, perhaps celebrate our good luck, not forgetting good management, together.[43]

Mary's chief companions now were Imlay's American colleagues: Mark Leavenworth, who could be counted on to deliver parcels to and from the Barlows; Colonel Blackden, who was exasperating when he drank. An American named Richard Codman sailed the first part of Mary's *French Revolution* across the Channel to Joseph Johnson, who could not write her back because of the French blockade.

The blockade also made it impossible for Johnson to send Mary money (his last check had arrived nine months earlier); so she now relied financially on Imlay, which perversely pleased her. Mary's autumn letters from Paris had been full of images of letting go—she imagined her heart resting on Imlay's heart, her body clinging to his "elm" for support.[44] She luxuriated in their mutual dependence and was "safe," she wrote Everina, "through the protection of an American. A most worthy man who joins to uncommon tenderness of heart and quickness of feeling, a soundness of understanding, and reasonableness of temper, rarely to be met with—."[45]

As the spring weeks passed, Mary's belly splayed, her ankles swelled. She went on shopping and cooking meals—just like other women. She took an interest in clothes. "If you see proper to send me anything, I mean a little dimity, white calico, or a light-coloured print calico, for a morning gown, do not send a stinted pattern," she instructed Ruth Barlow. "I have found some linen Shirts for Mr. I. so do not want any."[46] There was no more talk of gloomy moods threatening her fetus, who was "lively," even when Imlay left on a short business trip to Paris. For the trip *was* short. Mary barely had time to write in her playful *barrier* voice:

Do not call me stupid, for leaving on the table the little bit of paper I was to inclose.— This comes of being in love at the fag-end of a letter of business.— You know, you say, they will not chime together.— I had got you by the fire-side, with the *gigot* smoking on the board, to lard your poor bare ribs—and behold, I closed my letter without taking the paper up, that was directly under my eyes!—What had I got in them to render me blind!— I give you leave to answer the question, if you will not scold; for I am

Yours most affectionately

MARY[47]

Sometime in April, Mary finished her 235-page work on the French Revolution,[48] tracing the "progress of society" from ancient times through the fall of Louis XVI. The first chapter moves rapidly from the Roman Empire to the Crusades to the wars of Louis XIV and the "debauch[ed]"[49] court of Louis XV. Louis XVI and Marie Antoinette appear in Chapter 2, which follows the last days of the old regime, with its rising deficits and succession of incompetent ministers—Colonne, displaying "wild prodigality," the "weak and timid" Brienne, and Necker, whose halfhearted measures Mary declares "disastrous."[50] Then comes the king's opening of the Estates-General, the defection of the Third Estate, and the creation of France's first National Assembly. Midway through the book, the Bastille falls.

Then the *French Revolution* turns more speculative. In this passage, for instance, Mary contemplates the juncture between domestic and social happiness, while revealing her own deep attraction to France:

It is a mistake to suppose that there was no such thing as domestic happiness in France, or even in Paris. For many French families, on the contrary, exhibited an affectionate urbanity of behaviour to each other, seldom to be met with where a certain easy gaiety does not soften the difference of age and condition. The husband and wife, if not lovers, were the civilest friends and the tenderest parents in the world—the only parents, perhaps, who really treated their children like friends; and the most affable masters and mistresses. . . . Besides, in France, the women have not those fractious, supercilious manners, common to the

English; and acting more freely, they have more decision of character, and even more generosity.[51]

She comes to the (for her) remarkable conclusion that

it is perhaps in a state of comparative idleness—pursuing employments not absolutely necessary to support life, that the finest polish is given to the mind, and those personal graces, which are instantly felt, but cannot be described: and it is natural to hope, that the labour of acquiring the substantial virtues, necessary to maintain freedom, will not render the French less pleasing, when they become more respectable.[52]

Pleasure, which was rigidly bound to virtue in Mary's earlier works, now takes on a goodness of its own; clearly, the author of the *French Revolution* has experienced a joy that has nothing to do with helping others. And yet how much misery she perceives, under both the old and the new order. How far she has come since, setting off for Paris in 1792, she mocked "the shallow herd who throw an odium on immutable principles, because some of the mere instrument[s] of the revolution were too sharp."[53] Mere instruments indeed. The *French Revolution* declares violence is an absolute evil. And while Mary draws a balanced picture of Mirabeau and of the king, righteous anger is her dominant tone. The queen is a "profound dissembler"; the Parisians are shallow and cruel. "It may be questioned whether Paris will not occasion more disturbance in settling the new order of things, than is equivalent to the good she produced by accelerating the epoch of the revolution," Mary writes, raising the point that the world might be better off if there'd never been a French Revolution. And in one of her most rueful passages, she questions benevolence itself:

Unfortunately, almost every thing human, however beautiful or splendid the superstructure, has hitherto, been built on the vile foundation of selfishness; virtue has been the watchword, patriotism the trumphet, and glory the banner of enterprize; but pay and plunder have been the real motives.[54]

Here Mary seems to have come full circle from the optimism of *Rights of Men*. Yet, for all its rancor, the *French Revolution* speaks to an embattled idealism: "When the effervescence, which now agitates the prejudices of the whole continent, subsides, the justness of the principles brought forward in the declaration of the rights of men and citizens" will remain to ennoble a stabilized Europe, she feels sure.[55] And if *French Revolution* is not the great work Mary had envisioned the previous summer, it is a landmark for Mary, who stuck to it as she moved from Neuilly to Paris to Le Havre, carried a child, and watched the Terror spread through France.

IN THE WINTER of 1794, the Convention turned on both Danton's Indulgents, who wanted to damp the Terror and liberalize the economy, and their nemeses the Hébertists (named for Jacques-René Hébert, the head of the Paris Commune), who cried out for more beheadings and tighter price controls. Robespierre accused the two factions of merely feigning opposite views while in fact plotting together to undermine the Jacobins. And though his suspicion was preposterous, it had been stoked by an actual conspiracy where delegates of the Convention—including Fabre d'Eglantine, a close friend of Danton's—were appointed to liquidate the Indies Company, and wound up bribing its directors and speculating in its stock. Meanwhile, the French economy deteriorated, and when the Jacobins loosened price controls, hoping to stimulate business, Hébert accused them of exploiting the poor and called for an all-out assault. But too few of the

Hébertists dared to defy Robespierre. The Jacobins easily quashed their rebellion, and sent the offenders to the scaffold on March 24.

With the extremists gone, Robespierre now focused his anger on the freewheeling Indulgents. "The word virtue made Danton laugh," Robespierre sulked.[56] He demanded that Danton endorse righteousness by denouncing Eglantine for his part in the Indies Company scandal. Danton refused and was promptly tried and condemned, as were his fellow Indulgents. Spotting them all in their tumbril as she passed the Pont Neuf, Helen Maria Williams thought they seemed "indifferent to their fates." And Williams could not muster up much remorse over their departures (Danton, after all, had denounced her Girondist friends). But the leering crowd did appall her. To endure such indignity, she believed, "would be worse than death itself."[57]

A few weeks after Danton's death, Mary celebrated her thirty-fifth birthday, on April 27. Six days later, she was "still very well; but imagine it cannot be long before this lively animal pops on us—and now the history is finished and every thing arranged I do not care how soon."[58] On May 14, the "animal" popped out, spry and healthy. It was a girl, and Mary named her Fanny after the great love of her youth.

Unlike Fanny Blood, Fanny Imlay was robust. "My little girl begins to suck so *manfully* that her father reckons saucily on her writing the second part of the R——ts of Woman," Mary boasts to Ruth.[59] And what a remarkable head she has! Mary exults. Indeed, Ruth had so ill calculated "the quantity of brains [Fanny] was to have, and the skull it would require to contain them," that the baby caps she sewed for the child are far too small.[60] And not only is Fanny a superior specimen of babyhood, but her mother has flabbergasted the old-fashioned neighbors by rising from bed the day after giving birth. By her sixth day, she feels "so well that were it not for the inundation of milk, which for the moment incommodes me, I could forget the pain I endured. . . . —

Yet nothing could be more natural or easy than my labour—still it is not smooth work— I dwell on these circumstances not only as I know it will give you pleasure; but to prove that this struggle of nature is rendered much more cruel by the ignorance and affectation of women. My nurse has been twenty years in this employment, and she tells me, she never knew a woman so well—adding, Frenchwoman like, that I ought to make children for the Republic, since I treat it so slightly— It is true, at first, she was convinced that I should kill myself and my child; but since we are alive and so astonishingly well, she begins to think that the *Bon Dieu* takes care of those who take no care of themselves.[61]

Mary's comments on the baby's father are a bit starchier: "The constant tenderness of my most affectionate companion makes me regard a fresh tie"—the baby—"as a blessing," Mary wrote Ruth. She wrote too of her lover's impatience with French shipping policies, for it seems that even in the clamor of Fanny's arrival, Imlay could be distressed by business cares.

Mary, on the other hand, was totally caught up in her marvelous infant. At seven weeks, Fanny was "not only uncommonly healthy, but already, as sagacious as a child of five or six months old, which I rather attribute to my good, that is natural, manner of nursing her, than to any extraordinary strength of faculties,"[62] Mary told Ruth. But, of course, Mary did believe her daughter extraordinarily clever and talented.

Gilbert was ill and had been "for some weeks past, and during the last few days he has [been] seriously feverish. His mind has been harass[ed] by continual disappointments—sh[ips] do not return, and the government is perpetually throwing impediments in the way of business." Loyally, Mary purported to share Imlay's "disquietude," though it was perfectly clear she wished Imlay could forget his fevers and ship delays and enjoy the miracle of Fanny's life. But Gilbert was not to be bound by Mary's wishes.

And so in their private life, in the spring and summer of 1794, there was an abundance of milk and joy and irritation and illness.

IN PARIS, both the Hébertists and the Dantonists were out of the picture, and there was an appearance of harmony at the Convention, where the former "Plain" contingent was now ridiculed as a "Marsh" land, and the Mountain wielded absolute control. Robespierre staged elaborate festivals of the Supreme Being to reinstate Catholicism and pushed through the dire law of the 22 Prairial—forbidding political prisoners to hire attorneys or call witnesses, and limiting their verdicts to acquittal or death. The Grande Terreur set in, and beheadings increased. ✳

"The French will carry all before them—" Mary wrote Ruth, "but, my God, how many victims fall beneath the sword and Guillotine! My blood runs cold, and I sicken at thoughts of a Revolution which costs so much blood and bitter tears."[63] Corruption was again afoot. Delegates Jean-Lambert Tallien and Joseph Fouché were exploiting their power in the provinces to amass private fortunes. And on July 26, Robespierre rose from his president's chair at the Convention to denounce these culprits, who (the following morning) managed to turn the tables and attack Robespierre himself. "Down with the tyrant!" cried the delegates, suddenly emboldened. A majority voted for Robespierre's arrest. At this point, the architect of the Terror rushed for refuge among his hard-core supporters at the Hôtel de Ville—but the momentum was against him. At 2 A.M. on July 28, he submitted to the general will of France.

Later that day, Robespierre and sixteen of his staunchest acolytes rolled off to the guillotine. "Though I was standing above a hundred paces from the place of execution, the blood of the victims streamed beneath my feet," one viewer noted. "What surprised me was, as each head fell into the basket, the cry of the people was no other than a repetition of '*A bas le Maximum!*'"—heralding not the return of justice or stability, but the end of an unpopular tax.[64]

On August 1 the Convention repealed the law of 22 Prairial. Thirty-five hundred prisoners were released from prison, and the rituals of normal life returned. By September, "Paris, the refuge of barbarism, and the den of carnage, once more excite[d] the ideas of taste, elegance, refinement, and happiness,"[65] Helen Maria Williams wrote. The Terror was past.

In Le Havre, three-month-old Fanny caught a bad case of small-pox, a "dreadful disorder," said Mary, who, ignoring the superstitious neighbors, "determined to follow the suggestions of my own reason and saved her much pain, probably her life . . . by putting her twice a day into a warm bath."[66] Fanny's smallpox was a terrible scare for Mary, a reminder that her child was mortal and prey to chance. And the child's father was not around to fuss over Fanny's blighted skin or calm her mother. Once more, business had rushed Gilbert Imlay from home.

CHAPTER NINE

*T*his time, Imlay had gone to Paris. He needed to chastise a business associate who'd committed some "knavery"[1] and to look into new commercial prospects now that Robespierre was dead. He would be back soon, Gilbert once again promised Mary, but he no longer soothed her with talk about making just 1,000 pounds so they could buy a farm in America. He wanted "a certain situation in life," which demanded wealth.[2]

"Pray ask some questions about Tallien—I am still pleased with the dignity of his conduct," Mary wrote Imlay on August 20, 1794, soon after he left Le Havre. She also wanted Imlay to inquire "whether as a member declared in the Convention, Robespierre really maintained a *number* of mistresses."[3] The answers were disappointing. The same Tallien who now nobly condemned the Terror as "an instrument of tyranny" and demanded, "What does it matter to me if a man was born noble if his conduct is good?"[4] had two years earlier ordered the death of Bordeaux's wealthiest citizens, then helped himself to their jewels. Meanwhile, the terrible Robespierre was an impeccable family man and even a good person by his own lights. So sorting out heroes and villains in France was as confusing as ever. And while Parisians of all classes rejoiced at the end of the blood-shed, perfect liberty and equality eluded them still. Indeed, as they rushed to open new dress shops or queued for the theaters, Parisians were acting very like Voltaire's long-suffering optimist Candide, who finally determines just to cultivate his own garden. The larger world is too wicked to assail.

But Mary Wollstonecraft found little comfort in her domestic cir-cumstances. Her letters to Imlay during his 1794–1795 absence are more bitter and desperate than those of the previous year. Then, she had been a childless woman creating an important book that she hoped would make money. Now, she was a mother dependent both emotionally and financially on a capricious man.

Later, Mary acknowledged that she suspected Imlay had fallen out of love with her by the time he left Le Havre. But at the time, she pre-tended to believe he was called away by greed. "The demon of [com-merce] will ever fright away the loves and graces," she resumes her crusade against business in a first letter to Imlay in Paris. She'd come from dinner with a boarish merchant in an ugly house that "smelt of commerce from top to toe," she complains, adding peckishly that "business is the idea that most naturally associates with your image, I wonder that I stumbled on any other."[5]

Soon after, she is informing Imlay that she wants him only if he wants her: "Your attention to my happiness should arise *as much* from love, which is always rather a selfish passion, as reason—that is, I want you to promote my felicity, by seeking your own. . . . Unless the attachment appears to me clearly mutual, I shall labour only to esteem your character, instead of cherishing a tenderness for your person."[6]

But since Mary could not stop loving Imlay, she had to convince herself that he loved her still—even when, instead of returning to Le Havre, he set off alone for London in the early fall. All my "emotion

is on the same side as my reason, which always was on yours—"
Mary wrote. "Separated, it would be almost impious to dwell on
real or imaginary imperfections of [your] character.— I feel that I
love you."[7]

Mary wrote also of Fanny, "the little damsel," who was "almost
springing out of my arm. . . . Poor thing! When I am sad, I lament that
all my affections grow on me, till they become too strong for my
peace, though they all afford me snatches of exquisite enjoyment—
This for our little girl was at first very reasonable—more the effect of
reason, a sense of duty, than feeling—now, she has got into my heart
and imagination, and when I walk out without her, her little figure is
ever dancing before me."[8]

But it was the rare moment when Mary managed to steal out without Fanny. Mostly, she took her baby everywhere because there was
no one to watch her at home. Guiltily, Mary admitted there were
times when she felt a "slave" to her lively infant.

Nonetheless, Mary's mind was free and elastic. When she'd tucked
Fanny in at night or at nap time, she had the leisure to look out at the
boats wandering in and out of the Le Havre port and to speculate
philosophically. Her ideas had changed considerably since *Vindication*. Then, she'd felt so sure of the perfectibility of mankind. Now,
she wondered. And unlike Rousseau, who advocated rigorous attention to one's offspring while sending his own babies off to foundling
homes, Mary demanded a theory consistent with her own decisions.
Before she had come to France, Mary had scorned romance and mistrusted the imagination, especially woman's imagination, which
sketched such "dangerous pictures" of marital bliss.[9] Reason alone
was the spur to progress, she'd felt then. Now, without demeaning
reason, she spoke eloquently of dreams and sensual feelings. In an
August letter, Mary for the first time refers to romance as a partner to,
rather than an enemy of, thought. "I will allow you to cultivate my
judgement, if you will permit me to keep alive the sentiments in your

heart, which may be termed romantic," she tells Imlay. And in one of the loveliest passages in all her writing, she muses:

> Believe me, sage sir, you have not sufficient respect for the imagination—I could prove to you in a trice that it is the mother of sentiment, the great distinction of our nature, the only purifier of the passions—animals have a portion of reason, and equal, if not more exquisite, senses; but no trace of imagination, or her offspring taste, appears in any of their actions. The impulse of the senses, passions, if you will, and the conclusions of reason, draw men together; but the imagination is the true fire, stolen from heaven, to animate this cold creature of clay, producing all those fine sympathies that lead to rapture, rendering men social by expanding their hearts.[10]

In September, Mary decided to return to Paris. The journey was "the most fatiguing . . . I ever had."[11] Four times, the carriage tipped. And Mary's current servant was useless during the crisis and afterward couldn't even manage to take Fanny off her hands. "I still continue to be almost a slave to the child," Mary complained to Imlay, but quickly added that Fanny was "a sweet little creature" whose "eyes are not the eyes of a fool—I will swear."[12]

Fanny relished urban living. Her favorite activities, Mary reported, were "looking at me," riding in a coach, glimpsing a French scarlet waistcoat, and hearing loud music. These pleasures abounded throughout Paris, where cheerfulness pervaded and having fun was in favor once more. Salons reopened, church bells rang, and theaters filled. Baggy trousers and red wool hats were decidedly outré. Men strutted out in tight-waisted pants and high collars, while women wore transparent dresses and décolletage. It was fashionable to stand out again. Madame de Staël wrapped herself in stoles and a turban; Tallien's wife had her gowns slit to the thigh.[13]

1. (*right*) An unglamorous portrait of young Mary Wollstonecraft (by an unknown artist).

2. (*bottom*) The Wollstonecrafts moved to Beverley in 1769 and settled in Wednesday's Market, which looked out over this Gothic church, the Beverley Minster.

3. Mary's favorite pupil, Margaret Kingsborough, in later life.

4. (*below, left*) Mary Wollstonecraft's 1788 moral tales for children, *Original Stories from Real Life*, was illustrated by William Blake. This haunting lithograph accompanies a story about the terrors of poverty.

5. (*below, right*) Joseph Johnson, one of the greatest publishers of his era, changed Mary's life when he promised to pay her to write. He became her best friend and mentor.

6. (*below, bottom right*) Moody, passionate, and arrogant, the bisexual artist Henry Fuseli became Mary Wollstonecraft's first great love.

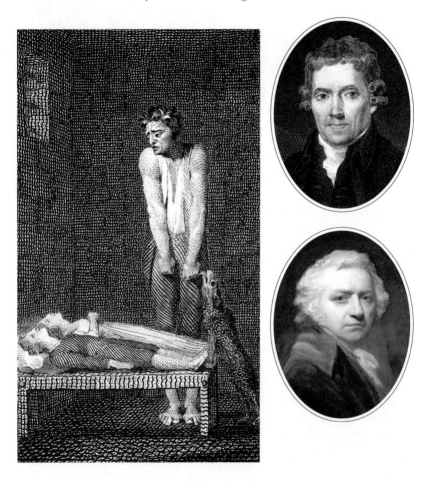

7 & 8. When Mary first arrived at St. Paul's Churchyard at the end of the summer of 1787, Anna Laetitia Barbaud (*left*) and Helen Maria Williams (*right*) were already established essayists and poets in the competitive publishing world.

9. Henry Fuseli gave his close friend Joseph Johnson this painting, *The Nightmare*, to hang in his dining room.

10. (*right*) This 1791 portrait commissioned by William Roscoe of Liverpool portrays Mary as the formidable woman author, with powdered curls; tensed, crooked fingers; and a mouth pinched with determination to have her way.

11. (*below*) When Mary arrived in Paris in December 1792, the guillotine was already busy decapitating "enemies of the Republic" across from the Tuileries Palace, formerly the home of kings.

12. (*facing page*) Manon Roland wrote hundreds of letters to newspapers defending the cause of the moderate Girondist partisans—always anonymously. For she believed a woman's ideas were demeaned by her public signature, just as her womanhood was diminished by an ambition to succeed in the world.

13. (*left*) Painted at the same time as the Roscoe portrait, this painting by John Opie shows Mary in a softer mood.

14. (*below, right*) Mary's 1792 *A Vindication of the Rights of Woman* was the first feminist manifesto in the history of human rights. One of *Vindication*'s most enthusiastic fans was fellow feminist Mary Hays, who signed this copy of the book.

A

VINDICATION

OF THE

RIGHTS OF WOMAN:

WITH

STRICTURES

ON

POLITICAL AND MORAL SUBJECTS.

By MARY WOLLSTONECRAFT.

LONDON:

PRINTED FOR J. JOHNSON, N° 72, ST. PAUL'S CHURCH YARD.

1792.

15. (*left*) Mary first met the young American poet-activist Joel Barlow and his wife, Ruth, at Joseph Johnson's in London. Their friendship deepened when Mary's American lover, Gilbert Imlay, and Barlow became business partners in France during the Terror.

16. (*below*) Thomas Paine's *Rights of Man* made him an honorary French citizen with a seat at the Convention in Paris, while he was condemned as a traitor by the British authorities and mocked as a fool in the anti-Jacobin press.

17. (*below, right*) Thomas Holcroft, eleven years older than his intimate friend William Godwin, was known as an "insatiable talker," who was also "dynamic," loyal, emotional, politically radical, and a seeker of truth.

18. (*below, left*) Elizabeth Inchbald captivated William Godwin when he met her after the triumph of his *Enquiry Concerning Political Justice* in the spring of 1792. She was said to look like a mixture of a milkmaid and a duchess, and Godwin frankly admired both her beauty and her spiteful wit.

19. (*bottom*) William Godwin was so infatuated with Amelia Alderson, known as the "Belle of Norwich," that he walked around carrying her shoe.

20. (*below, left*) William Godwin, Mary's husband and the father of Mary Shelley, began life as a Dissident minister but soon rejected faith in favor of Enlightenment thought.

21 & 22. (*below, right*) This later portrait of Mary Wollstonecraft by John Opie was painted during her second pregnancy and now hangs in London's National Portrait Gallery beside Richard Rothwell's portrait of Mary Shelley (*bottom*).

"Not to have suffered persecution during the tyranny of Robespierre, is now to be disgraced,"[14] wrote Helen Maria Williams. There were *bals de victimes* for relatives of the Terror's victims—widows cropped their hair and twined thin red ribbons around their necks to signify blood.[15] Newspapers advocating all points of view returned to the stands. "[The Parisians] write now with great freedom and truth, and this liberty of the press will overthrow the Jacobins,"[16] Mary predicted to Imlay.

Still, the Jacobins were not yet finished. Marat remained a national hero. His body was lowered into the Panthéon on September 21. Mary took Fanny to enjoy the accompanying festivities (though privately she mourned for her own martyrs, such as Condorcet, who had been discovered and arrested and died in his jail cell—probably from swallowing poison—before Robespierre's demise). And though they were quiet for now, the radical women would rise once more, in the upcoming May, to lead a siege on the Convention, to call for the Mountain to return to power, and to demand death for the new regime. It would take the military to defeat them, reflecting the growing power of the French armed forces. But defeated they would be, so thoroughly that in the spring of 1795 the Convention banned all unaccompanied women from its meetings and forbade more than five females to walk together in the street.

BUT IN THE FALL of 1794, Mary was free to walk with whomever she wanted. She moved into her old St-Germain apartment, hired a promising nursemaid named Marguerite, and quickly struck up a friendship with a German family, who shared Mary's passion for education and swapped tips with her about teething, early morning wake-ups, and the amount of time a child should nurse. While the German family was "just above poverty, I envy them—" Mary wrote Imlay. "She is a tender, affectionate mother—fatigued even by her attention.— However, she has an affectionate husband in her turn, to render her care light, and to share her pleasure. . . . I will own to you that, feeling extreme tenderness for my little girl, I grow sad very often when I am playing with her, that you are not here, to observe with me how her mind unfolds, and her little heart becomes attached!"[17]

Many of Mary's old friends had left the country—the Christies for first Switzerland and then England; the Barlows to Hamburg, where Joel had found work. The Schweizers remained. Once, while Mary composed a letter to Gilbert, Madeleine Schweizer sat beside her, reading Imlay's first book. "She desires me to give her love to you, on account of what you say of the negroes," Mary informed the author.

In her journal, Madame Schweizer was less flattering about Mary:

I was very fond of Mary Wollstonecraft . . . and should have liked to regard her with constant affection, but she was so intolerant that she repulsed those women who were not inclined to be subservient to her; whilst to her servants, her inferiors, and the wretched in general, she was gentle as an angel. Were it not for her excessive sensibility, which too often gains the upper hand, her personality would be exquisite. I passed one evening with her in the country. The blending of the varying tints of colour in the sky were of a marvellous poetic beauty. Mary was sitting with [a baron] beneath a tree gilded by the rays of the setting sun. I was opposite them, and was so enraptured by the scene that I said . . .: "Come Mary,—come nature lover,—and enjoy this wonderful spectacle—this constant transition from colour to colour!" But, to my great surprise, Mary was so indifferent that she never turned her eyes from him by whom she was at the moment captivated.[18]

So mothering and lovesickness did not keep Mary from (in her old friend George Blood's words) "assuming the Princess" and charming barons or counts, as in the case of Count von Schlabrendorf, who was out of prison and continued to adore her. There was also a certain judge she found attractive, and handsome Claude-Joseph Rouget de l'Isle, author of the "Marseillaise," whom Mary would be "half in love with" if Imlay did not return soon.

She made a new friend named Archibald Hamilton Rowan, an Irish patriot whom the British had unjustly accused of sedition and thrown into jail. He had escaped and, leaving his wife and eight children behind in Ireland, fled to Paris, where he arrived in the last days of the Grand Terror and remained after the death of Robespierre, waiting to be exonerated by the British king.[19] Rowan was forty-two and breathtakingly handsome. He first spotted Mary walking with Marguerite and Fanny in the fall of 1794. "[A friend] whispered to me that she was the author of the 'Rights of Woman.' I started! 'What!' said I within myself, 'this is Miss Mary Wollstonecraft, parading about with a child at her heels, with as little ceremony as if it were a watch she had just bought at the jeweller's. So much for the rights of women,' thought I."[20]

But Rowan and Mary quickly established a close rapport. "I got a dish of tea and an hour's rational conversation, whenever I called on her,"[21] Rowan recalled. Their talks were often intimate. Once, Mary dismayed Rowan by announcing that love was the only justification for perpetuating a marriage. If so, he wondered, would he lose his far-off wife? No, Mary assured him, "for . . . when a person whom we have loved [is] absent, all the faults he might have [are] diminished, and his virtues augmented in proportion."[22] They surpassed each other boasting of their partners. Mary's "account of Mr. Imlay made me wish for his acquaintance; and my description of my love made her desirous of your acquaintance," Rowan wrote his wife[23] in Ireland.

Also in Ireland, still governessing, was Mary's sister Everina, who'd lately received a series of shocking reports. First, in the spring of 1794,

Mary's letter from Le Havre arrived, implying that she was in love with an American. A few months later, Charles wrote from Philadelphia announcing that Mary was married and had a child. "I own I want faith—nay I doubt my senses," gasped Eliza. But when Joseph Johnson (who'd consulted with the repatriated Christies) confirmed Charles's report, Eliza expected to be summoned to Paris at any moment. She hired a fifty-year-old escaped royalist (who reminded her of Joseph Johnson and had "the manners of a gentleman blended, with great simplicity of character") to perfect her French.[24]

And, if this weren't enough, Charles invited Eliza to join *him* in Philadelphia: "In the autumn I will remit you 100 pounds . . . which will pay your passage to this country and you shall have a room in my house, and a quiet horse to ride—or it will go hard with me. If you can resolve to leave England you may rest assured of everything in my power being done to render life comfortable to you—and that elegant ease you have often longed for I will assure you."[25] Good-bye, Upton Castle! Eliza exulted. If her Paris plans failed, she would embrace the New World.

Eliza quit her governess job and moved into nearby Pembrokeshire. "Three and a half [years] I lingered in this dungeon [Upton Castle]. Yet I am sad—," she told Everina, for parting from the family's little boy[26] was "like losing a limb. . . . This is the *Last* child I ever *Love!*" she vowed.[27]

Meanwhile, Everina received a baffling note from Mary, telling her "You must, my dear Girl, have received several letters from me, especially one I sent to London with Mr. Imlay." But the sisters had not received Mary's letters, nor had Imlay contacted them in the two and a half months since he'd left France. Also perplexing was Mary's offhanded suggestion that Everina visit Paris in the springtime. "If possible in Spring, my Everina, why not have gone [to Paris] with Mr. *Imlay* [now] could he have written to us!" Eliza exclaimed.

Why not, indeed? Eliza promptly wrote to Imlay in care of Joseph

Johnson at St. Paul's Churchyard. And here is the tortuous letter she
received in reply:

My dear Madam

Mr. Johnson gave me your acceptable favor inclosing one to
Mrs. Imlay saying it was for her; which leaving me ignorant of
being included I could not return an immediate answer. Since
which time I have been out of Town. I hope this circumstance
will appear to you a sufficient apology for my silence, and that
you will be pleased to consider it a good reason for preventing a
forfeight of that claim to humanity, or at least respect, I esteem
for a person so affectionately loved by my dear Mary as yourself
which you say had already been impressed on your mind— As
to your sister's visiting England, I do not think she will previous
to a peace, and perhaps not immediately after such an Event.
However be that as it may we shall both of us continue to cherish feelings of tenderness for you and a recollection of your unpleasant situation, and we shall also endeavor to alleviate its
distress by all the means in our power—the present state of our
fortune is rather pre[carious]— However you must know your
sister too well—and I am sure you judge of that knowledge too
favorably to suppose that whenever she has it in her power that
she will not apply some specific aid to promote your happiness.
I shall always be happy to receive your letters, I shall most likely
leave England the beginning week. I will thank you to let me
hear from you as soon as convenient and tell me ingenuously in
what way I can serve you in any manner or respect. I am in but
indifferent spirits occasioned by my long absence from Mrs. Imlay and our little girl while I am deprived of a chance of hearing
from them

    Adieu yours—

    G. Imlay

So Imlay "cherish[ed] feelings of tenderness" for Mary's sisters, but had no plans to meet them. He'd love to help them out—some other time. And he'd "always be happy to receive your letters" but was leaving the country. What a muddle of downright deceit and unctuous dissimulation, not to mention bad grammar. And to add to the insult, when Eliza in a fury wrote Imlay that she needed neither him nor his wife and was positively bent on leaving for America, Imlay failed to reply.

The above note to Eliza is one of Imlay's few surviving letters. How different he sounds here than in his books. While the author is compassionate and idealistic, the correspondent is avid only to avoid trouble. The first is forthright, while the latter is abstruse. Mary alludes to another disparity between the two Imlays in one of her increasingly unchecked outbursts. "Reading what you have written [in your books] relative to the desertion of women, I have often wondered how theory and practice could be so different."[28]

If Imlay's letters to Mary were half as sly as his reply to Eliza, it must have been hard work convincing herself that he intended to return. Still, she was too proud to confide her doubts to her sisters and, rather than lie, simply ignored them during the terrible winter of 1795.

It was the coldest winter of the century. The Seine and all the Paris water fountains froze. Coal was a luxury one stood hours on line to purchase, and wood was so scarce women and children chopped logs from the trees in the Bois de Boulogne. When, in December, the Convention abolished more price and wage controls, the cost of bread shot up, and the value of the currency plunged. People died because they couldn't afford bread or fuel for their fires, or they killed themselves—suicide rates rose drastically. Wolves howled at the gates of Paris. And the traditional recourse of the poor, the Church, was so devastated by the Terror that it could do little to help.

Mary caught a cold and was feverish and coughing as madly as when she'd first arrived from London. Only now she was responsible for a shivering infant and had to drag herself from bed and walk great distances to find wood. "This however is one of the common evils which must be borne with—bodily pain does not touch the heart, though it fatigues the spirit,"[29] she wrote Imlay. Indeed, while Mary freely confided her mental suffering, she was proud of her strong body and despised admitting any physical need. She admitted her need now—in early January—because she wanted Imlay to pay for a servant to relieve her and Marguerite—who was now part of the family—from wood carrying. He would agree, she knew, which made asking all the harder: Imlay's eagerness to pay Mary's bills merely underscored his emotional negligence.

Mary had expected her lover in late December and so was "tormented by fears" at Christmastime when some British ships sank in a Channel gale. For once, it was a relief to learn that business had kept Imlay safely in London. But "How I hate this crooked business!" she was soon again expostulating, ". . . This intercourse with the world, which obliges one to see the worst side of human nature! Why cannot you be content with the object you had first in view [the farm in America] when you entered into this weary labyrinth?"[30] More than ever, she despised her financial dependence. She was determined to find a way to support her child and herself. "I have two or three plans in my head to earn our subsistence; for do not suppose that, neglected by you, I will lie under obligations of a pecuniary kind to you!— No; I would sooner submit to menial service."[31]

Fanny did not catch Mary's cold or gloomy perspective. All through the blighting winter, she made the normal progress. She began crawling and grew two teeth. She sucked from Mary's breasts and gnawed at crusts of bread and biscuits. She was like a squirrel, the way she husbanded her treats. And "after fixing her eye on an object for some time, [she darted] on it with an aim as sure as a bird of prey."[32] She had more spirit than physical beauty. She looked like Imlay, her mother thought.

In February 1795, Mary, still feverish and with her cough worsening, believed she had tuberculosis and began seriously to plan for the worst. She moved in with her German friends, who said they would bring up Fanny with their own child should Mary die. Mary "conjured" Imlay "by all you hold sacred" to accede to this plan.[33]

"Brought up here my girl would be freer,"[34] wrote Mary, showing some stirring of her old faith in the French, as well as an increasing aversion to England. Meanwhile, Imlay continued to hem and haw about returning to Paris, while his French associate maddened Mary with announcements of fresh delays.

In late winter, Mary threatened Imlay that if he delayed any longer she would refuse to accept his money. His failing to love her would impoverish and probably kill her, in other words. So in February, Imlay went through the motions of inviting Mary to join him in England. But the formal tone of his letter infuriated Mary, who suspected he would be off again as soon as she and Fanny came. "Am I only to return to a country, that has not merely lost all charms for me, but for which I feel a repugnance that almost amounts to horror, only to be left there a prey to it!"[35] Then Imlay rephrased the offer: "Business alone has kept me from you.—Come to any port, and I will fly down to my two dear girls with a heart all their own."[36]

So in April 1795, Mary, Fanny, and loyal Marguerite left Paris. Once again, Mary was in good health. "Here I am in [Le Havre]," she wrote Gilbert, "on the wing towards you, and I write now, only to tell you, that you may expect me in the course of three or four days; for I shall not attempt to give vent to the different emotions which agitate my heart. . . . I cannot indulge the very affectionate tenderness which glows in my bosom, without trembling, till I see, by your eyes, that it is mutual."

For once accepting conventional wisdom, Mary weaned Fanny so she'd be prepared to make love. "I did not wish to embitter the renewal of your acquaintance with [Fanny], by putting [the weaning] off till we met," she delicately wrote. "It was a painful exertion to me," for she relished suckling. But "I thought it best to throw this inquietude with the rest, into the sack that I would fain throw over my shoulder."[37] She was indulging hope.

In Le Havre, Mary packed up her clocks and linens and asked "the good people here" to sell her furniture. After two and a half years in France, on April 9, 1795, she boarded a boat heading home. Then the "awkward pilot" grounded the ship in the harbor! She had to disembark and go back to town and wait some more. "With the heart and imagination on the wing you may suppose that the slow march of time is felt very painfully," she wrote Hamilton Rowan, and flirtatiously continued: "If you were to pop in I should be glad, for in spite of my impatience to see [Gilbert Imlay], I still have a corner in my heart, where I will allow you a place, if you have *no objection*."

But her last words from France were oddly apprehensive. "Take any precaution to avoid danger,"[38] Mary warned her Irish friend.

PART THREE

The New Order

CHAPTER TEN

*T*he England Mary returned to had been struck by the same merciless cold that had devastated France. "So long and so severe a winter . . . was never known in this country,"[1] Joseph Johnson wrote an author in America. In London as in Paris, thousands had starved and died from food shortages. The poor rioted in the streets or hissed and threw stones at King George III as he rode by in his warm carriage on the way to the opening of Parliament. Pamphlets with threatening titles like *King Killing* and *Happy Reign of George the Last* circulated.[2] And, along with the king, the leader of Parliament, William Pitt, was blamed for England's hardships. But so too were the French Revolution and the French war, which was consuming England's resources.

English radicals were called Jacobins (though their sympathies were for the most part with the Girondists), and English politics was now firmly divided between Jacobin and anti-Jacobin factions. Jacobin men refused to powder their hair, which they cut short, and the women wore flowing robes like the simple chemises Mary had admired in Paris. Many Jacobins joined the London Corresponding

Society, known as the LCS. Its leader was John Thelwall, who drew thousands to his fiery lectures. But the LCS's mission was peaceful reform; there was no talk of regicide or revolution.

So it was a surprise when in 1794 Pitt arrested twelve LCS members on grounds of high treason. Though he was not himself a member, the writer William Godwin—author of the now famous 1793 *Political Justice*—had deeply influenced the philosophy of the LCS, which sought to follow his strategy of gradual reform. Four days before the LCS trial, Godwin published an anonymous article in the *Morning Chronicle* arguing the reformers' absolute innocence according to the principles of British justice. The defendants were swiftly exonerated—thanks to Godwin, many thought. Still, the division between Pitt and the LCS widened. Pitt suspended habeas corpus and backed the anti-Jacobin Church and King clubs; John Thelwall, writing in his weekly *Tribune*, raged against government policy: "Moderation! Moderation! A compromise between right and wrong: I detest it."[3]

And while the poor starved and the politicians contended, a new class of self-made men was quietly emerging in Great Britain. Abundant natural resources coupled with the skill to capitalize on technological advancements made England the fastest-industrializing country in Europe. Its first factory was a 1719 silk mill driven by a central waterwheel. Cotton and metal works swiftly followed. Copper was wrung from the Cornish countryside, coal from Yorkshire and Wales. As consumer demand grew, canals were dug to speed up inland transport, and the Royal Navy shepherded export abroad.

As the eighteenth century progressed, invention increasingly stoked production. Henry Cort's "reverberatory furnace" accelerated the creation of wrought iron, rotary steam engines propelled bigger and better flour and cotton mills, and Edmund Cartwright's power loom transformed cotton factories and incited a great riot by displaced hand loomers when it first appeared at Grimshaw's Manchester factory in 1792. The hand loomers lost their jobs, but demand for cheap labor in the metal trades, transportation, weaving, and all the services quickened. As populations shifted from the farms to the city, a labor force of trammeled children appeared on the English landscape, and entrepreneurs like John Christian Curwen, Richard Arkwright, and Josiah Wedgwood grew rich as lords.

While these newly rich basked in their enhanced social stature, they hastened to distinguish themselves from aristocrats in the domestic sphere. They scorned decadence and praised traditional values.[4] Women were extolled as the family's moral agents, while raising virtuous children became the wifely equivalent of thriving at work. In this context, needless to say, women demanding their own rights to achieve were anathemas—or Amazons, as they were snidely called.

With their allusions to reason and sensibility rather than the common sense British conservatives championed, radical women were mocked as would-be Parisians. Hannah More (who'd derided *Vindication*) summed up the anti-Jacobin position: "Under a just impression of the evils which we are sustaining from the principles of *modern* France, we are apt to lose sight of those deep and lasting mischiefs which so long, so regularly, and so systematically we have been importing from the same country, though in another form and under another system." In other words, such mischiefs as female vanity, intellectual aggressiveness, and loose morals.[5] Even liberal Maria Edgeworth, in her 1795 *Letters for Literary Ladies*, belittles the campaign for sexual equality. "Do not . . . call me 'a champion for the rights of women,'" she remarks. "I am more intent upon their happiness than ambitious to enter into a metaphysical discussion of their rights."[6] She has rarely met a woman fit to compete with a man, and as for those few superior creatures: "Prodigies are scarcely less offensive to my taste than monsters."[7]

In the spring of 1795, blithe platitudes about dutiful wives suffused the popular weekly *The Spectator*, and new editions of Reverend

James Fordyce's and Dr. John Gregory's benighted female conduct books sold briskly in the stores. As for the radicals: Mary's friend Mrs. Barbauld continued to applaud Dissident causes, and Joseph Johnson published a flurry of books on France, including Madame Roland's *Memoirs,* Mary's *French Revolution,* and *Letters and Essays, Moral and Miscellaneous* by a new author named Mary Hays, who in a meeker voice advanced Mary's points. To their credit, Jacobin and anti-Jacobin women overlapped more than their male counterparts. At moments, conservative women could sound almost like radicals, and there were radicals who questioned their own most cherished ideals. In one of her essays, Hannah More, for instance, deviates from her diatribe against female intellectuals to exhort girls to study philosophy rigorously, while Mrs. Barbauld takes time from delineating an enlightened education to admit:

> The education of your house, important as it is, is only a part of a more comprehensive system. Providence takes your child where you leave him. . . . Affections soften the proud; difficulties push forward the ingenious; successful industry gives consequence and credit, and develops a thousand latent good qualities.[8]

Mary came home to a country deeply confused about change, reform, and relations between the sexes. She traveled to London with Fanny and Marguerite only, for Imlay did not "fly down to my two dear girls" when their boat landed safely at Brighton on Saturday, April 7, 1795. That day Mary wrote Imlay:

> Here we are, my love, and mean to set out early in the morning; and, if I can find you, I hope to dine with you to-morrow; I shall drive to ———'s hotel, where ——— tells me you have been—and, if you have left it, I hope you will take care to be

there to receive us. . . . I have brought with me . . . a girl [Mar-
guerite] whom I like to take care of our little darling. . . . But
why do I write about trifles?—or any thing?— Are we not to
meet soon?— What does your heart say!

    Yours truly

    MARY

  I have weaned my [baby], and she is now eating away at the
white bread.[9]

So Mary reiterated that she was sexually available, then drove to
meet the rising businessman she'd kissed good-bye eight months before. The forward movement of the carriage raised her spirits. Again,
she dared to look forward to happiness—though the truth struck her
the moment she spotted Imlay. This man no longer loved her. The
ramifications of that loss were overwhelming, and she did not grapple
with them immediately, or indeed for a long time to come. Nor did
Imlay press her with details—such as the fact that he'd taken up with
a young actress from a company of traveling players. No, his "explanations" were vague enough that Mary could agree to move into a
furnished house Imlay had let for her on Charlotte Street near the
British Museum, not far from the Christies, who'd settled at Finsbury
Square. But then what were Mary's alternatives? She was a penniless
unwed mother in a country far more circumspect about marriage
vows than France.

  For a while, Imlay made a show of living with his family, though he
was constantly out for one reason or another. There was no other
woman, he promised. He was torn between devotion to his family
and a yearning for "the zest of life."[10] His morals were "exalted,"[11] he
informed his child's mother, and explained that whatever became of
their love, he would give her half his earnings—which infuriated
Mary.[12] Imlay's "attentions . . . to Mary were formal and con-
strained."[13] Probably, they never slept in the same bed. Fanny called

Imlay "Papa" and mimicked her mama's admonishments to him, such as "Come, come!" and "Will you not come and let us exert ourselves?"[14] There are no records of Imlay's reactions to year-old Fanny, though it is in the spring of 1795 that Mary stops referring to Fanny as *ours*. From now on, she will be *the child* or *my child*. Looking back, Mary began to perceive Fanny's birth as the start of her marital troubles. ("Despair since the birth of my child, has rendered me stupid,"[15] she would write Imlay that summer.) Mary's correspondence to Imlay ceases between April 11 and May 22—presumably because they are under the same roof—and when it starts up, there have been more "cruel explanations," and Imlay has moved out.

MARY HAD explanations of her own to make that spring to her sisters, especially Eliza, who lumbered on with her French in Pembrokeshire. Eliza had argued about politics with her royalist tutor and they were now on more "formal" terms, she informed Everina. So whatever private ideas she may have indulged of a close friendship, or more, with the man who reminded her of Joseph Johnson were dashed. Worse, when Eliza finally heard from her brother Charles, he merely recounted a long list of his own problems, saying nothing about Eliza's move to Philadelphia or even the 100 pounds he'd promised to send.[16]

Still, better news came from James, now an officer in the Navy, who had met Imlay in London and found him "a fine handsome fellow."[17] James said that Imlay had made 100,000 pounds since he'd arrived in England, and that Mary would join him in London soon. "To have made *such* a fortune in a few months— It is so truly in the novel style my Everina—and so similar to Castles we have dwelt on in days of yore that I am actually afraid to Hope," Eliza wrote.

Still, hope Eliza did, and she on the spot forgot all her gripes against the famous authoress, noting: "I know no one deserving of *even so large* a fortune [as] Mary or more worthy of such a companion as Imlay." The latter's fortune, however, did not excuse his ill manners. "I am a little surprised that [Imlay] should not recollect, at this juncture, poor I—for he is in my debt—" mused Eliza, referring to his failure to reply to her letter. "But I am out of conjecturing and will have patience till the sky falls."[18]

So it must have come as quite a shock to Eliza when at the end of April she received a letter from Mary at Charlotte Street:

I arrived in Town near a fortnight ago, my dear Girl, but having previously weaned my child on account of a cough I found myself extremely weak. I have intended writing to you every day, but have been prevented by the impossibility of determining in what way I can be of essential service to you. When Mr. Imlay and I united our fate together he was without fortune; since then there is a prospect of his obtaining a considerable one; but though the hope appears to be well founded I cannot yet act as if it were a certainty. He is the most generous creature in the world and if he succeed, as I have the greatest reason to think he will, he will, in proportion to his acquirement of property, enable me to be useful to you and Everina— I wish you and her could adopt any plan in which five or six hundred pounds could be of use. As to myself I cannot yet say where I shall live for a continuance it would give me the sincerest pleasure to be situated near you— I know you will think me unkind—and it was this reflection that has prevented my writing to you sooner, not to invite you to come and live with me— But Eliza it is my opinion, not a readily formed one, the presence of a third person interrupts or destroys domestic happiness— Accepting this sacrifice there is nothing I would not do to promise your comfort— I am hurt at being obliged to be thus explicit and do indeed severely feel for the disappointments which you have met in Life. . . . Do pray write to me immediately and do justice to my heart. I do not wish to endanger my own peace without a certainty of securing yours— Yet I am still your most sincere and affectionate friend.

MARY[19]

Had Eliza read between lines like "I do not wish to endanger my own peace," she might have detected her sister's insecurity or re-membered the "Princess"-like pride that had checked Mary's confi-dences in the past. But Eliza was in no frame of mind to divine *Mary's* predicament. Her own hopes were blasted; once again her powerless-ness was thrown in her face. "Good God . . . to be thus insulted . . . how have I merited such pointed cruelty!" Eliza exploded in a letter to Everina in Dublin. When, she demanded, had she ever asked to live with Mary or "to interrupt *their Domestic* happiness!"

"Are your eyes open at last?" Eliza continues and vows that never again will she "torment our amiable friend in Charlotte Street. . . . Alas! Poor Bess."[20]

Mary's letter to Eliza is dated April 23. On the twenty-seventh, she writes more contritely to her younger sister: "You will perhaps accuse me of insensibility" for not writing sooner; but she's had a violent cold and furthermore "was at a loss what I could do to render Eliza's situation more comfortable." Imlay has not yet made the great for-tune they all anticipated. "When a sufficient sum is actually realized I know he will give me for you and Eliza five or six hundred pounds, or more if he can." Again, she insists she can't offer Eliza asylum, but does not now dwell on her marital bliss. Imlay is merely "my present attachment."

"I am above concealing my sentiments though I have boggled at uttering them," she avers.

The effect of this second note was to further antagonize both sis-ters. Nor was their anger softened when a friend informed them that Joseph Johnson "said he *never* saw Mary so *well* or so happy as at pre-

sent."[21] Eliza dramatically renounced all her ambitions for a better future, insisting she'd accept whatever lowly position Everina could
procure. "Remember I am as fixed as my misery and nothing can
change my present plan,"[22] she wrote at the end of April, though by
May 8 she'd had second thoughts. "Would to God we were both in
America with Charles," she wrote of the blundering brother who
now seemed a paragon of dependability compared to Mary. "Do you
think it would be possible for us to go from Dublin in an American
ship to Philadelphia— This is my only HOPE."[23] Practical Everina ignored Eliza's scheme and urged her instead to come immediately to
Dublin, where yet another tedious governessing job awaited her. But
Eliza lingered for a month in Pembroke, mulling over a different fate.

As ELIZA was baffled by Mary's reticence, Mary pronounced herself
stupefied by Imlay's indifference. His cheerfulness drove her to dis-
traction, and, during the month of May, she waged a campaign to ruffle him: disputing, complaining, and raging whenever he gave her the
chance. Mary spent hours pouring her heart out to sympathetic Rebecca Christie. And she pulled herself together to visit friends she
hadn't seen in years. Surprisingly, she paid a call on Henry Fuseli,
maybe to boast of her consummated love affair and her fine daughter,
or to flout conventional morality, or to find sympathy. Mary herself
could not explain her motives. Nor could she bring herself to write so
much as an article for Joseph Johnson. She felt irritable and was given
to bursts of energy and attacks of despair. Though she was physically
in England, part of her still lived out the French Revolution, which
every day seemed more like the French war on the world. In October, France would annex Belgium, solidify its hold on Holland and
the Rhineland, and move to attack northern Italy. There would be a
new, less democratic constitution and an executive council of five directors increasingly under military sway. It seemed that all the early

idealism of the French Revolution was to end in mere territorial expansion.

Still, whatever the flaws of the French, Mary found little to recommend the stolid British with their prosaic low brick buildings, graceless manners, and obsession with virtuous wives. Even the well-pavemented London streets Mary had so missed in Paris were little solace now when there were so few places she wished to walk. It was a bittersweet joy to meet again with Joseph Johnson, working away in St. Paul's Churchyard, with his asthma and goodness and practical mind. He was the embodiment of constancy, like the cupola of St. Paul's flying above his window and the dinner list of familiar Jacobins and literati congregating weekly in his lopsided dining hall. Yet, Mary was different. In a foreign land, she had grasped and lost great happiness. Their friendship was as warm as ever, but Mary may initially have demurred from confiding in Johnson about Imlay's perfidy. And it is possible that enough pleasure still lingered in her expressive face for Johnson to honestly claim her "well" and "happy." And if not, then he chose to hide from the world her misery and shame.

Another friend particularly anxious to support Mary at this time was the Dissident writer Mary Hays, whom Mary had first met during the summer of 1792 before she had left for Paris. Two years younger than Mary Wollstonecraft, Mary Hays shared her fascination with Rousseau and Locke and also defended the increasingly embattled literature of "sensibility" against the tyranny of common sense. Coleridge described the older Mary Hays as "ugly," but she was zealous and intelligent and probably attractive in her youth. At least one man, John Eccles, fell passionately in love with her and she with him. Mary Hays's adolescent love letters to Eccles are the epistolary equivalent of Ann Radcliffe's Gothic novels. A typical passage reads:

The passions are common to all, but the affections, the lively sweet affections, the only source of true pleasure, are the portion of only a chosen few. . . . Half the world have no senses, at least no one but of the animal and vegetable kind; to these species of beings, love and sentiment are quite unnecessary. . . . I envy not their dull insipid calmness—rather would I suffer all those heart-rending, exquisite distresses, which too often flow from sensibility than possess that stoical indifference which though it may exempt them from pain, yet at the same time precludes them from the sweet, the pleasurable sensations which those hearts experience who are susceptible to the finer feelings of humanity.[24]

Hays was seventeen in 1779 when she and Eccles fell in love. Eccles's father forbade them to marry because Hays had no money and Eccles had no work. For a year, they simply gazed at each other in Dissident meetings and wrote ardent letters, which Hays's sister Betsy reluctantly trundled from house to house. Then Eccles's father relented. A wedding date was set. Suddenly, Eccles contracted a fever. "Ah! My dear Mama, it would indeed be a hard trial to part with my Eccles *now*, when every obstacle is removed, for the business is now quite settled, and there seems nothing to prevent [the wedding's] taking place, unless this illness of my Eccles should terminate in a decline," Hays wrote—presciently.[25] For John indeed died soon after, and for years Hays mourned. Then, in her mid-twenties, she recovered sufficiently to immerse herself in literature and philosophy. She published magazine stories and, in 1792, a well-received Dissident pamphlet that won such eminent admirers as the scientist Joseph Priestley and the poet George Dyer.

It was George Dyer who brought Mary Hays a copy of *Vindication*. Hays was awed by Mary's achievement and longed to become her friend. A first meeting took place in 1792 at Joseph Johnson's home.

Afterward, Mary invited Hays to breakfast at her place on Store Street. "I was extremely gratified by this interview," Hays reported. "This lady appears to me to possess the sort of genius which Lavater calls the one to ten million. Her conversation, like her writing, is brilliant, forcible, instructive and entertaining. She is the true disciple of her own system, and commands at once fear and reverence, admiration and esteem."[26]

Mary clearly enjoyed preaching a bolder feminism to her wide-eyed admirer. In November of 1792, Mary cautioned Hays against the typically female obsequiousness that suffused the preface to Hays's new book, *Letters and Essays, Moral and Miscellaneous* (published by Joseph Johnson in early 1793). "Let me remind you that when weakness claims indulgence it seems to justify the despotism of strength," she shrewdly observed. And:

> You must be aware, Madam, that the *honour* of publishing, the phrase on which you have laid a stress, is the cant of both trade and sex; for if really equality should ever take place in society the man who is employed and gives a just equivalent for the money he receives will not behave with the obsequiousness of a servant. . . . Disadvantages of education &c ought, in my opinion, never to be pleaded (with the public) in excuse for defects of any importance, because if the writer has not sufficient strength of mind to overcome the common difficulties which lie in his way, nature seems to command him, with a very audible voice, to leave the task of instructing others to those who can.[27]

Then Mary Wollstonecraft went off to Paris, and Mary Hays moved away from her family and into a home of her own on Gainsford Street near the Tower Bridge. It was here she read about William Godwin's *Political Justice* and pluckily wrote the author asking if he would lend her a copy. Godwin complied, and a friendship developed, based on their shared philosophical interests and Hays's emotional needs. Hays told Godwin of her burning love for a man she refused to identify, fearing that he would reject or, worse still, laugh at her. Godwin could not calm Hays with his admonishments to reason. The passion persisted. Indeed, Hays was more than ever obsessed with this mysterious male in April 1793, when Mary Wollstonecraft came home to London, heartbroken. Pain is a great equalizer, and Mary Hays and Mary Wollstonecraft had far more in common now than when last they had met.

In an obituary for Wollstonecraft, Hays would astutely interpret her friend's despair in May 1795, after Imlay left Charlotte Street: "The degree of calamity is to be estimated rather by the susceptibility of the sufferer, than by the apparent magnitude of the event."[28] But at the time, no one comprehended the depth of Mary Wollstonecraft's misery—except, perhaps, her devoted servant Marguerite, and Imlay, whom she had informed the previous winter that she was "dead to hope."[29] Now, in May, she wrote him: "It seems to me that I have not only lost the hope, but the power of being happy.—Every emotion is now sharpened by anguish.—My soul has been shook, and my tone of feelings destroyed."

"I am a nothing," she said.[30]

Throughout her months in Paris, Mary had lived for her daughter, but now even Fanny could not tempt her from the longing to be done with the world. Swallowing an overdose of laudanum, a form of opium, would kill you, and this Mary did some time near the end of May.

Her Anglican religion condemned suicide, of course, but for the past seven years the Enlightenment had been Mary Wollstonecraft's God. And while Locke deplored the taking of one's own life, most of the *philosophes* and deists defended it as an expression of free will, while dying for love or fine feeling was ennobled in literature like Goethe's *Sorrows of Young Werther* and popular romances like Herbert

Croft's *Love and Madness* (1780), which fictionalized the suicide of the seventeen-year-old indigent genius Thomas Chatterton.[31] Joseph Johnson's author Charlotte Smith wrote poems about suicide, while his most famous poet, William Cowper, attempted many times to kill himself. England was called the suicide capital of the world because of its tolerance for self-killing—albeit on the grounds that anyone who didn't want to live was mad.[32] Mary was not mad, but she was seriously depressed—inconsolable.

Mary would describe an attempted suicide by laudanum in a set of notes for the ending of her 1797 novel *Maria*. Here the heroine, Maria, is persecuted by her dastardly husband and deserted by a lover she adores. Overwhelmed by sorrows, Maria determines to die. She swallows laudanum and is gratified by the onset of "calm." Yet her eyes won't close. Scenes from her life pass before her to "prevent her sinking into the sleep of death." Maria thinks of her two dead children. If they were alive, could she have left them alone in this evil world? No answer comes to her, but the effects of the drug increase:

> Her head turned; a stupor ensued; a faintness— "Have a little patience," said Maria, holding her swimming head (she thought of her mother), "this cannot last long; and what is a little bodily pain to the pangs I have endured?"

Still, true resignation eludes her. The figure of a beloved servant, Jemima, appears in her mind's eye. Jemima has a "little creature" with her. "Behold your child!" Jemima proclaims. Maria faints and vomits. Restored to life, she learns that one of the children she presumed dead is alive and standing at her side.

> [Maria] remained silent for five minutes, crossing her arms over her bosom, and reclining her head—then exclaimed: "The conflict is over!— I will live for my child!"

Mary had written Imlay a suicide note, and he arrived in time to save her. Mary also had written to Joseph Johnson, "warmly in your praise," she later assured Imlay, "to prevent any odium being thrown on you."[33] Like so many attempted suicides, Mary's swallowing laudanum may have been halfhearted, a cry for attention and for help. Certainly, she did not regret her failure. Like Maria, "She determined to continue to exist."[34]

If it accomplished nothing else, Mary's suicide attempt excited Imlay's guilt, his fear of social humiliation, and maybe a spasm of remembered love. He stood fairly warned that he ignored her misery at his own peril.

Of course, knowing Mary Wollstonecraft, Imlay could never have expected that she would leave him peacefully. But it was reasonable for him to hope that, once she was back in London, she would turn some of her ferocious energy from love to work. It was surprising to him that Mary could not or would not resume her writing career. What she badly needed, Imlay saw, was some engrossing new employment. Recently, he had lost valuable cargo in Scandinavia. Now he proposed that Mary travel to Sweden, Norway, and Denmark to track it down. She agreed, and on May 19, Imlay composed a letter—as convoluted and crabbed as his earlier note to Eliza—entrusting his "best friend and wife . . . Mrs. Imlay" with the legal right to act on his behalf.[35] Imlay furthermore promised Mary that he would meet her somewhere in Europe at the end of the summer. By then, he would have made an ultimate decision whether or not they should share their lives.

SOMETIME DURING the first week of June, either just before or (probably) just after Mary headed off on her journey, a letter arrived at her London address. The letter was written by Eliza, who "linger[ed] in Wales . . . anxiously await[ing]" a reply from her older sister. "This suspense almost drives me mad," Eliza told Everina in the middle of June.[36] Though Eliza's letter no longer exists, we can surmise that she asked Mary to find an alternative to the dreadful new governess position Everina had procured for her in Dublin. Eliza must have implored the author of *Vindication* to save her from the humiliation of her class and sex. Until her recent bizarre behavior, Mary had always been a loyal sister. When they had both been poor, Mary had nursed addled Eliza to health and rushed her away from a miserable marriage. Now Mary was rich and happily married. Surely, she would not desert "Poor Bess."

Since Eliza knew nothing of Mary's depression or suicide attempt or flight from London, she had every reason to expect Mary would receive her note and write back soon. But one week passed, then a second, while Mary traveled northward, away from her own problems, and Eliza was not rescued. At the end of a third week, Eliza gave up and left for the Dublin position. She would never see France or America, nor is there any record that she ever wrote Mary again. From Eliza's point of view, Mary's silence was a grave betrayal. She would remember it years later, when Mary's own daughter needed help. And it is true that Mary never contacted either Eliza or Everina during her long summer in Scandinavia. But what they didn't know was that before she left London, Mary had urgently pressed Imlay to send her sisters the share of his fortune that she refused to take for herself.[37]

CHAPTER ELEVEN

The problem that now drew Mary to Scandinavia had begun the fall before, when one of Imlay's ships had vanished off the coast of Norway, carrying silver worth 3,500 English pounds. The Danish government (which ruled Norway) brought criminal charges against the ship's captain, Peder Ellefsen, in January of 1795, and an inquiry against him was still in progress as Mary headed north.

"Know all men . . . that Gilbert Imlay citizen of the United States of America residing at present in London do nominate constitute and approve Mary Imlay my best friend and wife to take the sole management and direction of all my affairs and business," Imlay began his letter introducing Mary to the Scandinavian officials. And he went on high-handedly to explain his wishes in a most confusing style:

Considering the aggravated distress is the accumulated losses and damages I retained in consequence of [Ellefsen's] disobedience of my instructions I desire the said Mary Imlay will clearly ascertain the amount of such damages, taking first the advice of

persons qualified to judge of the probability of obtaining satisfaction or the means said Ellefsen or his connections, who may
be proved to be implicated in his guilt, may have on powers of
being able to make restitution.[1]

In other words, Mary should travel through Gothenburg to consult
with Imlay's Swedish agent Elias Blackman and determine how much
Ellefsen or his prominent business family could in fact afford to pay.
Ellefsen was known as a rogue and a daredevil. Mary was to attempt
to mediate a reasonable deal with him and, only if that failed, seek
justice from the courts.

She was thirty-six when she set off for Scandinavia. She was disillu-
sioned with the French Revolution, heartsick for Imlay, and unable to
write, which meant she could neither express nor support herself as
she liked. The port of Hull near Beverley in Yorkshire was the first
stop on her journey. She arrived on June 10, depressed by yet another
separation from Imlay and "extremely fatigued with the child," who
was teething and had clung to her in the carriage all the night before.[2]
Even sprightly Marguerite failed to beguile Fanny away from her exhausted mother. And now that it was day, Fanny was larking about
mimicking a mail boat whistle while Mary felt irritable and full of bitter thoughts.

"We are here in a comfortless sort of tomb-like house," she complained to Imlay. And she implored him to tell her his true feelings,
though it is clear in all her letters from this period that what she really
wants is good news:

Are we ever to meet again? and will you endeavour to render
that meeting happier than the last? Will you endeavour to re-
strain your caprices, in order to give vigour to affection, and to
give play to the checked sentiments that nature intended should
expand your heart? . . . Examine now yourself, and ascertain

whether you can live in something like a settled stile. Let our confidence in future be unbounded; consider whether you find it necessary to sacrifice me to what you term "the zest of life"; and when you have once a clear view of your own motives, of your incentive to action, do not deceive me![3]

Soon after she arrived in Hull, Mary found a captain of a cargo boat bound for Elsinore who was willing to drop her in Gothenburg, but then ill winds kept the boat in harbor until June 21. While she was waiting to embark, Mary made a day's pilgrimage to her childhood home of Beverley. Twenty years had passed since her father's reck-lessness had driven her from the verdant park and the lively Guild-hall and the adolescent girls gossiping in the Minster near her fashionable Wednesday's Market house. Then, she'd been awed by proper people like Jane Arden's family. Now, she was proud to stand apart. For though she boasted to Imlay that she "ran over my favourite walks, with a vivacity that would have astonished you," nonetheless Beverley "did not please me quite so well as formerly— It appeared so diminutive; and, when I found that many of the inhabi-tants had lived in the same houses since I left it, I could not help won-dering how they could thus have vegetated, whilst I was running over a world of sorrow, snatching at pleasure, and throwing off prejudice."

Mary's voyage from Hull was filled with mishaps. The sea was rough; Marguerite, whose "timidity always acts as a feeler before her adventuring spirit," became hopelessly motion sick, so the full burden of entertaining Fanny harassed Mary once again. Then, just south of Gothenburg, the winds suddenly died, and the boat stood motionless. Mary watched for sailors to rescue her—in vain. For, as she shrewdly notes in the travel *Letters* she would publish the following winter: "The [Swedish sailors] being paid by the king, and scantily . . . will not run into any danger, or even quit their hovels, if they can possibly avoid it, only to fulfil what is termed their duty. How different is it on the English coast, where, in the most stormy weather, boats immediately hail you, brought out by the expectation of extraordinary profit." Perhaps without realizing it, Mary is celebrating the powerful profit motive. She is also struggling to emerge from her depression and to erase memories of the Terror in France.

Reacting to a seascape near her becalmed cargo ship, Mary exclaimed, "I gazed around with rapture and felt more of that spontaneous pleasure which gives credibility to our expectation of happiness, than I had for a long, long time before. I forgot the horrors I had witnessed in France, which had cast a gloom over all nature, and suffering the enthusiasm of my character, too often, gracious God! damped by the tears of disappointed affection, to be lighted up afresh, care took wing while simple fellow feeling expanded my heart."[4]

But not for long. When Mary was safely on shore and walking toward the carriage that would take her to Gothenburg, she tripped on some jagged rocks, smashed her head, lost consciousness, and woke up "confused" and with a huge, bloody contusion swelling her face.[5] Then, when, still smarting from her fall, she reached Gothenburg—"a clean airy town" with "canals running through each street"—she was seized by the sudden conviction that Imlay was lost to her. "My heart is so oppressed, I cannot write with precision," she wrote him on July 1.[6] But by July 7, as Fanny played happily with some young Swedes in the garden, Mary was looking at the bright side again, writing: "My dear friend! I cannot tear my affections from you and . . . think of you till I make allowance for the very defects of [your] character, that have given such a cruel stab to my peace."[7]

As after her break with Fuseli, Mary slept fitfully and was tormented by nightmares and night fevers, though her head slowly healed. And the beauty of the Swedish landscape buoyed her spirits, "teasing her out of thought," as Keats would say of art. "Nothing," Mary exclaims, ". . . can equal the beauty of the northern summer's evening and night if night it may be that only wants the glare of day. . . . I could write at midnight without a candle."[8]

Mary was less pleased with the Swedish people. Generalizing from decidedly limited experience, she found them hard-drinking over-eaters who knew nothing of science or literature, feigned French manners, grossly mistreated women and servants, and frittered away the day with "tiresome forms and ceremonies" rather than striving to do good.

Though Mary was staying with Imlay's agent Elias Blackman, her letters rarely allude to business. Fanny, however, is frequently mentioned. To spare Fanny and Marguerite arduous travel through Norway, Mary had arranged for them to remain behind in Gothenburg, where she would collect them on her way home. But now, as her departure day approached, Mary dreaded this first separation from her daughter. "I grow more and more attached to my little girl," she writes Imlay.[9] And in *Letters* she anguishes eloquently about her daughter's future:

> You know that as a female . . . I feel more than a mother's fond-ness and anxiety, when I reflect on the dependent and oppresed state of her sex. I dread less she should be forced to sacrifice her heart to her principles, or principles to her heart. With trembling hand I shall cultivate sensibility, and cherish delicacy of senti-ment, lest, whilst I lend fresh blushes to the rose, I sharpen the thorns that will wound the breast I would fain guard— I dread to unfold her mind, lest it should render her unfit for the world she has to inhabit— Hapless woman! What a fate is thine.[10]

The cultivation of female sentiment and reason, which *Vindication* had presented as the key to equal rights for women, now struck Mary Wollstonecraft as treacherous. Love and Revolution had tempered her bold theories. Maybe everything was not possible. Maybe nothing was possible, she mused in her darkest moments. With all her gifts, she'd have nothing to live for, she felt sure, if at the end of the summer Imlay confessed that he was no longer in love with her and wanted to part for good.

For now, though, Mary threw herself into Imlay's business. Two weeks after she'd arrived, she left Gothenburg for Strömstad, then took an open boat across the North Sea to eastern Norway, stopping briefly in Larvik before finding a one-horse carriage whose bibulous driver whisked her off to Tönsberg. On this site of Norway's oldest settlement, she would try to recover Imlay's boat and silver through the intercession of Mayor Jacob Wulfsberg, a member of the original commission investigating Peder Ellefsen. Here she would spend three of the most intensely thoughtful weeks of her life.

Tönsberg was a shipping and whaling town, with rushing fjords, rolling farmland, corridors of pine and fir and aspen trees, two churches, and the ruins of an ancient castle. Mary pronounced the landscape "beautiful," though less "romantic" than Sweden's. Still, she preferred the soft, musical Norwegian language, and while the culture was as intellectually deficient as Gothenburg's, the Norwegian people were more industrious and the government wise. For Mary, Mayor Jacob Wulfsberg—who had a long, agreeable face and bright red nostrils—personified Norway's egalitarian spirit.

"You will be surprised to hear me talk of liberty," Mary writes, "yet the Norwegians appear to me to be the most free community I have ever observed. . . . The mayor[s] . . . can do much good, but little harm, as every individual can appeal from their judgement; and as they may always be forced to give a reason for their conduct, it is generally regulated by prudence." Liberty did not require a guillotine in Norway. Murder was the only capital offense. Lesser crimes drew imprisonment and hard labor, though any third-time offender became a slave to the state for life. Still, "The number of these slaves do not, I am informed, amount to more than a hundred" out of a population of 800,000, Mary rationalized.

Like its penal code, Norway's agrarian economy impressed Mary. Sharecroppers were nonexistent. Every farmer owned the land he cultivated. And while merchants, captains, and farmers were all, it seemed, content to be ruled by the benign king of Denmark and his enlightened minister Count Bernstorff, they were also intrigued by the Revolution in France. "They sing, with great glee, many republican songs, and seem earnest[l]y to wish that the republic may stand."[11]

Here is a glimmer of Mary's old passion for the Revolution and zeal for improvement. It was the end of July, and she was living quietly on the sea in a small planked wooden seafarer's inn painted red with yellow trim outside and blue within. (Norwegians believed that blue kept flies away, which it probably did since they laced the paint with arsenic.)[12] Typical for its era, the house bore an orange tile roof and rested on a stone foundation. Heavy logs anchored the porch that protruded over the sea. For the first time since *The French Revolution*, Mary was writing a book—*Letters Written During a Short Residence in Sweden, Norway, and Denmark*—and writing eloquently, seamlessly interweaving specific details about little-known Scandinavia with her responses to people and views. In the tranquillity of a nightless summer, with no boisterous child or straying lover to distract her attention, Mary had the leisure to reflect.

"Nature is the nurse of sentiment—the true source of taste;—yet what misery, as well as rapture, is produced by a quick perception of the beautiful and sublime, when it is exercised in observing animated nature, when every beauteous feeling and emotion excites responsive sympathy, and the harmonized soul sinks into melancholy, or rises to extasy, just as the chords are touched, like the aeolean harp agitated by the changing wind,"[13] writes Mary the emerging Romantic, three years before William Wordsworth published *Lyrical Ballads*.

And as she scrutinizes the diligent Norwegians and exults in their landscape, her perspective on the evolution of culture shifts. Gone is her blind hatred for business. She begins to see labor, more than reason, as the spur to progress: "I never, my friend, thought so deeply of the advantages obtained by human industry as since I have been in Norway. The world requires, I see, the hand of man to perfect it; and as this task naturally unfolds the faculties he exercises, it is physically impossible that he should have remained in Rousseau's golden age of stupidity." Yet, the source of joy continues to elude her. Does happiness reward "the high-wrought mind" or "unconscious ignorance? Is it the offspring of thoughtless animal spirits, or the elve of fancy continually flirting round the expected pleasure?"[14]

Mary began sleeping better in Tönsberg. She developed new tastes, like a passion for the "elegant" beech tree, which she'd formerly dismissed as too thin and straight-backed.[15] She learned to row a boat, and, with a young pregnant companion at the other oar, traveled through bands of soft-shelled starfish—"like thickened water, with a white edge"[16]—to a rivulet just outside town.[17] Here she swam in clear water smelling of healing minerals. She walked and walked and went to the Church of St. Maria, which had no windows on its northern wall because of the Norwegian superstition that evil spirits came from the north. As a miserable child, Mary had believed that a just heaven would redeem her present suffering. Then, in her early thirties, the afterlife had become less important for her as she embraced the French Revolution with its promise of justice on earth. Now, when she found it hard to believe there was justice anywhere, her own vitality affirmed God's presence: "It appears to me impossible that I should cease to exist, or that this active, restless spirit, equally alive to joy and sorrow, should only be organized dust—ready to fly abroad the moment the spring snaps, or the spark goes out, which kept it together. Surely something resides in this heart that is not perishable—and life is more than a dream."[18]

Through Mayor Wulfsberg, Mary was invited to the Danish earl of Jarlsberg's stately redwood mansion; she went to dinners at stylish Rossegården with its saucy columned doorways, where Tönsberg's wealthiest merchant lived. Soon she knew most of fashionable Tönsberg, with their "golden locks"[19] and rotting teeth. As in Sweden, the rich drank and ate too much and underpaid their servants: "A young woman, who is wet nurse to the mistress of the inn where I lodge, receives only twelve dollars a year, and pays ten for the nursing of her own child; the father had run away to get clear of the expence." Most of the wealthy men were merchants or sea captains who spoke tolerable English but had little to say. For once, Mary preferred the women, who knew no English, but loved to dance and sing, and addressed Mary with animated gestures. Since they despised exercise, it amazed them that Mary walked for pleasure; and they grieved to learn she traveled all alone. Mary grew attached to these pretty, warmhearted creatures. Often she sat with them and the men on the Rossegården porch and bellowed out revolutionary songs.

Many days, Mary sat by herself, "reclining in the mossy down under the shelter of a rock" near the battered remains of a thirteenth-century fort and castle. The rare regional stones here, called *rombeporfyr*, are laced with leaflike marks from an ancient volcano. Today the sweeping park is filled with dandelions the size of small sunflowers and overgrown grass poking up between gray and red boulders. Farther out are the deep blue fjords and arching mountains, of which Mary writes: "With what ineffable pleasure have I not gazed—and gazed again, losing my breath through my eyes."[20]

And then three weeks have passed, and her summer in Tönsberg is over. Writing nothing about the progress of her business dealings, at the end of the first week in August, Mary prepares to leave. She is sorry to go and daunted by her next brief visit, in Larvik. "My head turned round, my heart grew sick, as I regarded visages deformed by vice," she writes of her meeting with local lawyers. She is similarly disdainful of Larvik's best-known home, Herregården, a grand mansion built in 1677 where the Danish governors live. The exterior is simple wood and looks Norwegian, but the inside is a hodgepodge of Continental styles replete with faux marble and gold: the epitome of showy extravagance, in Mary's view.

From Larvik, Mary traveled by sea toward the last place Imlay's boat had been spotted—Risör. The farther south she journeyed, the more extreme the Norwegian landscape became. The rocks jutted higher, the trees grew taller, the fjords clamored more thunderously as she headed down the coast. "The view of this wild coast, as we sailed along it, afforded me a continual subject for meditation. I anticipated the future improvement of the world and observed how much man had still to do, to obtain of the earth all it could yield."[21]

To Mary's dismay, Risör consisted of some two hundred dwellings sprawled under a high rock and pinched between boulders. "Talk not of bastilles! To be born here was to be bastilled by nature," she writes, though the view of the town is "fine."[22] She has come to work on the Ellefsen affair but says nothing of the outcome.

Every day now, the darkness came on sooner. "June and July are the months to make a tour through Norway . . . but towards the middle, or latter end of August, the clouds begin to gather, and summer disappears almost before it has ripened the fruit of autumn." Mary's final stop in Norway was Christiania (Oslo today). And while she praises its harbor and "uncommonly fine" landscape, Mary despises the boxy wood houses and feels restless in the tasteless villas where business acquaintances invite her to dine. She has headaches again and is contemplating the coming autumn. Soon she will embrace her beloved Fanny in Gothenburg. Soon too she will behold Imlay and learn if her absence has produced a miracle, and if he wants to live with her again. A brooding tone returns to Mary's writing. Despotism exists in Norway after all, she discovers, when she finds that the grand bailiffs of Christiania are "political monsters" from Denmark who reward their lackeys and exploit the local judges. A group of tricky merchants remind her that commerce is dehumanizing. And while Mary had admired Norway's penal code from a distance, the experience of meeting actual chained prisoners in a Christiania fortress disgusts her.[23]

It is time to go. Yet, at the last minute Mary pauses. Suddenly, she wants to draw out her journey, to travel north to a picturesque Norwegian community where she's heard that a people of unusual virtue and intelligence reside. Thinking of these people impels her to analyze the evolution of her own philosophy, from the triumphant fall of the Bastille six years earlier, when a perfect world seemed possible, to the present, when all is uncertainty in both the world and her private life. A summer in Norway has revitalized her health and restored some of her former optimism. But though she is tempted again to embrace an ideology of social improvement, she is checked by her hard-won knowledge of human nature—and of how hard it is to change:

> The description I received of [these people] carried me back to the fables of the golden age: independence and virtue; affluence without vice; cultivation of mind, without depravity of heart; with "ever smiling liberty"; the nymph of the mountain—I want faith! My imagination hurries me forward to seek asylum in such a retreat from all the disappointments I am threatened with; but reason drags me back, whispering that the world is still the world, and man the same compound of weakness and folly, who must occasionally excite love and disgust, admiration and contempt.[24]

BY THE TIME Mary had retrieved Fanny in Gothenburg and traveled to Copenhagen, her last stop for business, she sounded nearly as distressed as when she had set out from London in June. "I am weary of travelling—yet seem to have no home—no resting place to look to." Apparently, she had failed to resolve Imlay's business dispute. Still, she'd done her best. Before leaving England, she had convinced Imlay to meet her in Switzerland or Hamburg when her job was finished. But now Imlay procrastinated, and his vague promises to meet her *somewhere* brought only "fresh proofs of your indifference," which Mary nonetheless refused to accept as evidence that their affair was through. Four months of traveling had not diminished her desire for the wayward American. All her bathing and boating in Tönsberg now seemed part of a hopeless campaign to win him back. Thoughts of suicide recurred. "How often, passing through the rocks, I have thought, 'But for this child, I would lay my head on one of them, and never open my eyes again!'"[25] she declares, painting herself as a pathetic creature. Yet, from *Letters* we know she retained her energy and peevishness as she surveyed the ruins of Copenhagen, devastated by a fire the previous June.

The "dust and rubbish" oppressed her. She blamed the rich for letting the flames get out of hand. And she condemned the entire Danish population as provincial. Danish businessmen were "domestic tyrants," their wives were ignorant and their children "spoilt." After meeting the powerful minister Count Bernstorff, so revered by the Norwegians, she decided he was less anxious to do good than to avoid trouble. The current king was just a "machine of state," though Mary's sympathy flew to "poor" Queen Matilda, who in 1766 had been forced to marry the retarded former Danish king. Later, when the queen fell in love and had a daughter with a brave and influential social reformer, the Danes beheaded her lover, and at twenty-four she died of grief.[26]

Grief was much on Mary's mind these days. Imlay's letters were increasingly cool, and calculated to offend her. He refused to make any decisions about their future, telling her *she* could decide if she wished, and he flagrantly broke his promise to meet her in Hamburg. She pursued him still. Just three years earlier, in *Vindication*, Mary had demeaned romantic love, calling it "the common passion, in which chance and sensation take place of choice and reason."[27] Now she was as desperate for romance as any of the women she had mocked in her books.

"I am strangely deficient in sagacity,"[28] she admitted, and in early October she informed Imlay that she was leaving the continent for the second time that year: "What have I to do here?"[29] Imlay was in England.

England, though . . . The very idea oppressed her. Again, Imlay failed to meet her boat at Dover, though he found her a place to stay in London and continued offering financial support. He spoke of duty, but never of desire. He denied that he was living with another woman, though Mary overheard the servants tittering about his new love. On October 8, the author of *Vindication* ordered her cook to reveal the identity and address of Imlay's mistress. Then, armed with righteous indignation, Mary strode off to assail this home breaker with her crimes. But whatever transpired, it was Mary who left the meeting devastated. "I would encounter a thousand deaths, rather than a night like" the one that had just occurred, she wrote Imlay.[30] She informed him that she meant to end her life.

Like so many would-be suicides, Mary craved the power to punish. "Should your sensibility ever awake," she lectured Imlay, "remorse will find its way to your heart; and in the midst of business and sensual pleasure, I shall appear before you, the victim of your deviation from rectitude." But Mary was less eager to hurt Imlay than to escape her own mental suffering; so she would not, as in her haphazard suicide attempt the previous spring, consume laudanum, which could be vomited up. She would hurl herself into the Thames. Even thoughts of Fanny could not deflect her. On October 10, Mary composed a suicide note instructing Imlay to give the maid all her clothes and the cook the wages owed her. ("Do not mention the confession [about

Imlay's mistress] which I forced from her.") Fanny and Marguerite should be sent to the loving German couple she'd befriended in Paris. Away from England, Mary convinced herself, Fanny would be happier. As for Mary herself:

> Let my wrongs sleep with me! Soon, very soon, shall I be at peace. When you receive this, my burning head will be cold. . . . I go to find comfort, and my only fear is, that my poor body will be insulted by an endeavor to recall my hated existence. But I shall plunge into the Thames where there is the least chance of my being snatched from the death I seek.[31]

Mary dressed "elegantly"[32] and began walking along the river toward the remote Battersea Bridge. When she arrived and found people milling, she hailed a boatman, who rowed her farther still from central London to Putney Bridge in Fulham, where she'd stayed with Fanny Blood's family the year after her mother died. Her mother's last words had been "A little patience and all will be over," but Mary was not patient. And while her mother had endured a long and excruciating illness, Mary was determined to perish like her friends at the guillotine: swiftly. She felt calm and reasonable

On Putney Bridge, torrential rain was pouring down.[33] It occurred to Mary that wetting her clothes might help her to sink, and she spent a half-hour walking back and forth across the empty little wooden bridge, drenching her hair and garments. Then she leapt into the Thames—and got a terrific jolt from the sheer physical pain of plunging into icy water. Despite the rain, her clothes buoyed her. She tugged them to her, but they wouldn't let her sink. She bobbed. Her head went up and under. Suffocation began. The pain was unbearable. It was almost worse than living. It *was* worse, she thought before she lost consciousness and the waves drew her two hundred yards from the bridge.

Some men boating on the outskirts of London had watched her jump into the river, and now chased after her and pulled her on board. There she lay, a senseless creature shrouded in evening clothes, until, miraculously, the boatmen revived her and rowed her to shore. They carried her to the nearby Duke's Head tavern. A doctor came and declared she would survive. So her worst fear had transpired: she'd been "snatched from death." And by now, Mary's absence was worrying Marguerite and Fanny. Imlay received Mary's suicide note and traced her to the Duke's Head. There, Rebecca Christie picked up Mary in a carriage and took her, Fanny, and Marguerite to the Christie home at Finsbury Square. Mary thanked no one for their troubles. Rather, she bitterly lamented that her "fixed determination to die" had been thwarted.[34] Not even maternal affection could restore Mary's desire to live.

And after she was well enough to move into her own house in the Christies' neighborhood, Mary was still insisting she'd been "inhumanly brought back to life." Her decision to die had been "one of the calmest acts of reason."[35] When Imlay wrote that he had no idea "how to extricate ourselves out of the wretchedness into which we have been plunged," Mary answered, "You are extricated long since." So the placations and incriminations resumed. If Imlay offered money, Mary perceived "tenderness for your own reputation" rather than concern for her happiness.[36] "Even your seeing me, has been to oblige other people, and not to sooth my distracted mind,"[37] she sighed. Still, however "ignobly"[38] the real Imlay behaved, Mary clung to the memory of a peerless lover: "You know best whether I am still preserving the remembrance of an imaginary being," she taunted him, though in fact most all Mary's friends knew just as well as Imlay that he'd behaved like a cad.[39] To make matters worse, Imlay could not or would not rebuff Mary in person. So the few times they met, he was kind and soothing, abetting her false hopes.

Mary's reaction to the Terror was candidly to reassess the French

Revolution. But she hadn't the emotional strength to reassess her life with Imlay, so she just stumbled on day to day. In a variation on the Fuseli affair, Mary briefly entertained the idea of a ménage à trois with Imlay and his mistress. "If we are ever to live together again, it must be now," Mary insisted.

> We meet now, or we part forever. You say, You cannot abruptly break off the connection you have formed. It is unworthy of my courage and character, to wait the uncertain issue of that con- nection. I am determined to come to a decision. I consent then, for the present, to live with you, and the woman to whom you have associated yourself. I think it important that you should learn habitually to feel for your child the affection of a father. But, if you reject this proposal, here we end. You are now free. We will correspond no more. We will have no intercourse of any kind. I will be to you as a person that is dead.[40]

At first, Imlay humored Mary and even took her house hunting. But he inevitably about-faced, at which point Mary stepped up her rem- onstrances. "You torment me," he accused her, and Mary continued tormenting Imlay, writing him even when he traveled with his mis- tress to Paris; and she became as enraged as a married woman when an acquaintance of Joseph Johnson's proposed marriage to *her*. Clearly, she considered herself a wronged wife, not an available un- wed mother. And she rebuked her faithful publisher when he admon- ished her to calm down. "Dr. Johnson's cares almost drove him mad—but I suppose, you would have quietly told him, he was a fool for not being calm, and that wise men striving against the stream can still be in good humor,"[41] she bristled.

So even Joseph Johnson, the paragon of tolerance, grew exasper- ated by Mary's self-destructive obsession. Furthermore, he resented that Mary refused to accept Imlay's financial support, leaning on him instead. In mid-November, Johnson wrote to ask for help from Mary's brother Charles in America. (Recently, Charles had fulfilled his old promise to set up a small fund for Eliza, so there was reason to hope he'd pity Mary as well.)

> She has been deserted by Mr. Imlay whose affairs are in a very deranged state; she has herself and child to support by her literary exertion and you will not be surprised to learn has occasion to apply to me long before her productions can be made productive.

Johnson loyally adds that Mary "deserves more than most women, and cannot live upon a trifle; she has suffered much from the infamous behaviour of Imlay, both in her health and spirits, but she has a strong mind and has in great measure got the better of it."[42] Charles never replied.

So if Mary's correspondence suggests that nothing but Imlay and the past occupied her during the fall of 1795, Johnson observes that she is beginning to conquer her passion and move on. It was at this time, after all, that she forged ahead on the demanding task of compiling and editing her letters from Scandinavia, readying them for publication in the new year. The finished book reads almost like an epistolary novel. Its narrator is a brave and unconventional woman traveler, troubled by an unhappy affair with an unspecified American and keenly receptive to both landscapes and ideas. "We reason deeply when we forcibly feel,"[43] Mary writes in a letter from Denmark, summing up her book's thesis.

And Mary refuses to apologize for dwelling on her own circumstances, declaring in the preface: "A person has a right . . . to talk of himself when he can win on our attention by acquiring our affection. Whether I deserve to rank amongst this privileged number, my readers alone can judge—and I give them leave to shut the book, if they do not wish to become better acquainted with me." And tellingly, there is much sorrow but no regret in the letters that follow. In *Rights of Men* four years earlier, Mary had argued that the French Revolution was worth fighting, whatever its final consequence, because "the exercise of our faculties," and not the fulfillment of a particular goal, "is the great end." *Letters* applies the same logic to love.

In January, Mary wrote her Irish friend Hamilton Rowan that she lived only for her child, "for I am weary of myself."[44] But she also began, warily, expanding her London visits beyond Finsbury Square and St. Paul's Churchyard. She dined out in company with Rebecca Christie and on January 8 went on her own to Mary Hays's tea. The inseparable friends William Godwin and Thomas Holcroft were also present. This was Godwin's second meeting with Mary Wollstonecraft. Beforehand, he had with characteristic self-approval informed his hostess:

I will do myself the pleasure of waiting on you on Friday, and shall be happy to meet Mrs. Wollstonecraft, of whom I know not that I ever said a word of harm, and who has frequently amused herself by depreciating me. But I trust you acknowledge in me that reality of a habit upon which I pique myself, that I speak of the qualities of others uninfluenced by personal consideration, and am as prompt to do justice to an enemy as to a friend.[45]

He would not regret his noblesse oblige.

CHAPTER TWELVE

William Godwin's father and uncle and grandfather were all Dissident ministers, stolid Calvinists preaching divine retribution and original sin. How remote they seem from the progressive nonconformists Mary knew at Newington Green and St. Paul's Churchyard. Life for Godwin's parents was bleak and threatening: you battled both the hateful world and the evil within. As a child, William absorbed his parents' direful view of human nature. Until he was twenty-six, he "believed in the doctrine of Calvin, that is, that the majority of mankind were objects of divine condemnation, and that their punishment would be everlasting."[1]

William was born the seventh of thirteen children in the Fens of Cambridgeshire on March 3, 1756. He was small and sickly. His preoccupied mother sent him off for two years to a wet nurse and then handed him over to his father's cousin's care. For this cousin—Miss Godwin, who later married and became Mrs. Sothren—righteousness did not preclude pleasures. She took him on outings to plays, fostering a lifelong love of theater. While his parents admonished him about good and evil, she "watched over"[2] his imagination—the source of all "genuine morality" and "profound feeling," he would later declare.[3] When he was four, in 1760, William and Miss Godwin followed the rest of the family to Guestwick near Norwich, where William's father, John, took up a new ministership. Here he would preach for the rest of his life.

Godwin recalled his father as brusque and distant; his mother (from a landed family comfortable enough to afford their own carriage) was stern but could tell an amusing tale. According to family lore, precocious William read by four and at five donned his grandfather's wig and played the inveighing Dissident minister on his kitchen high chair.[4] *Pilgrim's Progress* and *Accounts of the Pious Deaths of Many Godly Children*[5] were his earliest books; he longed to follow in his father's footsteps. Far more than his siblings, William possessed a fierce Calvinist intellect and a zeal for accomplishment. So, at eleven, he was sent to study as the only pupil of a prominent Dissident reverend (one Samuel Newton) in Norwich, where he remained until 1770, when he was fourteen years old. His father died two years later, and the year after that his mother enrolled him in the Hoxton Dissenting Academy, arguably England's finest school.

At Hoxton, Godwin studied history as well as religion, for like the heroes of his novels *The Adventures of Caleb Williams* and *St. Leon*, he was insatiably curious. And for all the doom and gloom of his Calvinist upbringing, he exuded hope: "No effort, no invention of mine shall be left untried,"[6] he declared. Indeed, he was so conspicuously ambitious and gifted that his friend James Marshall predicted he'd become a Cabinet member.[7] Godwin had no patience with idle conversation and was "noisy"[8] in debate, though his normal manner was reserved and unassuming, with an awkward pedantry that belied his inquisitive mind. He was middle-sized, "slender and delicate,"[9] with soft brown eyes, a clear flushed complexion, and an unusually large nose, or "oh, most abominable nose!" as the poet Robert Southey later assailed it. Most women found Godwin attractive enough.

During his second year at Hoxton (unbeknown to Godwin), the Wollstonecraft family moved into the neighborhood, where Mary began her own haphazard tutelage under her eccentric neighbor Mr. Clare. In 1779, while Mary was governessing in Bath for Mrs. Dawson, Godwin graduated from Hoxton and accepted a Dissident ministership, at the town of Stowmarket in Suffolk. Here he first experienced the oppressiveness of rule by the majority when he chose to administer holy sacraments before he was officially ordained. Church doctrine is actually ambivalent about this practice, but the neighboring ministers unanimously condemned it, and Godwin refused to submit to their view. He continued ministering as he liked until he was forced to resign two years later.

Then, rather than immediately seeking a new congregation, he went to London. Somehow he'd never read the *philosophes*. Now he took up a controversial new work, Baron d'Holbach's *Système de la Nature*, whose premise is that man should obey the dictates of nature and his own intellect because God does not exist. D'Holbach's atheism shocked even liberal thinkers. But pious Godwin was less appalled by the attack on religion than intrigued by d'Holbach's other bold concepts, and he set out to immerse himself in the theories of Rousseau, Voltaire, and Helvétius, reading about rule by reason and the general will. And while the Enlightenment vision of happiness flew in the face of everything Godwin had learned since childhood, it found an answering voice in his own optimistic temperament and faith in the triumph of talent and hard work.

So Godwin was experiencing something of a religious crisis when, a half-year after leaving Stowmarket, at the end of 1782, he accepted his second minister's post, at Beaconsfield in Buckinghamshire. Seven months later, he was peremptorily dismissed. This time, it was not because of a technical disagreement but because his sermons blatantly celebrated reason—which offended the determinist Beaconsfield Dissidents, as it would have offended Godwin's own father and *his* father before.

Another decade would pass before Godwin openly rejected religion, but his conversion to progressive Enlightenment thinking was relatively swift. And yet he missed his old vocation. "Habit is more potent than any theoretical speculation," he would write in his novel *St. Leon.*[10] And to his mother, Godwin explained: "You seem to regret my having quitted the character of a dissenting minister. To that I can only say with the utmost frankness . . . that the character quitted me when I was far from desiring to part with it."[11] Throughout his life, Godwin retained the sobriety of a minister, but he never again sought a minister's post. From Beaconsfield, he moved to London and, after briefly flirting with the idea of teaching, set out to pursue a literary career.

Godwin's Hoxton friend James Marshall was already in London eking out a hack writer's living. Godwin moved in with him and soon was churning out essays, plays, translations, even a few mildly erotic novels, and literary reviews at a guinea a page for John Murray's *English Review*, a precursor of Joseph Johnson's *Analytical Review*. Suddenly, he was thrust from the minister's threadbare stability to the havoc of Grub Street. Landlords refused to renew his three-month leases, and he frequently had to be bailed out of debtor's prison, or to bail out Marshall. With no Joseph Johnson to smooth his progress, Godwin encountered fierce competition and changed publishers almost as often as he changed residence.

Then in 1784 he got his first steady work writing the historical section of the liberal *New Annual Register*, owned by George Robinson, who operated the largest publishing house on the Row. Robinson guaranteed Godwin sixty guineas a year and stimulating duties, such as scurrying off to Parliament to hear his favorite Whig, Edmund

Burke, eloquently promote democratic causes, and immersing himself in news on events in France or the Irish economy. For his report was to embrace all major world events. And Godwin's own world expanded as he began socializing with his progressive colleagues, the most conspicuous of whom was Thomas Holcroft, soon to be Godwin's best friend.

Thomas Holcroft, eleven years older than Godwin, was an abrasive, "insatiable talker," who was also "dynamic,"[12] loyal, emotional, politically radical, and a seeker of truth. Godwin's daughter, Mary Shelley, would deem him "stern and irascible."[13] And Holcroft was a disputatious but "purely speculative politican," according to his friend William Hazlitt:[14] "He believed that truth had a natural superiority over error, if only it could be heard, that if once discovered, it must, being left to itself, soon spread and triumph." He also believed pain was in the mind and refused medical treatment.

Holcroft's frontispiece in his *Memoirs* shows a virile, fair-haired man, eagerly hunched forward and clutching a pair of eyeglasses with faintly ridiculous ardor while his deep eyes stare challengingly ahead. Like Godwin, Holcroft looked up to no one. Like Mary Wollstonecraft, he'd had a sentimental father who could suddenly turn abusive and "beat me up, pull my hair up by the roots, and drag me by the ears along the ground till they ran with blood."[15] When Holcroft was six, his father lost his shoemaker's job and was reduced to peddling. Holcroft's own first job was as a stable boy, and though he soon moved on to acting and then writing, his gruff manner clung. The poet Samuel Coleridge describes a typical first meeting with this prickly individual.

Holcroft, Coleridge recalls, had for some time been stealing glances at him over the rim of his newspaper when

At last, he rose, advanced to me with the paper in his hand, and began "Sir! I apprehend, that you are the Author of this

Sonnet on Kosciusko?" I bowed assent. "Sir! it is a very bad composition—a very wretched performance, I assure you." I again bowed; and with a smile that expressed a little surprise at the oddness, but no offense at the harshness of this volunteer address, made some modest reply admitting the too probable appropriateness of the criticism. "Nay, but Sir! do not misunderstand me— It is a poem of genius—a proof of great Genius, Sir! You are certainly a man of Genius, Sir! My name is Holcroft—and I should be glad to have you at my house next Sunday to dine with me and . . . Mr. Godwin, the sublime Philosopher!"[16]

Coleridge called Holcroft "ignorant as a scholar," an unfair judgment, for Holcroft taught himself well. He succeeded as a hack because he could write anything, but theater was his niche. And by the time he met Godwin, Holcroft's translation of Beaumarchais's *Marriage of Figaro* had played at Covent Garden and his original comedy *Duplicity* at Drury Lane. Curiously, most of Holcroft's plays are purely conventional farces or comedies of manners, peopled with scheming poseurs and naughty rich people, that bear no connection to his radical thoughts.[17]

In 1788, two years after they met, Godwin and Holcroft developed an "extremely intimate"[18] friendship. Despite their dissimilar backgrounds, they possessed a number of common traits: both were gregarious and hated small talk, but thrived on righteous indignation. Increasingly, they were admired or scorned as a pair. And though Holcroft had a family, he and Godwin managed to meet almost daily and dined together once or twice a week. They committed themselves to absolute honesty since "the smallest reserve is deadly to [friendship]."[19] And both were "unspeakibly gratif[ied]"[20] by the experiment, though there were times when emotional Holcroft bridled or moped at his friend's frank judgments. Once Holcroft "lay wakeful and ruminating full three hours on the injustice and wrong nature of [Godwin's] remarks"[21] about his new play. Although they soon made up just like lesser mortals, Godwin in particular continued to insist that truth was sacred. Thus, some years later he would serenely inform his new wife, Mary Jane Godwin, that the reason he was enthralled by her love letter was because it reminded him of his dead first wife.[22]

Secure in his position at the *New Annual Register*, in the late 1780s Godwin moved north from the dank warrens around Grub Street to a little house by a peaceful church and graveyard on Cumming Street in Somers Town. He settled into the routines he would follow for most of his long career: he woke between seven and eight, got up and read from the work of a classical author, and ate breakfast alone before sitting down at his desk. Here he threw himself into writing between nine and noon and then stopped, Mary Shelley explained, because "he could not exceed this measure of labour with any advantage to his own health, or the work at hand. While writing *Political Justice*, there was one paragraph that he wrote eight times over before he could satisfy himself. . . . On this occasion a confusion of the brain came over him and he applied to his [doctor] friend Anthony Carlisle . . . who warned him that he had exerted his intellectual faculties to their limit. In compliance with his direction, Mr. Godwin reduced his hours of composition."[23]

An old woman came to clean each morning. During the afternoon, Godwin either read or visited with a widening social circle, including his publisher George Robinson, the poet Helen Maria Williams, the Dissident Dr. Aikin, and his daughter Mrs. Barbauld, Mary's friend. He retained his childhood passion for theater and went to plays when he could.

In 1789, Godwin applauded the fall of the Bastille in the *New Annual Register*, and he was present at the crucial meeting of the Revolution Society at which Dr. Price championed the insurgent French.

Though Godwin had admired Edmund Burke when he had allied with liberals Sheridan and Fox in Parliament, Godwin was now infuriated by Burke's attack on France and applauded Thomas Paine's rousing rebuttal, *The Rights of Man*. On November 13, 1791, at Godwin's request, Joseph Johnson invited Paine and Godwin to dine at St. Paul's Churchyard. As usual, Godwin sought to dominate the conversation, but an irritating female kept frustrating his plans. Here is how Godwin recalls this first meeting with Mary:

> The interview was not fortunate. Mary and myself parted, mutually displease [*sic*] with each other. I had not read her Rights of Woman. I had barely looked into her Answer to Burke, and been displeased, as literary men are apt to be, with a few offenses against grammar and other minute points of composition. I had therefore little curiosity to see Mrs. Wollstonecraft, and a very great curiosity to see Thomas Paine. Paine, in his general habits, is no great talker; and, though he threw in occasionally some shrewd remarks, the conversation lay principally between me and Mary. I, of consequence, heard her, very frequently when I wished to hear Paine.[24]

When Godwin enthused about Voltaire, Mary informed him "that praise, lavished in the way that I lavished it, could do no credit either to the commended or the commender." She deplored his religious skepticism and left Godwin convinced that, for all her grammatical shortcomings, she was a master at "seeing every thing [*sic*] on the gloomy side, and bestowing censure with a plentiful hand." Speaking with Holcroft that same night over supper, Godwin magnanimously declared Mary "a person of active and independent thinking,"[25] while Mary derided Godwin whenever his name came up. Maybe she disliked his snorting laugh and combativeness as well as his opinions. "We met two or three times in the course of the following year, but made a very small degree of progress toward a cordial acquaintance," Godwin writes.[26] Then Mary went to France, and Godwin quit the *New Annual Register* and received advance money from George Robinson to write a major political work.

For Godwin was never content as a writer of commissioned reviews and essays. He yearned to plumb the depths of his talents. "In the first fervour of my enthusiasm, I entertained the . . . imagination of 'hewing stone from the rock' which, by its inherent energy and weight, should overbear and annihilate all opposition and place the principles of politics on an immoveable basis."[27]

These are Romantic words, though Godwin's "hewing" required sixteen months of dogged perseverance, and he drew upon the hardship of his childhood as well as Enlightenment thought. So *An Enquiry Concerning Political Justice* combines a Calvinist fervor for rectitude with Enlightenment faith in human stamina. It is a major work, at once naïve and noble, making a heroic case for personal responsibility and the rewards of an improving world. "I hold my person as a trust in behalf of mankind,"[28] Godwin declaims, twisting Locke's precept to stress man's duty rather than his privileges. But "it is necessary that every man should [think] by himself," not lean on the general will.[29]

Sixty years before Karl Marx, Godwin perceives justice as a voluntary redistribution of property. "Each man has a perfect claim upon everything the possession of which will be productive of more benefit to him than injury to another." Conversely, a man should relinquish what would give more pleasure to someone else. Why? Because "if there be any truth more unquestionable than the rest, it is that every man is bound" to do the right thing. Doing right, of course, requires knowledge. Knowledge has made great bounds since the invention of the printing press, and the world would be wiser still if there were no governments. Government should vanish, Godwin declares, sounding like an early anarchist, though a curious one, since he deplores forced change as heatedly as does Edmund Burke. Revolution is "at war with the existence of liberty," Godwin surprisingly insists, and furthermore, in most cases (the current Revolution in France being an exception),[30] unnecessary since "everything may be trusted to the tranquil and wholesome progress" of time.[31]

Time and again, Godwin needles his reader, claiming, for instance, that "it is impossible not to see the beauty of equality," even, presumably, if you are a king. And he refuses to allow for human weakness, insisting that if there were a fire and you could choose to save someone in your family or the great philosopher François Fénelon, you would unhesitatingly choose Fénelon because he can contribute more to the common good. Friendship is "one of the most exquisite gratifications,"[32] but sexual pleasure is overrated and marriage "evil,"[33] because it permits one person to monopolize another's life.

Political Justice was published in February 1793 and became the rare book that touches the nerve of the moment. Although George Robinson priced it dearly, no serious thinker was deterred. Soon anyone who was anyone was spouting Godwin's ideas—particularly his theory that justice would triumph by its own merit. After all, the book appeared in London stores just a month after the beheading of Louis XVI. As France increasingly sought freedom through bloodshed, it was reassuring to read there could be liberty without death.

Political Justice made Godwin an immediate celebrity. "Tom Paine was considered for the time a Tom Fool to him; Paley an old woman; Edmund Burke a flashy sophist," the essayist William Hazlitt wrote. "Truth, moral truth, it was supposed had . . . taken up its abode [in Godwin]. . . . 'Throw aside your books of chemistry,' said Wordsworth to a young man . . . 'and read Godwin on Necessity.'"[34] And "with the first blush and awkwardness of success," Godwin's "dictatorial, captious, quibbling pettiness of manner"[35] vanished. He was improving personally as well.

In 1793, Godwin, author of *Political Justice*, was thirty-seven, and Mary, author of *Vindication,* was thirty-four. Both were sincerely committed to making the world better. Both also were famous and much in demand at swank affairs. While Mary was off in Paris consorting with expatriates and leaders of the French Revolution, Godwin dined in London with Whig lords, prominent liberal industrialists like the Wedgwoods, and pretty women eager to expand their minds.

In the spring of 1793, while Mary was falling in love with Imlay, Godwin, who'd formerly shown no sexual interest in anyone, was playing at love with the "Fairs," as he called beautiful women like Elizabeth Inchbald, whose play he had recently helped revise.[36]

Mrs. Inchbald was said to look like a mixture of a milkmaid and a duchess. She'd been born poor but raised herself through talent and good looks. Now in her early forties, widowed and surrounded by admirers, she guarded her spotless reputation and was also something of a snob. Mrs. Inchbald immediately captivated Godwin, who visited her again on May 22 and regularly after that. Calling on "Inchbald" was very different from calling on good Mary Hays or Mrs. Barbauld. For a start, Mrs. Inchbald was not a particularly good person. She was spiteful, devious, and had a brutal wit, which greatly intrigued Godwin, for all his righteousness. Usually, Inchbald encouraged Godwin's awkward flattery, though she could turn on a dime and become "cold and cunning,"[37] the poet Coleridge observed.

Godwin's other "Fairs" included the actress Mary Robinson and the aspiring young writer Amelia Alderson—"the Belle of Norwich"—a doctor's daughter with a shapely figure, dense auburn hair, soft eyes, and a "beaming countenance." "All around and about her was the spirit of youth, and joy and love,"[38] an early biographer effused. Godwin was so infatuated with Amelia that he completely forgot his horror of courtship and small talk, as Miss Alderson makes clear in a letter to a friend:

> It would have entertained you to see [Godwin] bid me farewell. He wished to salute me, but his courage failed him. . . . "Will you give me nothing to keep for your sake and console me [in my] absence," murmured out the philosopher, "not even a slipper? I had it in my possession once, and need [not have] returned it!" This was true, my shoe had come off and he had put it in his pocket for some time.

And besides cherishing a woman's shoe in his pocket, Godwin has become a purveyor of gossip:

> Mrs. Inchbald says the report of the world is that Mr. Holcroft is in love with her, *she* with Mr. Godwin, Mr. Godwin with *me,* and I am in love with Mr. Holcroft! A pretty story indeed! . . . Godwin . . . says Mrs. I always tells him that when she praises *him* I praise Holcroft. . . . She appears to be jealous of G's attention to [me] and makes him believe I prefer H. to him.[39]

Godwin cut his long minister's tresses just before he wrote *Political Justice.* Afterward, he began actively working on his pulchritude, so that one day Miss Alderson found him "with his hair *bien poudré,* and in a pair of new, sharp-toed, red morocco slippers, not to mention his green coat and crimson under waistcoat."[40] Still, he remained the erudite philosopher.

And also, after 1794, an esteemed novelist. That year he published his first serious work of fiction, *Things as They Are; or, The Adventures of Caleb Williams.* This book was intended as a companion to *Political Justice*, but it can stand on its own as a gripping novel of ideas.

Set in the British countryside, *Caleb Williams* tells the story of an insatiably curious youth—the eponymous narrator—who is relentlessly persecuted by his master, the most illustrious landowner in town. This landowner, Squire Falkland, is justly revered for his virtue and intellect. What few suspect is that he has the tragic flaw of pride. Indeed, Falkland is so jealous of his reputation that, when the novel begins, he has murdered a neighbor because the man insulted him and has permitted an innocent peasant and his son to die for his crime. Inside, Falkland seethes with self-loathing, while to the world he seems distracted and sad. Still, his wealth and reputation place him above suspicion of wrongdoing until the honorable but poor Caleb Williams comes to work as a secretary in his house.

There, Caleb discovers a trunk containing evidence of the murder. And while Falkland confesses his guilt, he insists, first, that Caleb never reveal his master's secret and, second, that Caleb remain forever in his present job. Caleb agrees to the first but refuses to become Falkland's prisoner. So he runs away, but then Falkland invents false charges and has him arrested. When Caleb escapes from prison, Falkland tracks him down and slanders him to his neighbors so—whether he is posing as a humble Jewish writer in London or as a watchmaker in rural Wales—he can never keep a friend or a job. Divining no alternative, Caleb breaks his vow and brings charges against Falkland. Then, in a psychological twist, Falkland admits his ignominy, praises Caleb, and dies; while Caleb condemns himself for killing the heroic monster:

> I thought that, if Falkland were dead, I should return once again
> to everything that makes life worth possessing. I thought that, if
> the guilt of Falkland were established, fortune and the world

would smile upon my efforts. Both events are accomplished; and it is now only that I am truly miserable.[41]

Caleb Williams successfully fuses epic, Gothic, and realistic conventions and argues a seminal theme of *Political Justice*: that institutions are gravely flawed. The law, for instance, supports Falkland simply because of his seeming honor and prominence, while Caleb is mistrusted because he has no influence or wealth. A lowly birth also condemns Caleb to spend his talents simply fleeing capture. He has no energy left to effect positive change.

Godwin succeeds in sustaining a heightened narrative tension from start to finish. Both the gruesome prison and the yawning countryside are vividly evoked. And Caleb's many attempts to escape Falkland are so convincingly recounted that we wince at each of his failures—however predictable. What's more, the psychological revelations are skillfully wed to believable action. And, in Godwin's greatest triumph, Falkland emerges as both a terrifying monomaniac and an admirable man.

The *Critical Review* ranked *Things as They Are; or, The Adventures of Caleb Williams* above "all novels save Fielding, Smollett and Burney."[42] Hazlitt declared it unforgettable,[43] and it would indelibly influence the Romantics. But for now, *Caleb Williams* was infuriating the British anti-Jacobins, whose power was quickly mounting during the third year of war with France. Indeed, on May 12, 1794, the day Godwin finished his novel, Prime Minister Pitt suspended the right of habeas corpus. Five months later, a group of Godwin's friends, including Holcroft, were accused of high treason, which was punishable by death. Their crime, the state argued, was seeking to reform the British government. But, according to British law, seeking reform does not constitute high treason, Godwin discovered and persuasively argued in his famous letter to the *Morning Chronicle*. When the letter was reprinted and released as a pamphlet, it undermined the prosecution, and within a month all charges were dropped, though supporting France remained dangerous.

And Godwin continued to support France. He went on espousing radical ideas and attending radical dinners. He wore his hair short like the French sans-culottes. And his feelings underwent a sea change when he became friendly with Maria Reveley, wife of the radical architect Willey Reveley, whom Godwin knew through a mutual friend.

Born in England, Maria had been raised in Rome and Constantinople. She was open-minded, intelligent, very pretty, and sure of her appeal to men. She and Godwin dined together frequently, both with and without her husband. And on January 9, 1795, they met secretly on the island of Greenwich, where she frankly declared her love.[44] Abashed, Godwin rejected the idea of an adulterous liaison. Still, he was clearly moved. A few years later (when both Willey Reveley and Mary Wollstonecraft were dead), Godwin would beg Maria to marry him. And it was in a letter to Maria that he most fully expressed his views on women and men. "Can you fail to be aware of the inferences which you ought to draw from the respective characters of the two sexes?" he asked her.

> We are different in our structure; we are perhaps still more different in our educations. Woman stands in the need of the courage of man to defend her, of his constancy to inspire her with firmness, and at present at least of his science and information, to furnish to her resources of amusement. . . . Women richly repay us for all we can bring into the common stock, by the softness of their natures, the delicacy of their sentiments, and that peculiar and instantaneous sensibility, by which they are qualified to guide our tastes and correct our skepticism. For my part, I confess I am incapable of conceiving how domestic happiness could be so well generated without this disparity of character.[45]

So it was not a great champion of female equality that joined the author of *Vindication* for tea at Mary Hays's house on January 8, 1796; but it was an emotional man with a weakness for women who valued constancy and "the courage . . . to defend." Mary and Godwin were more comfortable with each other at this second meeting. Mary Hays must have predisposed Mary in his favor. And Mary's undisguised sorrow affected Godwin. He met her at another party six days later and was now sufficiently intrigued to begin reading her new book.

On January 25, Godwin notes in his diary that he has read the first seventy-eight pages of "Wolstencraft's Travels." Nine days later, he has finished Mary's *Letters* and decided, "If ever there was a book calculated to make a man in love with its author, this appears to me to be the book. [Mary] speaks of her sorrows in a way that fills us with melancholy, and dissolves us in tenderness, at the same time that she displays a genius which commands all our admiration. Affliction had tempered her heart to a softness almost more than human; and the gentleness of her spirit seems precisely to accord with all the romance of unbounded attachment."[46]

This "unbounded attachment" continued to distract Mary during the days and weeks after Mary Hays's tea. She wrote a heartbroken letter to Archibald Hamilton Rowan, confessing, "I am unhappy—I have been treated with unkindness—and even cruelty, by the person from whom I had every reason to expect affection— I write to you with an agitated hand— I cannot be more explicit— I value your good opinion—and you know how to feel for me— I looked for some thing like happiness—*happiness!* in the discharge of my relative duties and the heart on which I leaned has pierced mine to the quick."[47]

So finally, Mary could admit to herself that Imlay did not love her, but she could not bring herself to make the final break—though longer periods did elapse between their talks and letters. An especially long period had passed when, one night in February, Mary took Fanny for a walk to see the Christies, who happened to be entertaining Imlay in their parlor at the time. Hearing Mary's voice, Rebecca rushed to urge her to turn back. But Mary strode into the parlor, dropping Fanny at her father's feet. Mortified, Imlay convinced Mary to leave by promising to visit the following day, at which point—as usual—he spoke soothingly and left as soon as he could.

The day after Imlay's visit, Mary took off for a month to visit the Berkshire country home of her old friend Mrs. Cotton, where, despite a harsh letter from Imlay, she managed to enjoy a country spring. When she returned to London in March, Mary sent Imlay a note like myriad others she had written over the past two years, with the difference that now she intended to act on her words. "You must do as you please with respect to the child," she writes, urging Imlay to draw up some official document, probably the bond she later mentions, that would define his obligations to Fanny. And she promises:

It is now finished.— Convinced that you have neither regard nor friendship, I disdain to utter a reproach. . . . I now solemnly assure you, that this is an eternal farewell.— Yet I flinch not from the duties which tie me to life. . . . I have . . . thought in vain, if the sensations which lead you to follow an ancle or step, be the sacred foundation of principle and affection. [My morality] has been of a very different nature, or it would not have stood the brunt of your sarcasms.

Mary remains emphatic about her feelings:

The sentiment in me is still sacred. If there be any part of me that will survive the sense of my misfortunes, it is the purity of my affections. The impetuosity of your senses, may have led you to term mere animal desire, the source of principle; and it may give zest to some years to come— Whether you will always think so, I shall never know.

And she refuses to condemn Imlay outright:

It is strange that, in spite of all you do, something like conviction forces me to believe, that you are not what you appear to be. . . . I part with you in peace.[48]

And so she did. Sometime not long afterward, the former lovers spotted each other traveling, aptly enough, along the New Road. He was on horseback, she on foot. He got down and walked with her for quite a while, and they parted "without producing in her any oppressive emotion."[49]

And now she made plans to move out of Finsbury Square with all its painful associations. She had stored her furniture in 1792 when she had left the country. And, planning soon again "to leave England forever,"[50] she kept her belongings in storage and moved north to furnished rooms in a grassy area near the edge of London in Cumming Street, Pentonville, not far, as it happened, from Godwin's house in Somers Town.

On April 14, she felt cheerful enough to defy social etiquette and pay a call on this unmarried man.

CHAPTER THIRTEEN

*T*he week after Mary called on Godwin, Godwin invited her back to dine with some of his most impressive friends, including Elizabeth Inchbald and Thomas Holcroft. Mary fell decidedly short of Mrs. Inchbald's lofty moral standards, while Inchbald's sarcasms and haughty demeanor instantly put Mary off. Mary dubbed Mrs. Inchbald "Mrs. Perfection" and, in a May review of her novel *Nature and Art* in the *Analytical Review*, doubted that the author could keep the reader's attention "awake" since her "peculiar talent" was not wit but naïveté.[1]

Holcroft, on the other hand, was worldly and emotional. His wife had died, and he had fallen lustily in love with Mary the previous fall. Then, in a dramatic letter, Holcroft exceeded even his usual effusiveness, proclaiming:[2]

In you I think I discover the very being for whom my soul has for years been languishing: one who, the woman of reason all day, the philosopher that traces compares and combines facts for the benefit of present and future times, in the evening becomes the playful and passionate child of love: one who would realize all the fond raptures of my fanciful and ardent youth ҃. . . well, well, I never touched your lips; yet I have felt them, sleeping and waking.[3]

Mary discouraged Holcroft's passion, but liked his flair and forthright manner. They soon resumed a companionable friendship, though Mary kept the letter, which profoundly shook Godwin when he discovered it sometime in the months ahead.

Amelia Alderson was nearly as ardent as Holcroft in her rush to praise the new woman in Godwin's circle, writing Mary:

I remember the time when my desire of seeing you was repress'd by fear but as soon as I read your letters from Norway the cold awe which the philosopher had excited was lost in the tender sympathy call'd forth by the woman— I saw nothing but the interesting creature of feelings and imagination, and I resolved, if possible, to become acquainted with one who had alternately awakened my sensibility and gratified my judgement. I saw you, and you . . . have exceeded my expectations.[4]

Later, Amelia informed Mary that "a richish oldish bachelor" had heard of her "distressed circumstances" and wished to give her a small sum of money to allay her woes. Needless to say, Mary took umbrage and in high dudgeon refused the gift.[5]

While Mary never really trusted Amelia, she quickly warmed to Godwin's friends Maria Reveley and the writer Eliza Fenwick. Never before had she socialized with so many accomplished females. And new friends must have comforted her, for she lost contact with her brother Charles and Ruth Barlow, who no longer wrote. Eliza stuck to her vow of silence, and Everina, never much of a writer, corresponded less frequently than ever. But Mary's closest friend, Joseph Johnson, remained devoted, as did Rebecca Christie, whose husband, Thomas, was off on a long business trip in Surinam, where Imlay may have gone as well.

Mary's passion for Imlay had coincided with the most idealistic days of the French Revolution. Her feelings for Godwin developed during England's fourth year of war with France, as the Enlightenment waned and reaction against all progressive thought followed the violence of the Terror. While many of the lofty principles of 1789 lived on in France's 1795 Constitution, other reforms had been lost in the intervening years. Deputies were now chosen not by all citizens but by electoral assemblies composed exclusively of large property owners—in other words, less than half the number of people who had been eligible to vote in 1791. And the present Constitution demanded that *two-thirds* of the new Assembly be made up of current delegates, thus minimizing the possibility for change, which was unlikely anyway, given the growth of military power.

In England, Jacobinism was reviled and ridiculed. The novel of sensibility, touted just a few years earlier, was despised for its association with French *romans*. Indeed, as Amelia Alderson told Godwin, in the current climate it was courageous simply to admire Mary Hays's new novel, *Memoirs of Emma Courtney*, with its decidedly out-of-vogue emphasis on the emotional life.[6]

In the spring and summer of 1796, Mary Wollstonecraft and William Godwin met constantly, though he was still misspelling her name and calling on other "Fairs." Typical of Godwin's diary entries are "Dined at H's with Wolstencraft" (May 15) and "sup at Wolstencraft's" (May 28). Mary was in the process of writing a "comedy" about the French Revolution, which Godwin perused at the beginning of June. (In *Memoirs of Mary Wollstonecraft*, Godwin intriguingly notes that the play's serious scenes draw from Mary's own experiences,[7] but he deemed the overall piece too crude to publish and destroyed it at her death.) By July, she had "altered" it in light of his comments, and she had also, in her first extant letter to her future husband, suggested some alterations in *his* prose. For Godwin, it seems, had made an awkward attempt at a love letter. "I send you the last volume of [*La Nouvelle*] *Héloïse*, because, if you have it not, you may chance to wish for it," she begins jauntily, and continues:

> You may perceive by this remark that I do not give you credit for as much philosophy as our friend [Rousseau], and I want besides to remind you, when you write to me . . . not to choose the easiest task, my perfections, but to dwell on your own feelings—that is to say, give me a birds-eye view of your heart. Do not make me a desk "to write upon," I humbly pray—unless you honestly acknowledge yourself *bewitched*. . . . Of that I shall judge by the style in which the eulogiums flow, for I think I have observed that you compliment without rhyme or reason, when you are most at a loss what to say.[8]

In other words, Godwin was not a gifted suitor, which seemed to amuse Mary, who clearly relished her new role as expert on romance. As in France, she was widely admired. She no longer grasped at life; she had lived. Although going by Imlay's name (except with intimate friends) made her technically respectable, her uncommon experience gave her an exotic charm—as did the slight squint, or *louche*, she'd developed in one eye. A new acquaintance told Amelia Alderson he found Mary "very voluptuous-looking,"[9] while the poet Robert Southey declared her face "the best, infinitely the best [of the London literati]. . . . Her eyes are light brown, and though the lid of one is affected by a little paralysis, they are the most meaning I ever saw."[10] And the famous painter John Opie called on her so often it was rumored she would soon be Mrs. Mary Opie. (Opie ultimately married Amelia Alderson.) Yet, Mary favored Godwin despite his big nose.

GODWIN SPENT the month of July 1796 in Norfolk. His July 5 diary entry finds him "in Norwich with [his friend Robert] Merry." On July 7, penniless Merry was thrown into debtor's jail, a catastrophe, in Godwin's view. The nights of July 7, 8, and 9, Godwin slept at the home of Dr. Alderson and his daughter Amelia. Then, on July 10, Godwin wrote in his diary, "Propose to Alderson." These words have led many biographers to surmise that Godwin went to Norfolk to propose marriage to Amelia, and that it was only because she rejected him that he on July 13 made a second (similarly flawed) attempt to write Mary of love: "I love your imagination, your delicate epicurism, the malicious leer of your eye, in short every thing that constitutes the bewitching tout ensemble."

This interpretation makes Godwin uncharacteristically expedient, not to say deceitful, and perplexingly eager to embrace the institution of marriage, which he told everyone he abhorred. In *The Godwins and the Shelleys*, William St. Clair advances a more plausible explanation for the entry: that Godwin proposed not to Amelia, but to Amelia's father; that he wanted Dr. Alderson to help buy off Robert Merry's creditors so Merry could start a new life in America. This hypothesis makes perfect sense in light of Merry's predicament and is buttressed by a September 19 letter in which Merry informs Godwin that he intends to pay some money back to Dr. Alderson before he sails for the United States.[11]

Godwin would later recall that he spent most of his free moments in Norfolk thinking of Mary, while she at last took her furniture out of storage and moved with Fanny and Marguerite to Judd Place, on the

outskirts of Somers Town—much nearer to his home. "She had med-
itated a tour to Italy or Switzerland. . . . Now however she felt herself
reconciled to a longer abode in England, probably without exactly
knowing why."[12]

Mary may in fact have known her mind better than Godwin imagined. For on July 21 she writes of his recent letter: "the sentence I *liked*
best was the concluding one, where you tell me, that you were coming home, to depart *no more*."[13]

A flirtatious letter follows on August 2: "How can you find in your
heart to let me pass so many evenings alone . . . I did not wish to see
you this evening because you have been dining, I suppose, with Mrs.
Perfection, and comparison[s] are odious."[14] And on August 6, Mary
boldly addresses an envelope "Not to be opened 'till the Philosopher
has been an hour at least, in Miss Alderson's company, cheek by
jowl." The note inside reads:

Miss Alderson was wondering this morning whether you *ever*
kissed a maiden fair— As you do not like to solve problems, *on
paper*, TELL her *before* you part— She will tell *me* next—year—

Seven days later, on Saturday, August 13, Godwin kissed Mary, or
as he phrased it, "the sentiment which trembled upon the tongue,
burst from the lips." "It was friendship melting into love," Godwin
calmly states. But in fact there was nothing calm about the start of
their affair. It was a momentous step, both for Godwin, who was a vir-
gin, and for Mary, who had twice tried to kill herself because Imlay
withdrew his love.

And the day after they first made love, Godwin was so flummoxed
he behaved as if nothing had happened and, without so much as
sending a note to Judd Place, trundled off for his regular Sunday dinner at Holcroft's home. The following day, Monday, they made love
"chez moi.," Godwin reported in his diary (using the French he in-

evitably turned to in delicate situations and the period that was his code sign for consummated sex).[15] And Tuesday morning, Godwin, ungracious as ever, informed his lover: "I have been very unwell all night. You did not consider me enough in that way yesterday, & therefore unintentionally impressed upon me a mortifying sensation." Whatever sensations were or were not impressed "chez moi." the next evening, Mary awoke the following morning thoroughly depressed. She wrote Godwin:

> I have not lately passed so painful a night as the last. . . . Struggling as I have been a long time to attain peace of mind (or apathy) I am afraid to trace emotions to their source. . . . Is it not sufficient to tell you that I am thoroughly out of humor with myself? . . . Despising false delicacy I almost fear I have lost sight of the true. Could a wish have transported me to France or Italy, last night, I should have caught up my Fanny and been off in a twinkle, though convinced that it is my mind, not the place, which requires changing. My imagination is for ever betraying me into fresh misery, and I perceive that I shall be a child to the end of the chapter. You talk of the roses which grow profusely in every path of life—I catch at them; but only encounter the thorns.

In her final paragraph, she gets to the real source of her upset: "Full of your own feelings, little as I comprehend them, you forgot mine."[16]

And Godwin saw this was true. "I am a fool," he wrote back.

> . . . You do not know how honest I am. I swear to you that I told you nothing but the strict & literal truth, when I described to you the manner in which you set my imagination on fire on Saturday. For six & thirty hours I could think of nothing else. I longed

inexpressibly to have you in my arms. Why did I not come to you? . . . I feared still that I might be deceiving myself as to your feelings, & that I was feeding my mind with groundless presumptions.

"Do not hate me. Indeed I do not deserve it," he continues, and then, struggling for a connection between what he believes in the abstract and his confused new feelings, Godwin urges Mary:

Be happy. Resolve to be happy. You deserve to be so. Every thing that interferes with it, is weakness & wandering; & a woman, like you, can, must, shall, shake it off. Afford, for instance, no food for the morbid madness, and no triumph to the misanthropical gloom, of your afternoon visitor [Mary Hays]. Call up, with firmness, the energies, which, I am sure, you so eminently possess. . . . Send me word that I may call on you in a day or two. Do you not see, while I exhort you to be a philosopher, how painfully acute are my own feelings? I need some soothing.[17]

"You may come when you please," she replied.[18]
And a few days later, Mary felt sufficiently loved to confess:

I am sometimes painfully humble— Write me, but a line, just to assure me, that you have been thinking of me with affection, now and then— Since we parted—[19]

Then Godwin exhorted her:

Humble! for heaven's sake, be proud, be arrogant! You are— but I cannot tell what you are. I cannot yet find the circum-

stance about you that allies you to the frailty of our nature. I
will hunt it out.[20]

Mary begins teasing Godwin as she did Imlay. On August 24, for
instance, she puts her lover on his guard:

As you are to dine with Mrs. Perfection to day, it would be dangerous, not to remind you of my existence—perhaps—a word
then in your ear—should you forget, for a moment, a possible
accident with the most delightful woman in the world, your fealty,
take care not to look over your left shoulder— I shall be there.[21]

And Godwin answers:

I will report my fealty this evening. Till then farewell.[22]

FOR ALL MARY'S resolve to be cautious, by the end of August she
was already hoping Fanny and Godwin would "love each other." "Me
wants to see man," Fanny informed Mary at the beginning of September, and "Fannikin" soon began running notes from her working
mother at Judd Place to Somers Town, where "man" often stopped
writing to feed her biscuits and talk.

Inevitably, their social circles mingled. When Mary's friend from
Berkshire came to town, Mary rejoiced to Godwin, "You have almost
captivated Mrs. C[otton]." "Opie called this morning— But you are
the man— Till we meet joy be with thee— Then—what then?"[23] And
after spending a day with "Mrs. Perfection," Mary admitted, "if I do
not admire her more I love her better— She is a charming woman!"[24]

While the lovemaking was awkward for Godwin initially, he soon lost his diffidence and would remain eager for marital sex well into old age. He called Mary "Adorable maîtresse!" and himself her "boy pupil,"[25] while Mary titillated Godwin with reports of the marvel of her postcoital glow: "I have seldom seen so much live fire running about my features as this morning when recollections—very dear, called forth the blush of pleasure, as I adjusted my hair."[26] ("I wish I had been a spectator of the live fire you speak of,"[27] he wrote back.) She candidly admitted pleasure at "acting the part of a wife" when she washed his household linens. And sometimes she lost herself completely when he held her in his arms.[28] Other times, she simply felt lusty: "There is no flying from voluptuous sensations, I find, do what a woman can—can a philosopher do more?"[29]

By loving Imlay during the French Revolution, it had seemed to Mary that her happiness had a larger social significance. Now, in her letters to Godwin, Mary rarely mentions either the French or the British government. She is more concerned about the state of *them*; and specifically about sustaining love while working, living, and frequently socializing apart from each other. In *Political Justice*, Godwin despised the monopoly of marriage. And Mary was as determined as he to preserve her independence and keep their love secret while she struggled to meet Godwin as often as she could. That struggle was itself intoxicating—like Imlay's having to cross a barrier to reach her in Neuilly—though it could be hilarious at times, as suggested in Mary's rushed note to Godwin on September 28:

> I was detained at Miss Hay's, where I met Mrs. Bunn, as it was necessary for me to out stay her. But this is not the worst part of the story. Mrs. Bunn was engaged to dine at Opie's, who had promised to bring her to see me this evening— They will not stay long of course—so do as you please I have no objection to your drinking tea with them— But should you not like it—may I request you drink tea with M. Hays, and come to me at an early

hour. Nay, I wish you would call on me in your way for half an hour—as soon as you can rise from the table.[30]

In addition to her diligent nursemaid, Marguerite, Mary hired another servant, whose main mission, it appears from Mary's correspondence, was to run her mistress's social messages all over town. For Mary was full of energy and eager to see every new play and meet anyone worth knowing in London. Little gestures thrilled her; she told Godwin: "There is such a magic in affection that I have been more gratified by your clasping your hands round my arm, in company, than I could have been by all the admiration in the world, tho' I am a woman—and to mount a step higher in the scale of vanity, an author."[31] The more exuberant she felt, the more she wished everyone else joy. When it appeared that Mary Hays suspected her new liaison, Mary told Godwin: "[Mary Hays] has owned to me that she cannot endure to see others enjoy the mutual affection from which she is debarred— I will write a kind note to her today to ease my conscience, for when I am happy myself, I am made up of milk and honey."[32]

Mary was again contributing regularly to the *Analytical Review.* In a September 1796 article, she reiterates her ambivalence about the French Revolution, noting its "strange mixture of wisdom and folly, of generous actions and atrocities, and of sufferings and success."[33] She has not lost faith in the inevitability of progress, but it is shaken, while the idea of a personal God appeals to her more than it has in years. "I would [offer you] a God bless you—did you care for it,"[34] she provoked her atheist lover at one point. She lent him her family Bible, because "I do not intend to let you extend your skepticism to me."[35] Then, when she was very angry at Godwin, Mary demanded: "How can you blame me for tak[ing] refuge in the idea of a God, when I despair of finding sincerity on earth?"[36]

Unique as they were, they quarreled by the book. One morning, for instance, Mary coquettishly greets Godwin and *just like a woman* broadly hints that he should drop in on her that afternoon: "How do you do this morning—are you alive? It is not *wise* to be cold during such a domesticating season, I mean then to dismiss all my frigid airs before I draw near your door, this evening, and should you, in your way from Mr. Carlisle's, *think* of [stopping by]—why it would be a pretty mark of attention— And—entre nous, *little* marks of attention are incumbent on you at present."[37]

Just like a man, Godwin grumbles back: "Yes, I am alive. Perhaps I am better. I am glad to hear how enchanting and divine you will appear this evening.— You spoil little attentions by anticipating them."[38]

"To have attention I find it is necessary to demand it. . . . But, *never mind,*"[39] retorts Mary, stealing the last word.

For all her happiness, Mary was frequently exasperated with Godwin, and he was constantly perplexed by her. "I cannot tell what you are," he confessed at one point.[40] And when Mary predicted that he would leave her just like Imlay had, she "put an end to all my hopes," Godwin melodramatically answered. "I needed soothing, & you threaten me. Oppressed with a diffidence and uncertainty which I hate, you join the oppressors & annihilate me." He told her he was "afraid" of her, and she dreaded his disapproval.

Caring more than ever now about the plight of her own sex, Mary had begun a new novel tentatively called *Maria; or, The Wrongs of Woman.* Like *Mary,* it was highly autobiographical, and like *Original Stories,* deeply concerned with the poor. She was writing slowly and carefully for the first time, but "I seem to want encouragement,"[41] she told Godwin one day, and sent him a fragment of the novel, hoping he would like it and spur her on. Instead, Godwin informed Mary that there was a "radical defect" in her writing: "What you principally want is distinctness of narrative." There was too much "detail of feeling," her plot was muddled, and she painted everyone black or white.[42] Furthermore, her grammar was execrable. Mary was devastated by Godwin's judgments. And her long response reveals the continued centrality of work to her identity:

> What is to be done, I must either disregard your opinion, think it unjust, or throw down my pen in despair; and that would be tantamount to resigning existence; for at fifteen I resolved never to marry for interested motives, or to endure a life of dependence. You know not how painfully my sensibility, call it false if you will, has been wounded by some of the steps I have been obliged to take for others. . . . In short, I must reckon on doing some good, and getting the money I want, by my writings, or go to sleep for ever. I shall not be content merely to keep body and soul together— By what I have already written Johnson, I am sure, has been a gainer. . . . I am compelled to think there is some thing in my writings more valuable, than in the productions of some people on whom you bestow warm eulogiums— I mean more mind—denominate it as you will—more of the observations of my own senses, more of the combining of the imagination—the effusions of my own feelings and passions.[43]

Godwin realized he'd been overly harsh and went to Mary as soon as he got her letter. By that night, she could write him, "I have spent a pleasant day,"[44] so he must have tempered his criticism and also offered some help. For two weeks later, she is reminding him, "You are to give me a [grammar] lesson this evening," and with her old determination declaring, "Now you have led me to discover that I write worse, than I thought I did, there is no stopping short—I must improve."[45]

In the middle of September, "Poor Fannikin" came down with chicken pox. As her sweet face grew red and swollen, Mary thought back to the smallpox that had nearly killed her infant daughter in Le Havre the year she was born. "I write with [Fanny] in my arms— I have been trying to amuse her all the morning to prevent her scratching her face," anxious Mary told Godwin. When Mary went out, Fanny "did nothing but seek for me . . . and moan my absence, which increased her fever";[46] so Mary stayed home and nursed Fanny until she grew feverish and sick herself. Both patients soon recovered, but at the end of November, Mary was again suffering, now from a "*very* troublesome cough."[47] And then, on December 6, an "extreme lowness of spirits . . . cre[pt] over" her.[48] The next day, she berated Godwin for finding her only a low corner place at the theater while he watched the same play with Mrs. Inchbald from a choice seat high up. "I was a fool not to ask Opie to go with me,"[49] Mary snapped. And she took offense again a week later, when Godwin left a dinner party without waiting for her. Clearly, independence had its price.

Mary became increasingly cool and touchy and suggests she has already confided in Godwin that she believes she is pregnant when she writes on December 20: "Fanny says, *perhaps* Man come today— I am glad that there is no perhaps in the case.— As to other perhaps—they must rest in the womb of time."[50]

Three days later, Mary was hopeful about Godwin's feelings for the coming baby: "There was a tenderness in your manner, as you seemed to be opening your heart, to a new born affection, that rendered you very dear to me. . . . There are other pleasures in the world, you perceive, beside those know[n] to your philosophy." But she adds, "Of myself I am still at a loss what to say."[51] And on December 28, she tells him she is assailed by "painful recollections," doubtless of her experiences as an unwed mother at the end of the eighteenth century in the England of George III.

On December 31, Godwin tries to deflect Mary's anger by eliciting her sympathy:

You treated me last night with extreme unkindness: the more so, because it was calm, melancholy, equable unkindness. You wished we had never met; you wished you could cancel all that had passed between us. Is this—ask your own heart,—Is this compatible with the passion of love? Or, is it not the language of frigid, unalterable indifference? . . . You wished all the kind things you had written me destroyed.[52]

"This does not appear to me just the moment to have written me such a note as I have been perusing," Mary answers, refusing the bait.[53]

When the new year came and the author of *Political Justice* failed to propose marriage or any other scheme to spare Mary a second illegitimate birth, she became "sick at heart— Dissatisfied with every body and every thing."[54] She was also running out of money because Imlay failed to pay "the first half-year's interest of the bond given to me for Fanny."[55] And for the first time ever, Johnson refused to settle her bills. It was finally Godwin who swallowed his pride and requested a loan from his industrialist friend Thomas Wedgwood. Wedgwood sent fifty pounds to see her through the winter ahead.

In mid-January, it snowed, and Mary's petticoats dangled on the wet ground. "Poor Women how they are beset with plagues—within and without," she lamented.[56] Later in the month, still suffering from the "inelegant complaint, which no novelist has yet ventured to mention as one of the consequences of sentimental distress," Mary accused Godwin of doubting that she was sick.[57] On February 3, their friend Dr. Fordyce confirmed her pregnancy. And on February 12, Everina arrived for a visit on her way to a new position governessing for the Wedgwood children in Etruria, Staffordshire. Probably, Godwin had found Everina the job.

But Everina immediately disliked Godwin, seeing him as the monster who'd sunk Mary even further in the world's view, and Godwin resented Everina's gloomy refusal to talk to him. So now Mary found herself in the peculiar position of having to soothe rather than rebuke the lover who'd made her pregnant. She apologized profusely for her sister's rudeness, first blaming it on a bad cold. But when both Everina's cold and her hostility intensified, Mary had to stay at home alone with the sulky invalid, which made her long for the man she'd despised just days before. "Everina's cold is still so bad, that unless pique urges her, she will not go out today," Mary sighed on February 22. Further "torment" came from the family cat, Puss, who flew into a fit, crawled "up my chimney, and was so wild, that I thought it right to have her drown. . . . Fanny imagines that she was sick—and ran away." Mary says nothing of Fanny's reaction to her Aunt Everina, or of the aunt's initial feelings toward her illegitimate niece. This meeting would have a profound impact on both the child and the visitor, though it was a bitter time for Mary. "The evenings with [Everina] silent, I find very wearisome and embarrassing,"[58] Mary confessed to Godwin. The lovers were jubilant when, on the night of March 5, Everina at last judged herself well enough to take off.

And now a sauciness returns to Mary's letters to Godwin. "Should you call and find only books, have a little patience, and I shall be with you," she writes on March 11; and "so you goose you lost your supper—and deserved to lose it for not desiring [my servant] to give you some beef" on March 17. Why the teasing tone? The answer can only be that sometime during or shortly after Everina's visit Godwin has agreed to compromise his grand notions about the way things ought to be and deal as well as possible with "things as they are." And Mary has grown eager to embrace the institution she for over twenty years disparaged. Sheepishly perhaps, on the afternoon of March 29, they met (with James Marshall as their witness) at the sturdy little stone St. Pancras Church near their homes in north London and vowed to love each other 'til death did them part.

CHAPTER FOURTEEN

On April 6, 1797, Mary, Fanny, and Godwin slept in their new home in Somers Town, at No. 29, the Polygon—a development of handsome attached houses, shaped like its name, and reaching three stories high. The rooms were spacious, and there were gardens where Mary could stroll while Fanny romped to her heart's content. From now on, Mary's daughter would be Fanny Godwin. Soon she would forget the American who had darted in and out during the first two years of her life. Godwin was "Papa." And Godwin, who later described his children as his "favorite companions,"[1] became a devoted adoptive father. Years afterward, a visitor to the household observed that "Godwin, by nature as undemonstrative as possible, showed more affection to Fanny than to anyone else."[2]

After the move, Mary worked at home at the Polygon, while Godwin rented a nearby study where he turned up early each morning and remained until dinner or even after dinner sometimes. Mary and Godwin resolved to continue seeing friends of both sexes independently as well as together and to be far less dependent than the husbands and wives they had derided in their books. They saw themselves authoring the narrative of an enlightened partnership. Still, for all his good intentions, Godwin could be as dunderheaded as any husband. During her second week as Mrs. Godwin, Mary was forced to disabuse him of the idea that a wife does all the unpleasant chores: "Mr. Johnson, or somebody, has always taken the disagreeable business of settling with tradespeople off my hands— I am, perhaps as unfit as yourself to do it—and my time appears to me, as valuable as that of any other persons accustomed to employ themselves. . . . [I] feel, to say the truth, as if I was not treated with respect, owing to your desire not to be disturbed."[3] Godwin took her point.

And, for the most part, Mary was, as Godwin claimed, "a worshipper of domestic life."[4] She loved fussing over Fanny and concocting dinners. She enjoyed country outings and listening to Godwin read his essays by the fire after tea. Her vivacity and his steadiness proved fruitful contrasts. The narrator of Godwin's 1800 novel *St. Leon* seems to be describing Godwin and Mary when he muses: "It is impossible for two persons to be constituted so much alike, but that one of them should have a more genuine and instantaneous relish for one sort of excellence, and another for another. Thus, we added to each other's stores, and acquired a largeness of conception and liberality of judgement that neither of us would have arrived at if separate."[5]

When Hazlitt told Coleridge that he'd seen Mary "turn off Godwin's objection to something she advanced with quite a playful, easy air," Coleridge declared Mary the stronger partner, noting "the ascendency which people of imagination exercised over those of mere intellect."[6]

But Godwin and Mary proved equally unimaginative when it came to announcing their nuptials to the world. Godwin wrote Mary Hays with labored humor:

> My fair neighbor desires me to announce to you a piece of news
> which it is consonant to the regard that she and I entertain for

you, you should rather learn from us than from any other quarter. She bids me to remind you of the earnest way in which you pressed me to prevail upon her to change her name, and she directs me to add, that it has happened to me, like many other disputants, to be entrapped in my own toils; in short, we found that there was no way so obvious for her to drop the name of Imlay, as to assume the name of Godwin. Mrs. Godwin—who the devil is that?—will be glad to see you . . . whenever you are inclined to favor her with a call.[7]

In his announcement to Holcroft, Godwin neglected to disclose his wife's identity. "Your secrecy somewhat pains me,"[8] Holcroft understatedly replied. So much for unbounded confidence! And Mary was no less defensive. Her letter to Amelia Alderson is filled with lists of how she'll avoid or defy the author of *Political Justice*:

It is my wish that Mr. Godwin should visit and dine out as formerly, and I shall do the same; in short I still mean to be independent even to the cultivating sentiments and principles in my children's mind, (should I have more), which he disavows.[9]

And she is so eager to sustain her image as suffering for a great lost love that she all but apologizes for marrying a mere person: "The wound my unsuspecting heart formerly received is not healed. [But] I found my evenings solitary; and I wished, while fulfilling the duty of a mother, to have some person with similar pursuits, bound to me by affection; and besides, I earnestly desired to resign a name which seemed to disgrace me,"[10] she lamely explains. Her fate sounds dull indeed. But no duller, of course, than that of her husband, who was busy explaining how he'd married Mary out of a sense of duty, but would leave her as soon as he wanted, marriage vows or not.

On April 8, Mary sent Godwin to report the momentous events to

Joseph Johnson, who must have been displeased at some—probably financial—aspect of the marriage, for Godwin's diary reports "altercations" at St. Paul's Churchyard that day. And Johnson later told Mary's brother Charles that she was "happily married in every sense but one—no money on either side nor the means of procuring it but by literary exertion."[11] Or by borrowing from me, Johnson might well have added. But he was too much the gentleman, and besides, he was incapable of begrudging Mary love. So the day after Godwin's visit, Johnson returned to dine *en famille* at the Polygon along with Godwin's sister Hannah. Godwin's mother was delighted at the marriage, seeing it as a sign that he'd cast off some of his odder predilections and might now return to God.

Maria Reveley is said to have cried on April 4 when Godwin reported his marriage, but she quickly recovered, as did the Fenwicks. (The Reveleys' son Henry and the Fenwicks' daughter Eliza played frequently with Fanny now.) Elizabeth Inchbald, on the other hand, snubbed and insulted Mary on April 19, when the married couple appeared in her theater box, and though Godwin tried to sustain his private friendship with Mrs. Perfection, soon they were quarreling too. (Nonetheless, Inchbald continued to criticize Godwin's manuscripts astutely for years to come. And so keen was her appetite for gossip that in 1816, after years of silence, Inchbald dared to write her former friend, "I have some curiosity to know whether you have a daughter or an adopted daugher, or neither the one, or the other, in Switzerland at the present?"[12] She was referring, of course, to his daughter Mary's scandalous elopement with the married Percy Bysshe Shelley.)

Mrs. Sarah Siddons was another moralistic actress who had been eager to entertain Mary before her marriage and refused to see her now. For while Godwin had presumed a beloved Mrs. Godwin would be more socially acceptable than a deserted Mrs. Imlay in a century when divorce was impossible, Mary's marriage underscored what many previously had only suspected—that she had never been Imlay's wife, and Fanny was illegitimate. Mary's sister Eliza Bishop, with a dead daughter and no support from her husband, was more respectable in polite society because she was legally married to the father of her child. Certainly, Eliza and Everina felt threatened by Mary's marriage to Godwin—and not without cause, for Mary's notoriety offended Eliza's would-be employers and cost her an attractive job.[13]

And then there was a Miss N. Pinkerton, who took all the gossip about Mary's promiscuity as an invitation to flirt with her spouse. At first, Mary mocked Miss N. as just "another Fair in intellectual distress."[14] But soon she was accusing Godwin of encouraging her. "My old wounds bleed afresh— What did not blind confidence, and unsuspecting truth, lead me to—my very soul trembles sooner than endure the hundred[th] part of what I have suffer[ed], I could wish my poor Fanny and self asleep at the bottom of the sea."[15]

So Godwin learned Mary was not the wife to tolerate even playful flirtations. "I am fully sensible of your attention in this matter, & believe you are right,"[16] he penitently solaced his fretting wife, who promptly banned Miss Pinkerton from the Polygon. ("At length I am sensible of the impropriety of my conduct. Tears and communication afford me relief,"[17] Miss Pinkerton replied.) So ended their worst fight.

For the most part, life at No. 29, the Polygon, was tranquil. Mary and Godwin were both expecting a child and creating a marriage, which, of course, entailed tears and tantrums. Still, both knew they loved and were loved in an enduring way. Meanwhile, Fanny played at the Fenwicks' and the Reveleys', Godwin prepared a revised edition of *Political Justice*, and Mary sat for a second portrait by Opie while working hard on *Maria; or, The Wrongs of Woman*. By the end of the summer, a little more than the first of three proposed volumes was finished and revised.

And that third, like *Caleb Williams,* was a tirade against injustice. The book opens at a madhouse outside London where its three main characters reside. The first, Maria—we learn in a long exposition—is a beautiful wife in her mid-twenties, whose childhood was darkened by a tyrannical father like Edward Wollstonecraft and a scheming older brother like Ned. To escape home, she married her neighbor George Venables, a "model of perfection," she thought, until she discovered Venables had courted her for her uncle's money, since whatever his wife owned would be his. And Venables no sooner worked his way through Maria's dowry than he began demanding the small sums her devoted uncle periodically sent. Meanwhile, Venables slept with other women and paraded around the house in filthy clothes. Disgusted, Maria, like Eliza Bishop, fled the marriage, and, unlike Eliza, brought her baby along. When she failed to elude Venables in London, Maria resolved to travel to Lisbon, where her uncle was dying. By bequeathing his fortune to Maria's baby (who was single and thus permitted by British law to own property), the good man hoped to keep his inheritance out of Venables's grasp. But in a melodramatic turn of events, Venables kidnapped his daughter and drugged and incarcerated his wife.

The book's second and less well-developed character is another wronged and perfectly sane inmate named Henry Darnford, who calls himself "thoughtless" and "extravagant," but Maria dismisses his faults as "the generous luxuriancy of a noble mind" and falls in love with him on the spot. Though British, handsome Darnford tells Maria that he lived many years in America, whose "prudery"[18] and worship of commercial speculation he loathes.

Like Maria, Darnford despises the poverty that victimizes hapless souls such as the illegitimate madhouse guard Jemima, the novel's third and most intriguing character, who was raped and reduced to hard labor and prostitution before she at last found refuge cleaning a learned "gentleman's" house. Here she could read in the library and listen to her employer's brilliant friends converse. But when her master died, these friends rebuffed her pleas for help with platitudes like "misery [is] the consequence of indolence,"[19] convincing her that "the rich and poor [are] natural enemies."[20] She accepted the job at the madhouse as a last resort.

Darnford sums up the moral of Jemima's experience: "Though riches may fail to produce proportionate happiness, poverty most commonly excludes it, by shutting up all the avenues to improvement."[21]

The main plot development in this initial third of the novel is Jemima's visit to London, where she learns the devastating news that Maria's child is dead.

The later sections of *Maria* are roughly sketched in a twelve-page outline. Here, Darnford, Maria, and Jemima all flee the madhouse, and Maria and Darnford live out their fantasy of love for a short time until Darnford loses interest and moves on. "A fondness for sex often gives an appearance of humanity to the behaviour of men, who have small pretensions to the reality," Maria bitterly assesses Darnford's true character.[22] But she insists Darnford never seduced her, when her husband takes his battle to court. Here the judge scorns Maria's "French" notions of love and honor and condemns her to remain married to Venables for life.

At this point in the narrative, *Maria* abruptly finishes, but Godwin tacks on a few hastily written notes which he discovered on Mary's desk. One reads:

Sued by her husband— Damages awarded to him— Separation from bed and board— Darnford goes abroad— Maria into the country— Provides for her father— Is shunned— Returns to London— Expects to see her lover— The wrack of expectation— Finds herself again with child— Delighted— A discovery— A visit— A miscarriage— Conclusion.

Another has Maria

Divorced by her husband— Her lover unfaithful— Pregnancy—
Miscarriage— Suicide.

In a final and most fully described ending, Maria swallows laudanum, but recovers when Jemima appears leading a child she has
"snatched . . . from misery," Maria's daughter. Now the mother has
reason to live.

MARY WROTE *Maria* when she was as content as she'd ever been—
except, perhaps, during her first spring and summer in France with
Imlay. And yet it is her angriest and most radical work. More em-
phatically than *Vindication*, it condemns British law: for denying
women divorce; for perpetuating primogeniture; and, worst, for insisting on a rule that her own grandfather, the weaver, had sought to
undermine four decades earlier—that married women have no right
to possess property of their own.

Maria is furious as well at British mores. "I execrate . . . the institutions of society, which . . . enable men to tyrannize over women,"
Maria exclaims,[23] and the novel proceeds to condemn the exclusion
of women from meaningful work and their subjection to poverty at its
bleakest. Jemima is one of the first realistic lower-class protagonists in
British fiction, a rebuke to lucky Moll Flanders and all the "poor" girls
in Fanny Burney's novels who lack nothing more than carriages and
fine clothes. And *Maria* goes further than *Vindication* not just to pity
but to condone prostitutes who choose self-employment over slaving
for cruel taskmasters, and to excoriate "writers, professing to be
friends to freedom" whose hopeful theories refuse to acknowledge the
preponderance of despair.

As in *Mary*, autobiographical references abound. Maria's early experiences are obviously drawn from Mary's own youth. Darnford behaves like Imlay, and the needy daughter who deters Maria from suicide is clearly based on Fanny, while Eliza's long-ago escape from her husband, Bishop, is retraced in Maria's flight. Most intriguingly, the uncle's scheme to bequeath his money to Maria through her daughter, bypassing Venables, uncannily parallels the senior Edward Wollstonecraft's attempt to enrich his daughter and not her husband—the only indication that Mary ever saw her grandfather's will. Curiously, no character at all resembling Godwin appears, though Jemima does pointedly deride "advocate[s] for unequivocal sincerity" who delude themselves that any able person can find work.

Presumably, Mary visited real insane asylums that inspired *Maria*'s depictions of the madhouse, but Mary's ideas about the mind's fragility also emerge in passages such as this:

Maria was not permitted to walk in the garden; but sometimes, from her window, she turned her eyes from the gloomy walls, in which she pined life away, on the poor wretches who strayed along the walks, and contemplated the most terrific of ruins— that of a human soul . . . a mental convulsion, which, like the devastation of an earthquake, throws all the elements of thought and imagination into confusion, makes contemplation giddy, and we fearfully ask on what ground we ourselves stand.[24]

It is frustrating that two-thirds of *Maria* remains unfinished and that even this first third suffers from convoluted grammar and the absence of a forward-thrusting plot. Still, with its bold attack on British misogyny and its insistence that feelings are as crucial as thought, the novel is a major, even culminating work. Mary eloquently defends the importance of her subject in a letter to her painter friend George Dyson, who was, besides Godwin, the only person who saw and criticized her final work:

> I have been reading your remarks and I find them a little discouraging. I mean I am not satisfied with the feelings which seem to be the result of [your] perusal [of the manuscript]. I was perfectly aware that some of the incidents ought to be transposed and heightened by more harmonious shading; and I wished to avail myself of yours and Mr. G's criticism before I began to adjust my events into a story, the outline of which I had sketched in my mind at the commencement; yet I am vexed and surprised at your not thinking the situation of Maria sufficiently important, and can only account for this want of—shall I say it? delicacy of feeling by recollecting that you are a man— For my part I cannot imagine any situation more distressing than for a woman of sensibility with an improving mind to be bound, to such a man as I have described, for life—obliged to renounce all the humanizing affections, and to avoid cultivating her taste lest her perception of grace, and refinement of sentiment should sharpen to agony the pangs of disappointment. Love, in which the imagination mingles its bewitching colouring must be fostered by delicacy— I should despise, or rather call her an ordinary woman, who could endure such a husband as I have sketched—yet you do not seem to be disgusted with him!!![25]

How far Mary has come from *Vindication*, where she declared neglected wives made the "best mothers" and "an unhappy marriage" was "very advantagious to a family" and by extension to the larger world.[26] Now marriage *is* the larger world symbolically, and while *Maria* is far from optimistic about romantic love—Maria never finds a virtuous or even faithful lover—it does urge, "Whilst your own heart is sincere always expect to meet one glowing with the same sentiments; for to fly from pleasure, is not to avoid pain!"[27]

MARY HERSELF did not fly from pleasure, though past experience kept her on guard. Typical was her reaction to Godwin's June walking tour. This trip—to the Wedgwood house and china factory in Staffordshire—was planned in part to reinvigorate the Godwins' passion. Mary *was* more ardent at first, warmly writing her absent husband on June 6 that the baby whom they'd already decided was a boy and named William "frisk[ed] a little at being informed of your remembrance. I begin to love this little creature, and to anticipate his birth as a fresh twist to a knot, which I do not wish to untie." And: "Men are spoilt by frankness . . . yet I must tell you that I love you better than I supposed I did, when I promised to love you forever—and I will add what will gratify your benevolence, if not your heart, that on the whole I may be termed happy."[28]

And she remained happy for about a week as Godwin wrote her long, newsy accounts of his journey. On Saturday, June 10, for instance, he found Everina (now governessing for the Wedgwoods) "in high spirits," for her at least, and he bought Fanny the mug he'd promised her, while assuring Mary, "No creature expresses, because no creature feels, the tender affections, so perfectly as you do." He finishes his letter, saluting "the trio M, F, & last & least (in stature at least) little W" and promising to write again soon.[29] That he does, recording in fastidious detail everything that absorbs his interest as he leaves the Wedgwoods and presses on through Utchester and Derby and Elford: places that do not interest Mary in the least.

Godwin's trip was scheduled to last a week. When he'd been gone twice that time, on June 19 Mary berated him:

One of the pleasures you tell me, that you promised yourself
from your journey was the effect your absence might produce on
me— Certainly at first my affection was increased; or rather
more alive— But now it is just the contrary. Your latter letters
might have been addressed to any body—and will [only] serve to
remind you w[h]ere you have been.

And in the tone that she formerly reserved for Imlay: "Whatever
tenderness you took away with you seems to have evaporated in the
journey . . . unless you suppose me a stick or a stone, you must have
forgot to think—as well as to feel, since you have been on the wing."[30]
Godwin got the message and returned.

So Mary would always be Mary, but what she told Godwin in her
June 6 letter was true: "on the whole," she was happy, and productive as well. Besides *Maria,* she began conceiving a book, "On the
Management of Infants," and a series of "Lessons" for very young
children in which a mother uses concrete examples to instruct her
four-year-old girl. In Lesson X, for instance, she compares this
daughter to her newborn son and then to Betty, the housekeeper:

See how much taller you are than William. In four years you
have learned to eat, to walk, to talk. Why do you smile? You can
do much more, you think: you can wash your hands and face. . . .
Betty is making an apple-pye. You love an apple-pye; but I do
not bid you make one. Your hands are not strong enough to mix
the butter and flour together; and you must not try to pare the
apples, because you cannot manage a great knife.[31]

Twice, the mother in *Lessons* alludes to the child's grandmother.
"My mamma took care of me, when I was a little girl, like you," she
says. And: "When I was a child, my mamma chose the fruit for me, to
prevent my making myself sick." So Mary either permits herself the

luxury of imagining the sort of kindness she herself never received, or she truly remembers some of her mother's good points.[32]

The portrait John Opie painted of Mary the summer of 1797 observes her striking growth over the past five years. While she appeared as a twisting form (turning from a book, raising her eyes at a visitor) in his 1792 painting, she now faces straight ahead with her chin held high. No longer pale, her cheeks glow with good health, and a gauzy white gown exposes the roundness of her arms and breasts. She is obviously pregnant. And the fussy gray-white wig encircling Mary's face in the 1792 portrait is replaced here by her own wavy light auburn hair pulled back to expose a full, untroubled countenance. Her knowing eyes gaze vaguely off the picture plane.

"Baby William" was due at the end of August. While she'd boasted of her good health during her last months of pregnancy in Le Havre, Mary was now sick as often as she was well. But she felt sure the delivery would again be easy. She never expressed fears about dying in childbirth, though she knew, of course, that many women did—Fanny Blood, for instance (though Fanny was also dying from tuberculosis at the time). And although mortality rates were lower than earlier in the century, complications from pregnancy still caused a high percentage of female deaths.

The placenta, or afterbirth, was usually the culprit. If everything goes well, the placenta smoothly follows the baby out of the mother's vagina, allowing her blood vessels to close and the uterus to tighten and shrink. If the placenta is not soon expelled, however, the patient can die from hemorrhaging. And having the placenta manually removed was equally perilous in the eighteenth century, because doctors, not realizing they needed to wash their hands before touching a new patient, unknowingly introduced bacteria.

Male and female midwives were popular during Mary's time. The Godwins' family physician, Dr. Fordyce, especially praised female midwives and could see no reason for a doctor to be summoned except in an extraordinary case. "Let nature take its course" was a favorite adage of the era. Besides, many women preferred to be delivered by members of their own sex. So there was nothing unusual about Mary's ignoring Godwin's wish that she hire a doctor and instead choosing a midwife, Mrs. Blenkinsop, from the reputable Westminster Lying-In Hospital.

By August, Mary was eager "to regain my activity, and to reduce to some *shapeliness* the portly shadow, which meets my eye when I take a musing walk," she told James Marshall. On Friday, August 25, she had a false alarm, and then real labor pains began at 5 A.M. on Wednesday, August 30. She called for Mrs. Blenkinsop and wrote Godwin in his study:

> I have no doubt of seeing the animal today; but must wait for Mrs. Blenkinsop to guess at the hour. . . . Pray send me the news paper— I wish I had a novel, or some book of sheer amusement, to excite curiosity and while away the time— Have you anything of the kind?

A few hours afterward, she wrote again:

> Mrs. Blenkinsop tells me that Every thing is in a fair way, and that there is no fear of the event being put off till another day— Still, *at present*, she thinks, I shall not immediately be freed from my load— I am very well— Call before dinner time, unless you receive another message from me.

Mary went up to her room at 2 P.M. But the labor progressed slowly, and there is a trace of irritation in her final note to Godwin: "Mrs. Blenkinsop tells me that I am in the most natural state, and can promise me a safe delivery— But that I must have a little patience." "A little patience and all will be over" had been her mother's deathbed words. But it is doubtful Mary was having morbid forebodings, since she'd boasted to Godwin that she'd be down for dinner the next day. Now, though, she insisted Godwin must leave her to scream and moan with only Mrs. Blenkinsop as witness. Once the grand drama was over, she promised to perform "the interesting office of presenting the new-born child" to him.[33]

So Godwin dined at the Reveleys', had supper with the Fenwicks and James Marshall, then went and sat in his parlor, anxiously consulting his watch. When William turned out to be Mary ("Birth of Mary 20 minutes after 11," Godwin recorded in his diary on August 31), Godwin continued waiting. "It was not till after two o'clock on Thursday morning, that I received the alarming intelligence, that the placenta was not yet removed, and that the midwife dared not proceed any further."[34]

Immediately, he called in Mrs. Blenkinsop's colleague at Westminster, Dr. Poignard. The doctor came quickly. But now nearly four hours had passed since the birth, and the placenta—which is normally expelled in the first ten to thirty minutes—still clung to Mary's uterus, where it remained for quite a while even as Dr. Poignard pulled and Mary bled and fainted. It never dropped down whole. Dr. Poignard thrust his hand inside and picked it out in pieces. And how Mary suffered! She would have died that night, only she was determined not to leave Godwin, she informed her husband the next day. By then, she could laugh at her close call. Godwin had summoned in Dr. Fordyce, who concurred with Dr. Poignard that the danger had passed.

On Friday, Mary did not come down to dinner. But Joseph Johnson and Maria Reveley called and found both her and the baby well. She was less well by that evening, and no better on Saturday. Then, on Sunday morning, Mary appeared so greatly improved that Godwin walked all the way to Kensington with his lawyer friend Basil Montagu. He came home to find "a degree of anxiety in every face."[35]

Mary had had an attack of shivering and called for him. Ashamed that he had been out when she needed him, Godwin resolved to remain near the Polygon until his wife had completely healed.

So he was sitting by her Sunday night when suddenly "every muscle of the body trembled, the teeth chattered, and the bed shook under her."[36] The shivering lasted five minutes and was a struggle between life and death, Mary said afterward. Dr. Fordyce was once again sent for. The infection was burrowing in.

On the following day, Monday, September 4, Dr. Fordyce decided the baby should be given to a wet nurse because Mary's milk was no longer safe to drink. Puppies were brought in to lap her tumid breasts. Still, she stayed calm and even joked about the puppies. "Nothing could exceed the equanimity, the patience, and affectionateness of the poor sufferer. I entreated her to recover; I dwelt with trembling fondness on every favourable circumstance; and as far as it was possible in so dreadful a situation she, by her smiles and kind speeches, rewarded my affection," Godwin would write.[37]

And what of Fanny? Preoccupied with his own troubles, Godwin had little time to consider the bewildered three-year-old, who was sent off here and there to play with friends' children, and maybe rushed in between doctors for a few words with a mother whose face confirmed her worst fears. Amused all summer long with tales of a baby brother, Fanny was not prepared for a sister, or for death.

By now, John Fenwick, Basil Montagu, James Marshall, and George Dyson were sitting up all night with Godwin. Mary Hays and Joseph Johnson called often, and Elizabeth Fenwick never left Mary's side. "A favorite servant," probably Marguerite, was also with her. "It is not possible to describe the unremitting devoted attention of [Godwin] nor is it easy to give you an adequate idea of the affectionate zeal of many of her friends who were on the watch night and day to seize upon an opportunity of contributing toward her recovery or to lessen her sufferings," Eliza Fenwick later told Everina.[38]

But for all that, on Wednesday, when another good friend, Dr. Carlisle, was brought in on the case, Mary was clearly getting worse. She pressed Godwin to send for her Berkshire friend Mrs. Cotton to nurse her, and Godwin wrote the letter, but the doctors told him it was "useless" to send it off. "It was now decided that the only chance of supporting her through what she had to suffer, was by supplying her rather freely with wine," which Godwin was assigned to administer. He began at four in the afternoon and kept on until seven, anguishing all the while over his medical ignorance, and was he giving Mary too small or too large a dose? In one of his most poignant passages, Godwin recalls how, after he'd finished feeding Mary the liquor, "I happened foolishly to ask the servant who came out of the room, 'What she thought of her mistress?' she replied, that in her judgment, she was going as fast as possible."[39]

On Wednesday night, Louisa Jones, who would soon be hired to governess for Fanny and her younger sister, slept at the Polygon for the first time. On Thursday, Godwin wrote in his diary, "Dying in the evening," but Mary did not die, though on Friday, Godwin notes, she sometimes spoke as if she expected to perish. Other times, she was more hopeful or at least pretended she had hope. Godwin, who disapproved of her religion, reports with obvious relief that Mary never mentioned God during this period. But no one can say what thoughts sustained her as she prepared to leave the world. Saturday morning, Godwin set himself the terrible task of asking Mary how to educate the children without admitting he thought she would not live to do it herself:

Seeing that every hope was extinct, I was very desirous of obtaining from her any directions, that she might wish to have followed after her decease. . . . I . . . affected to proceed wholly upon the ground of her having been very ill, and that it would be some time before she could expect to be well; wishing her to tell me any thing that she would choose to have done respecting the children, as they would now be principally under my care. After having repeated this idea to her in a great variety of forms, she at length said, with a significant tone of voice, "I know what you are thinking of," but added, that she had nothing to communicate to me upon the subject.[40]

A thoroughly exhausted Godwin gave Carlisle instructions to alert him if Mary worsened and then slept briefly Saturday night, probably for the first time in a week. At 6 A.M. Carlisle came to wake him. Mary would live less than two hours more. "20 minutes before 8.———" was all Godwin could write in his diary for Sunday, September 10, 1797. He'd been married a little over five months. And his wife, who'd fought to make women men's equals, was dead at thirty-eight from giving birth to a baby girl. The irony escaped no one. And those who did not believe in progress could point to her case as proof that reproduction would forever subjugate the weaker sex.

Godwin was too devastated to attend Mary's funeral, but did compose the words inscribed on her headstone that still stands beside his, on a knoll at St. Pancras Church. He could not foresee that Mary's children would carry her torch into the future. But he did feel confident that a book that he didn't much like personally would spread her ideas to a changing world. So his epitaph reads:

MARY WOLLSTONECRAFT GODWIN
Author of
A Vindication
of the Rights of Woman:
Born 27 April, 1759
Died 10 September, 1797

But Mary herself had inadvertently written her own best eulogy in a letter earlier that summer:

Those who are bold enough to advance before the age they live in, and to throw off, by the force of their own minds, the prejudices which the maturing reason of the world will in time disavow, must learn to brave censure. We ought not to be too anxious respecting the opinion of others.— I am not fond of vindications.— Those who know me will suppose that I acted from principle.— Nay, as we in general give others credit for worth, in proportion as we possess it—I am easy with regard to the opinions of the *best* part of mankind. I *rest* on my own.[41]

EPILOGUE

After Mary's death, Godwin received an outpouring of condolence notes. "I have read daily notices of what I dreaded to hear," wrote Joseph Johnson,

> and nothing but Mrs. G's strength of constitution left me the faint hope of her recovery. You have a great but not an exaggerated sense of her merit; I knew her too well not to admire and love her. Your loss is immeasurable.[1]

Mrs. Cotton wrote in a shaky hand from Berkshire: "A paragraph in a paper has put me in an agony 'Death of My Dear Mrs. Godwin.'" And a shocked Archibald Hamilton Rowan rushed off a letter from America: "I hope the report [of Mary's death] is false: if true, let this convey my condolence to Mr. G."[2]

Godwin, who was too upset to attend Mary's funeral on September 15, sat alone in his old friend James Marshall's study, confiding in a letter to Dr. Carlisle, "Nothing could be more soothing to my mind than to dwell . . . upon [Mary's] virtues and accomplishments, and our mutual happiness past and in prospect. But . . . I dare not trust myself with it." Still, his courage returned quickly, and on September 24 he recorded in his diary that he'd written the first two pages of the

Memoirs of Mary Wollstonecraft—a frank account of Mary's deprived childhood, sexual awakening, two suicide attempts, and many emotional crises, as well as the enormous contributions she had made to women and the world.

By now, Fanny and infant Mary were both home at the Polygon, and doing well—especially the baby, Eliza Fenwick reported to their Aunt Everina in Dublin. That Fanny was less well than the infant is not surprising: she was three years old and could grasp her loss. To exacerbate matters, her biological father, Gilbert Imlay, briefly resurfaced, demanding back the "trust deed" he'd given Mary, which promised Fanny income from his bond. Godwin returned the deed, thereby assuming all responsibility for Fanny's upbringing. Meanwhile, Imlay, in his roundabout manner, begged Joseph Johnson to suppress his shameful behavior so he could hold up his head among mutual friends:

> I always like to be where I can be most useful—I believe the opinion of the world is always sufficiently secured by an upright and unequivocal conduct, though one should refuse to conform to some of its narrow and censorious maxims—I believe this observation will apply to my case—if so, I beseech you to reflect how brotherly and considerate a conduct it is, to begin the senseless cry of scandal, and incite the world to consider that conduct as faulty which I believe it is inclined to consider as innocent— observe also that what is done is irremediable, and that, if I were to change my situation upon such a remonstrance as yours, I should encourage, not silence the tongue of calumny.[3]

On this note, Gilbert Imlay disappeared from Fanny's life forever.

Mary Hays wrote Mary's obituary for the *Annual Necrology*. "The mind of Mary Wollstonecraft was not formed on common principles,"[4] she declared, and spoke eloquently of Mary's "impatience of injustice." Johnson published (along with *Maria* and other of Mary's writing fragments) Godwin's *Memoirs* in January 1798. *Memoirs* appalled average British citizens, who now despised everything that reminded them of the French Revolution's bloody Terror and military campaigns. Even Mary's great admirer the poet Southey was shocked by Godwin's allusions to her sexual experiences, while the anti-Jacobins denounced Mary as immoral and derided Godwin's eagerness to dwell on his wife's unseemly past. As with *Political Justice*, the *Memoirs* thrust Godwin into the limelight—but now he was ridiculed in satires like George Walker's novel *The Vagabond*, Maria Edgeworth's *Moral Tales*, and, most unkindly, in his old "Fair" Amelia Alderson's *Adeline Mowbray*, in which the central characters are outrageous parodies of Mary and himself.

Deeply humiliated by all the public attention, Godwin was also dealing with Mary's debts, which he repaid as best he could, mildly protesting at one point:

> The answer I have made to Mr. Cowie's letter [asking for money Mary owed him] is this: That I have surrendered the whole prosperity of Mrs. Godwin's posthumous works, without receiving a penny advantage from them, that I have paid or undertaken to pay her . . . debts, in addition to this, to the amount of about fifty pounds, that I was married to her five months; and that I have taken upon myself the care and support of her two children. More than this, under my circumstances, cannot, I think, be expected from me.[5]

Initially, the idea of raising children alone overwhelmed Godwin, but he hired his sister's friend Louisa Jones to housekeep and governess. He was soon calling his children his "favourite companions," while continuing his routine of writing all morning (he was now idealizing his life with Mary in the novel *St. Leon*), and frequently dining out.[6] Fanny astonished her governess by reading fluently at six. Mary too was precocious, but Godwin refused to race them ahead. "We should always remember that the object of education is the future man or woman," Godwin, sounding like Mary Wollstonecraft, replied to an inquiry about his teaching methods. "It is a miserable vanity that [will] sacrifice the wholesome and gradual development of the mind to the desire of exhibiting little monsters of curiosity." Let your children read fairy tales, he suggested. Awaken their imagination, for "This is the faculty that makes the man."[7]

In the summer of 1800, Godwin set out on a journey to Ireland to visit his lawyer friend John Curran, leaving Louisa Jones and James Marshall in charge of the house. Godwin missed his children. "It is the first time that I have been seriously separated from them since they lost their mother," he reminded Marshall, and asked his friend to buy Fanny a new spelling book and to reassure Mary that "I shall not give her away, and she shall be nobody's little girl but papa's."[8]

He wrote about meeting Mary Wollstonecraft's favorite pupil, the former Margaret Kingsborough, who was now the unhappy wife of an aristocrat, Lord Mountcashell, though she herself was a republican and a "singular" character—a fit subject for a farce, Godwin thought. He liked her so much that he twice invited himself back to dinner. Meanwhile, he had to force himself to visit Everina and Eliza, who were currently running a Dublin school. Though Eliza was certainly distressed by her undignified situation, she set out to charm Godwin, who enthused in a letter to Marshall, "I love Aunt Bishop as much as I hate (you must not read that word [to the children]) Aunt Everina."[9] The antagonism between Godwin and Everina persisted, but they bore with each other because of the children, particularly Fanny, whom Everina tried to adopt five years after Godwin's visit. Godwin refused to let her go.

Godwin aggressively pursued Maria Reveley after her husband died in 1799. She had, years before, told Godwin she loved him. "You cannot imagine how much, how entirely I love you," he wrote, and: "You have it in your power to give me new life, a new interest in existence, to raise me from the grave in which my heart lies buried."[10] But when Maria turned him down (giving no convincing explanations), Godwin was soon pursuing his neighbor, French-born Mary Jane Clairmont, mother of two young children—Jane (later called Claire) and Charles. Like Mary Wollstonecraft, Mary Jane soon became pregnant, and they married in December of 1801.

Intelligent, but narrow-minded and always eager to push her own children forward, Mary Jane was not, as Godwin had hoped, a comfort to his girls. "Mama and I are not great friends,"[11] Fanny diplomatically noted, while Mary freely expressed her dislike for Godwin's second wife during her teenage years. Most of Godwin's friends agreed, calling Mary Jane a "baby" and one-upping each other mimicking her tantrums. At times, even Godwin bemoaned Mary Jane's "baby sullenness,"[12] but he loved her passionately for the rest of his life.

They would always be haunted by money worries. When Godwin was fifty-one, in 1807, they decided to supplement his meager writing income by opening a children's bookstore and publishing house: the Juvenile Library. It was an appealing project, and friends like Coleridge and Charles and Mary Lamb contributed first-rate books. But publishing was a risky venture, and as Godwin feared from the outset, he was no businessman.[13] So rather than staving off financial disaster, the Juvenile Library lost money and thrust the Godwins further into debt. Godwin was tormented by his fear of debtor's prison. His writing suffered, his patience strained.

"Though philosophy supports in great matters it seldom vanquishes the trivial every day-ishes of life," Margaret Mountcashell sagely noted.[14] There were days now when philosophy itself exasperated Godwin. Asked whether he had raised his family according to Mary Wollstonecraft's educational theories, he snapped, "Having formed a family establishment without . . . provision for the support of a family, neither [the current] Mrs. Godwin nor myself have leisure enough for reducing novel theories of education into practise."[15]

He also, apparently, hadn't the time to sustain his former strict impartiality toward the children. Wanting someone to lean on, Godwin turned to amiable Fanny, making her his cook and gardener and peacemaker, failing to do justice to her increasingly expressive writing, her keen critical faculties, and her shrewd political views. Mary had the finer intellect, Godwin rationalized as he failed to prepare Fanny for a satisfying future. And though the sisters loved each other equally, Mary *was* the star.

Godwin makes this clear in his reply to a letter inquiring about Mary Wollstonecraft's daughters:

Of the two persons to whom your enquiries relate, my own daughter is considerably superior in capacity to the one her mother had before. Fanny, the eldest, is of a quiet, modest, unshowy disposition somewhat given to indolence (which is her greatest fault) but sober, observing, peculiarly clear and distinct in the faculty of memory and disposed to exercise her own thoughts and follow her own judgements. Mary, my own daughter, is the reverse of her in many particulars. She is singularly bold, somewhat imperious and active in mind. Her desire of knowledge is great and her perseverance in every thing she undertakes, almost invincible. My own daughter, I believe, is very pretty. Fanny is by no means handsome but in general prepossessing.[16]

In 1812, the young married poet Percy Bysshe Shelley entered the Godwin household. Recently expelled from Oxford for declaring his atheism, Shelley, an admirer of both *Vindication* and *Political Justice*, was just the man to rekindle Godwin's passion for ideas. Moreover,

Shelley was due to inherit a fortune, which he was prepared to borrow against to promote worthy causes. And what cause could be worthier than beleaguered William Godwin? A crucial sentence in *Political Justice* now seemed written for Godwin himself: "Each man has a perfect claim upon everything the possession of which will be productive of more benefit to him than injury to another." Surely, Shelley would not be injured by financially freeing Godwin to pursue philosophy. But because Shelley's father was taking steps to curb his son's spending, raising the money proved harder than he'd supposed.

In the midst of Shelley and Godwin's financial negotiations in the spring of 1814, Mary Godwin came home from a long stay with friends in Scotland. Shelley was twenty-one. Mary was sixteen. Both were beautiful and creative, with sweet tempers and searching minds. On June 26, Mary led Shelley to her mother's grave at St. Pancras Churchyard and kissed him. The next day, they promised to love each other forever.

When Shelley told Godwin he planned to elope with Mary, Godwin was thunderstruck and ordered Shelley to return to his wife. But Shelley did not, and at 4 A.M. on July 28, 1814, he and Mary and her stepsister Claire stole off for the Continent, where Mary Wollstonecraft had loved Gilbert Imlay and given birth to his child. Over the next seven years, Mary and Shelley traveled, bore children, and wrote masterpieces of the Romantic era, while always attempting to solace Godwin, who initially refused to write them. When he finally did, it was not to Mary but to Shelley, demanding the money Shelley had promised him and that Godwin believed was rightfully his.

Fanny—who'd stayed home out of loyalty to her father—was often dispatched to convey Godwin's wishes. She was thrust into the role of go-between, with sincere affection both for her father and for Mary and Shelley. She wrote Mary: "You know the peculiar temperature of Papa's mind . . . ; you know he cannot write when pecuniary circumstances overwhelm him; you know that it is of the utmost consequence, for *his own* and the *world's sake* that he should finish his novel; and is it not your and Shelley's duty to consider these things, and to endeavour to prevent, as far as lies in your power, giving him unneccesary pain and anxiety?"[17]

Meanwhile, she constantly defended the purity of Mary and Shelley's love to Godwin, who was, as always, full of affection for "poor" Fanny, but had less time than ever to consider her needs.

Fanny, however, did not lose sight of herself even in the current maelstrom. She confided in Mary about her feverish depressions, but also about conversations with the famous Godwinian socialist Robert Owen and about a gallery outing where she had seen "the finest specimens of Murillo, the great Spanish painter . . . and two very fine Titians" besides. She begged Shelley to send copies of his latest poems, exclaiming, "It is only the poets that are eternal benefactors of their fellow-creatures, and the real ones never fail of giving us the highest degree of pleasure."[18] Fanny was enormously pleased when her mother's childhood friend George Blood came to visit: "Everything he has told me of my mother has increased my love and admiration of her memory. . . . George Blood seems to have loved and venerated her as a superior being. This has in some degree roused me from my torpor. I have determined never to live to be a disgrace to such a Mother," she wrote Mary.[19]

Fanny had to contend with very dim prospects. *Vindication* had brought about little social change, and her career options were as limited as her mother's had been. She had her mother's depressive tendencies but none of her rambunctious determination. She could not betray Godwin by joining Mary, Claire, and Shelley, and yet she was a burden at home, as "Mama" constantly reminded her. Her aunts debated whether or not they should risk bringing her to teach at their Dublin school in light of this latest family scandal. They could not help feeling a certain satisfaction that now the tables were turned and

Mary's daughter needed *them*. And for her part, Fanny—after a stimulating, cultured childhood with her interesting father in London—dreaded narrow-minded Ireland, teaching, and her bitter aunts. "My Aunt Everina will be in London next week, when my future fate will be decided," she dolefully informed sympathetic Mary. "I shall then give you a full and clear account of [how] my unhappy life is to be spent."

But she never did describe the meeting with Everina. Instead, on the morning of October 9, twenty-two-year-old Fanny dressed in a blue striped skirt, a white blouse, and a brown coat with fur trimming. She threw a matching hat over her long dark hair, and informing no one of her departure, boarded a mail coach to Bath, where her mother years before had taken her first job. It happened that Mary and Shelley were also in Bath at the moment, yet Fanny did not stop to see them, but journeyed on first to Bristol, then to Swansea, in Wales. Here she checked into the Mackworth Arms inn and ate dinner. She told the chambermaid she was tired and intended to go right to bed.

Sometime that night, Fanny Godwin, née Imlay, followed her mother's example and swallowed laudanum to extinguish her mental pain. Unlike Mary Wollstonecraft, Fanny succeeded and was dead when the hotel staff broke down her door the following morning. She'd left the laudanum bottle on a table beside a note:

I have long determined that the best thing I could do was to put an end to the existence of a being whose birth was unfortunate, and whose life has only been a series of pain to those persons who have hurt their health in endeavouring to promote her welfare. Perhaps to hear of my death will give you pain; but you will soon have the blessing of forgetting that such a creature ever existed as . . .[20]

By the time journalists were allowed in, Fanny's name had been torn from the corner of the letter, but to anyone who knew of the family, her identity was not hard to guess. Fanny's note spoke of her desire to disappear, yet the undergarments she died in were marked "MW" for Mary Wollstonecraft—tying Fanny to *Vindication* and to all women who refused to do as they were told. "I have determined never to live to be a disgrace to such a Mother," Fanny had insisted. Meanwhile, in Bath, Mary Godwin had begun to write *Frankenstein*. The revolution continued.

POSTSCRIPT

WILLIAM GODWIN continued to write for the rest of his life. He died in 1836, a month after his eightieth birthday, and was buried beside Mary outside St. Pancras Church.

EDWARD JOHN WOLLSTONECRAFT died in 1803 in Laugharne, Wales. His will, dated twelve years earlier, instructed Mary to pay his debts.

NED WOLLSTONECRAFT died young, at almost the same time as his wife in 1807. He left no will. His son Edward and daughter Elizabeth moved to Australia, where the family prospered. A suburb of Sydney is named Wollstonecraft.

EVERINA WOLLSTONECRAFT, frequently ill and plagued by financial worries, continued running the Dublin school with her sister until Eliza died in her late sixties. Everina then moved back to London and became, in her words, "painfully attached to Mary Shelley."[1] Everina continued to denounce Godwin whenever she got the chance, up to her death, a decade after Eliza's.

JAMES WOLLSTONECRAFT ran up debts and borrowed from both Godwin and Joseph Johnson.[2] He eventually rejoined the Navy and died in the West Indies the same year as Ned.

CHARLES WOLLSTONECRAFT remained in America, where he briefly ran a calico-printing business in Delaware with Mary's Irish friend Archibald Hamilton Rowan. During the war of 1812, he became a captain on the American side, and he is said to have died wealthy and old.

JOSEPH JOHNSON continued to publish books and to help needy authors like Godwin, even when his health deteroriated and he had to bring in a relative,

287

Rowland Hunter, to run the shop. When Johnson died in 1809, he left a will freeing Godwin from paying back the 200 pounds Johnson had lent him to start the Juvenile Library, and instructing him to spend the money on "Fanny Imlay."[3] Since Fanny was known to the world as Fanny Godwin, Johnson's calling her "Imlay" and excluding her sister Mary from the bequest seemed calculated to make a point.

MARGARET MOUNTCASHELL left her aristocratic husband and seven children to run off with George Tighe in 1804. Ten years later, they settled in Italy, where she raised their two daughters and became a close friend to Shelley and his friends. Margaret remained passionate about politics and education. In 1823, she published *Advice to Young Mothers on the Physical Education of Children*,[4] full of practical medical advice of the sort that Mary Wollstonecraft had advanced. She died in 1835.

The fate of Fanny's father is untraceable, but we do know that someone named Gilbert Imlay died in 1828 and was buried in a churchyard on the island of Jersey.[5] His epitaph conveys the passionate interest in human improvement that Mary believed her lover possessed:

> Stranger intelligent! should you pass this way
> Speak of the social advances of the day—
> Mention the greatly good, who've serenely shone
> Since the soul departed its mortal bourne;
> Say if statesmen wise have grown, and priests sincere
> Or if hypocrisy must disappear
> As phylosophy extends the beam of truth,
> Sustains rights divine, its essence, and the worth
> Sympathy may penetrate the mouldering earth,
> Recall the spirit, and remove the dearth,
> Transient hope gleams ever in the grave,
> Then silently bid farewell, be happy,
> For as the globe moves round, thou will grow nappy.
> Wake to hail the hour when new scenes arise,
> As brightening vistas open in the skies.[6]

NOTES

ABBREVIATIONS AND SHORT TITLES USED

Cave of Fancy—Mary Wollstonecraft, *The Cave of Fancy*

French Revolution—Mary Wollstonecraft, *An Historical and Moral View of the Origins and Progress of the French Revolution*

Lessons—Mary Wollstonecraft, *Lessons*

Letters—Mary Wollstonecraft, *Letters Written During a Short Residence in Sweden, Norway, and Denmark*

Maria—Mary Wollstonecraft, *Maria; or, The Wrongs of Woman*

Mary—Mary Wollstonecraft, *Mary*

Memoirs—William Godwin, *Memoirs of Mary Wollstonecraft*

Original Stories—Mary Wollstonecraft, *Original Stories from Real Life*

Political Justice—William Godwin, *An Enquiry Concerning Political Justice*

Rights of Men—Mary Wollstonecraft, *A Vindication of the Rights of Men*

SHC—*Shelley and His Circle*

Thoughts—Mary Wollstonecraft, *Thoughts on the Education of Daughters*

Vindication—Mary Wollstonecraft, *A Vindication of the Rights of Woman*

Wardle—Ralph M. Wardle, *Collected Letters of Mary Wollstonecraft*

All the works cited below appear in the text in their original form. I have neither updated the language nor corrected the spelling or grammar.

Notes

CHAPTER ONE

1. Edward Wollstonecraft's will, Public Record Office, London.

2. There are, however, speculations, based on information about an Irish Dixon family in Hugh Allingham's *Ballyshannon*, that Elizabeth Dixon's family were wealthy wine merchants.

3. *Memoirs*, p. 10.

4. *Mary*, p. 8.

5. My information on Beverley comes from three booklets: Pamela Hopkins, *Beverley: A Stroll through Twelve Centuries*; Philip Brown, *Old Beverley*; and Ian and Margaret Summer, *Beverley as It Was*; as well as my own observations during a visit to the town.

6. John Gregory, *A Father's Legacy to His Daughters* (London: John Sharpe, 1822).

7. Halsband, ed. *Selected Letters*, p. 237.

8. Letter from MW to Jane Arden, c. 6/4/1773–11/16/1774, Wardle, pp. 60–61.

9. Letter from MW to Jane Arden, c. 5/20–6/3/1773, Wardle, pp. 54–56.

10. Letter from MW to Jane Arden, c. 6/4/1773–11/16/1774, Wardle, pp. 59–60.

11. Letter from MW to Jane Arden, 11/16/1774, Wardle, pp. 63–64.

12. Letter from MW to Jane Arden, c. 5–6/1779, Wardle, pp. 64–65.

13. Letter from MW to Jane Arden, c. 5/20–6/3/1773, Wardle, pp. 54–56.

14. Letter from MW to Jane Arden, c. 6/4–7/31/1773, Wardle, pp. 56–60.

15. Ibid.

16. *Memoirs*, p. 15.

17. Letter from MW to Jane Arden, 10/17/1779, Wardle, pp. 68–70.

18. Letter from MW to Jane Arden, 5–6/1779, Wardle, pp. 65–68.

19. Ibid.

20. Letter from MW to Jane Arden, 4–6/1780, Wardle, p. 71.

21. Letter from MW to Jane Arden, c. late 1782–early 1783, Wardle, pp. 77–78.

22. Letter from MW to Jane Arden, 10/17/1779, Wardle, pp. 68–70.

23. Letter from MW to Eliza, 8/17/1780, Wardle, pp. 75–77.

24. See Sunstein, *A Different Face*, pp. 36–38.

25. Letter from MW to Jane Arden, late 1782–early 1783, Wardle, pp. 77–78.

26. Letter from MW to Jane Arden, c. 10/20/1782–8/10/1783, Wardle, p. 79.

27. See Tomalin, *Life and Death*, p. 36.

28. Letter from MW to Everina, autumn–early winter 1783, Wardle, pp. 81–82.

29. Letter from MW to Everina, 1/7/1784, Wardle, pp. 83–84.

30. Ibid.

31. Letter from MW to Everina, 1/12 or 1/19/1784, Wardle, pp. 85–86.

32. Letter from MW to Everina, 1/1784, Wardle, p. 84.

33. Ibid.

34. Letter from MW to Everina, 1/1784, Wardle, pp. 88–89.

35. Letter from Eliza to Everina, 8/17/1786, Pforzheimer Collection, reel 9.

CHAPTER TWO

1. See Burgh, *Human Nature.*

2. Letter from MW to George Blood, 7/20/1785, Wardle, pp. 92–94.

3. Dr. Price's neighbor, the future poet Samuel Rogers, remembered evenings when the clergyman appeared at his door wearing a dressing gown. "He would talk and read the Bible to us, till he sent us to bed in a frame of mind as heavenly as his own." See O. and M. Handlin, *James Burgh,* p. 42.

4. Letter from MW to George Blood, 7/20/1785, Wardle, pp. 92–94.

5. Letter from MW to George Blood, 7/3/1785, Wardle, pp. 89–92.

6. Letter from MW to George Blood, 7/20/1785, Wardle, pp. 92–94.

7. Letter from Fanny Blood to Eliza and Everina, 11/12/1785, Wardle, pp. 100–101.

8. Letter from MW to Eliza and Everina, 11/12/1785, Wardle, pp. 100–101.

9. *Memoirs,* p. 36.

10. Letter from MW to George Blood, 2/4/1786, Wardle, pp. 101–103.

11. *Thoughts,* p. 12.

12. Ibid., pp. 20, 21.

13. Ibid., p. 28.

14. Ibid., p. 30.

15. Ibid.

16. Ibid., p. 26.

17. Ibid., p. 32.

18. Letter from MW to George Blood, 5/1/1786, Wardle, pp. 104–106.

19. Letter from MW to George Blood, 1/17/1788, Wardle, pp. 169–170.

20. Letter from MW to George Blood, 7/6/1786, Wardle, pp. 109–111.

21. Letter from MW to Eliza, 9/23/1786, Wardle, pp. 113–116.

22. Letter from MW to George Blood, 8/25/1786, Wardle, pp. 111–112.

23. Letter from MW to Eliza, 9/23/1786, Wardle, pp. 113–116.

24. Letter from MW to Everina, 1/15/1787, Wardle, pp. 132–133.

25. Joseph Johnson's depiction of MW, Pforzheimer Collection, reel 9.

26. Letter from MW to Reverend Henry Dyson Gabell, 4/16/1787, Wardle, 149–150.

27. The Kingsborough estate was in Mitchelstown, near Cork.

28. Letter from MW to Everina, 10/30/1786, Wardle, pp. 120–122.

29. The artist who painted these portraits is unknown.

30. Letter from MW to Everina, 3/25/1787, Wardle, pp. 146–148.

31. Letter from MW to Eliza, 11/5/1786, Wardle, pp. 122–124.

32. Letter from MW to Everina, 3/25/1787, Wardle, pp. 146–148.

33. A grown-up Margaret Kingsborough would lavish praise on Mary, writing: "No person . . . can be more thoroughly [sure] of the injurious consequences of unkindness and tyranny to young minds [than myself], for few (I believe) more severely experienced the baneful effects and I am convinced that had it not been my peculiar good fortune to meet with the extraordinary woman [Mary] to whose superior penetration of affectionate mildness of manner I trace the development of whatever virtues I possess; I should have been in consequence of the distortion of my best qualities, a most ferocious animal." Instead, she dared to leave an unhappy first marriage and move to Italy, where she and her lover raised a second family. She wrote a child-rearing book full of Mary Wollstonecraft's favorite theories and befriended Mary's second daughter and her husband, Percy Bysshe Shelley, shortly before the poet drowned.

34. Letter from MW to Eliza, 12/22/1786, Wardle, pp. 131–132.

35. Letter from MW to Henry Gabell, late winter–early spring, 1787, Wardle, p. 136.

36. Letter from MW to Joseph Johnson, 12/5/1786, Wardle, pp. 129–131.

37. *SHC*, vol. 1, p. 79.

38. Letter from MW to Everina, 3/3/1787, Wardle, pp. 139–141.

39. Letter from MW to Everina, 2/12/1787, Wardle, pp. 137–139.

40. Letter from MW to Eliza, 6/27/1787, Wardle, pp. 154–156.

41. *Mary*, p. 7.

42. Ibid.

43. Ibid., p. 9.

44. Ibid., p. 10.

45. Ibid., p. 17.

46. Ibid., p. 53.

47. Ibid.

48. Letter from MW to Henry Gabell, 9/13/1787, Wardle, pp. 161–162.

49. *Mary*, p. 15.

50. Ibid., pp. 40–41.

51. Mary never explicitly states that Joseph Johnson is her benefactor, and it has been argued that Henry Gabell, George Ogle, or even Lord Kingsborough might have helped her out. Gabell, however, is a most unlikely guess, since he was working for a living and furthermore planned to marry soon. Mary tells Eliza she admires her champion; so this eliminates Ogle, whom she describes as "half-mad" and pitiable in the very letter where she mentions the gift. And Lord Kingsborough had neither the generosity nor, seemingly, the motivation to help his governess; while this act is typical both of Joseph Johnson's character and of all his future dealings with Mary.

52. Letter from MW to JJ, 9/13/1787, Wardle, p. 159.

CHAPTER THREE

1. Knowles, *Life and Writings*, p. 164.

2. Museum of the City of London, exhibit on the eighteenth century.

3. John Pendred, *The London and Country Printers, Booksellers, and Stationers Vade Mecum* (1785), quoted in Brewer, *Pleasures*, p. 138.

4. See *SHC*, vol. 1, p. 69, and Chard, "Joseph Johnson," p. 62.

5. Brewer, *Pleasures*, p. 156.

6. Letter from MW to Everina, 11/7/1787, Wardle, pp. 163–165.

7. See Brewer, *Pleasures*, pp. 125–197; Porter, *English Society*, pp. 239–240; Museum of the City of London, exhibit on the eighteenth century; Todd, *Sign of Angelica*, pp. 125–145.

8. The speaker is T. Constable, quoted in Chard, "Joseph Johnson," p. 63, n. 28.

9. By W. Sharpe after Moses Haughton, National Portrait Gallery, London.

10. Letter from MW to Everina, 11/7/1787, Wardle, pp. 163–165.

11. Aikin, "Biographical Account."

12. Most of my information on Joseph Johnson comes from Chard, "Joseph Johnson."

13. William Blake, *The Letters of William Blake*, ed. Geoffrey Keynes (London: Rupert Hart-Davis, 1956).

14. Letter from Joseph Johnson to Charlotte Smith, 11/25/1803, Pforzheimer Collection of Johnson's letters.

15. "Puff" here means "boast."

16. Letter from Joseph Johnson to Charlotte Smith, 11/25/1803, Pforzheimer Collection of Johnson's letters.

17. Letter from MW to Everina, 11/7/1787, Wardle, pp. 163–165.

18. *Cave of Fancy*, p. 195.

19. Letter from MW to George Blood, 9/11/1787, Wardle, pp. 157–158.

20. The story is "Gathering Flowers," in Trimmer *et al.*, *Easy Lessons*, pp. 220–221.

21. *Original Stories*, pp. 367–368.

22. Ibid., p. 380.

23. Ibid., p. 375.

24. Ibid., p. 422.

25. Letter from MW to Everina, 11/15/1787, Wardle, pp. 165–167.

26. Letter from MW to JJ, late 1787–early 1788, Wardle, pp. 167–168.

27. Letter from MW to Everina, 11/15/1787, Wardle, pp. 165–167.

28. National Portrait Gallery exhibit, 2/1998, catalogue p. 68.

29. Knowles, *Fuseli's Life*, p. 7.

30. Knowles, *Life and Writings*, p. 59.

31. Letter from WG to John Knowles (Fuseli's biographer), 9/8/1826, Pforzheimer Collection, reel 6.

32. Letter from Henry Fuseli to James Northcote, 9/29/1778, quoted in Knowles, *Fuseli's Life*, p. 51.

33. Ibid.

34. Tomalin, *Life and Death*, pp. 114–115.

35. Letter from MW to JJ, late 1787–early 1788, Wardle, pp. 167–168.

36. Letter from MW to Everina, 3/22/1788, Wardle, pp. 172–174.

37. Wardle, p. 174, n. 5.

38. Letter from MW to George Blood, 3/3/1788, Wardle, pp. 171–172.

39. Letter from MW to George Blood, 5/16/1788, Wardle, pp. 174–176.

40. Letter from MW to George Blood, 3/3/1788, Wardle, pp. 171–172.

41. Sunstein, *A Different Face*, p. 170.

42. The quote is from the advertisement in the first issue of the *Analytical Review* as reported by Tyson, *Joseph Johnson,* pp. 99–100.

43. Since few contributors to magazines like the *Analytical Review* ever signed their own names to their articles, there is a disagreement over which articles Mary in fact wrote. I ascribe to Ralph Wardle's theory, persuasively defended by Janet Todd and Marilyn Butler in their preface to Mary's *Analytical Review* articles in *Wollstonecraft*, that Mary wrote the reviews signed "M," "W," and "T." What most informed my decision was the presence of Mary's unmistakable style in all these articles.

44. *Analytical Review*, 6/1788. See Wollstonecraft, *Works*, vol. 7, p. 19.

45. *Analytical Review*, 7/1788. See Wollstonecraft, *Works*, vol. 7, pp. 22–27.

46. *Analytical Review*, 8/1788. See Wollstonecraft, *Works*, vol. 7, pp. 32–33.

47. Letter from MW to JJ, c. 7/1788, Wardle, pp. 178–179.

48. Letter from MW to George Blood, 2/28/1789, Wardle, pp. 181–182.

49. "A few facts": Joseph Johnson's history of Mary in London, Pforzheimer Collection, reel 9.

50. Letter from MW to JJ, c. mid-1788, Wardle, p. 178.

51. Letter from MW to JJ, late 1789–early 1790, Wardle, p. 186.

52. Letter from MW to JJ, c. mid-1788, Wardle, pp. 177–178.

53. This quote is from a statement by Joseph Johnson in the Pforzheimer Collection, reel 9. Johnson is speaking of his "trouble" as well as Mary's, for he helped her both morally and financially in this endeavor.

CHAPTER FOUR

1. Letter from Edmund Burke to Lord Charlemont, 8/9/1789, quoted in Burke, *Reflections*, introduction by Conor Cruise O'Brien, p. 13.

2. Letter from MW to Everina, 3/22/1788, Wardle, pp. 172–174.

3. Letter from MW to Joseph Johnson, late 1788, Wardle, pp. 179–180.

4. Letter from MW to George Blood, 2/28/1789, Wardle, pp. 181–182.

5. *Analytical Review*, in Wollstonecraft, *Works*, vol. 7, pp. 65–66.

6. Letter from MW to JJ, c. late 1788, Wardle, pp. 179–180.

7. *Analytical Review*, 2/1789, in Wollstonecraft, *Works*, vol. 7, pp. 82–83.

8. Ibid., 4/1789, p. 97.

9. Letter from MW to George Blood, 4/16/1789, and letter from MW to George Blood, 9/15/1789, Wardle, pp. 182–184.

10. St. Clair, *Godwins*, p. 41.

11. Letter from MW to George Blood, 11/19/1789, Wardle, pp. 184–186.

12. Price, *Discourse*, pp. 27–28.

13. Ibid., pp. 1–2.

14. Ibid., p. 32.

15. Ibid., pp. 20–21.

16. *Analytical Review*, 12/1789, in Wollstonecraft, *Works*, vol. 7, pp. 185–187.

17. The italics are Price's.

18. See n. 16. The ellipses indicate places where I have cut parts of Price's speech from Mary's full quotation.

19. *Analytical Review*, in Wollstonecraft, *Works*, vol. 7, pp. 202–203.

20. Letter from MW to JJ, late 1789–early 1790, Wardle, p. 186.

21. Letter from MW to Joshua Cristall, 3/19/1790, Wardle, pp. 187–189.

22. London *Times*, 3/22/1790.

23. The following quotes are taken from Mary's letters to Fuseli that John Knowles recorded in *Fuseli's Life*. The letters were subsequently destroyed.

24. *Thoughts on the Education of Daughters*, p. 29.

25. Knowles, p. 165.

26. Ibid.

27. *Analytical Review*, 5/1790, pp. 251–253.

28. Letter from MW to JJ, c. spring 1790, Wardle, pp. 189–190.

29. Letter from MW to Eliza, late 1790, Wardle, pp. 198–199.

30. Letter from MW to Eliza, 8/23/1790, Wardle, pp. 191–193.

31. Letter from MW to Everina, 8/23/1790, Wardle, pp. 191–192.

32. Mary is obviously alluding to Henry and Ann Gabell when she uses these words to denounce Adam and Eve in her letter to Everina, 9/10/1790.

33. Edmund Burke, *Reflections on the Revolution in France*, p. 97.

34. Ibid., p. 198.

35. Ibid., p. 330.

36. Ibid., p. 156.

37. Ibid., p. 374.

38. Ibid., p. 119.

39. London *Times*, 12/20/1790.

40. Mary Wollstonecraft, *The Rights of Men, Works*, vol. 5, p. 34.

41. Ibid., p. 14.

42. Ibid., p. 28.

43. Ibid., p. 16.

44. Ibid., p. 18.

45. *Memoirs*, pp. 52–53.

46. Letter from MW to Eliza, Saturday, late 1790, Wardle, pp. 198–199.

47. Letter from Dr. Price to MW, 1/17/1790, Pforzheimer Collection, reel 7.

CHAPTER FIVE

1. Letter from MW to George Blood, 10/6/1791, Wardle, pp. 201–202.

2. Letter from Eliza to Everina, 7/3/1792, Pforzheimer Collection, reel 9.

3. Letter from MW to William Roscoe, 10/6/1791, Wardle, pp. 202–204.

4. Ibid.

5. Letter from MW to George Blood, 10/6/1791, Wardle, pp. 201–202.

6. Letter from MW to Everina, 2/23/1792, Wardle, pp. 209–210.

7. Letter from MW to William Roscoe, 10/6/1791, Wardle, pp. 202–204.

8. Astell, *Serious Proposal,* p. 20.

9. Ibid., p. 11.

10. Ibid., p. 6.

11. Ibid., p. 157.

12. See Janet Todd's penetrating remarks on Mary Astell in *The Sign of Angelica.*

13. Ibid., p. 109.

14. *Vindication,* p. 206.

15. Soon after Wollstonecraft pubished *Rights of Man,* Macaulay wrote an answer to Edmund Burke's *Reflections.* Her book was called *Observations on the Reflections of the Right Honorable Edmund Burke on the Revolution in France* and spoke even more scathingly than Wollstonecraft of Burke's patriotic zeal. "I have always considered the boasted birthright of an Englishman as an *arrogant* pretension built on a *beggarly* foundation," she writes. "It is an arrogant pretension, because it intimates a kind of exclusion to the rest of mankind from the same privileges, and it is beggarly because it rests our legitimate freedom on the *alms* of our princes."

16. For biographical information on Catharine Macaulay, see Bridget Hill's *Republican Virago.* For analysis of Macaulay's work, read Janet Todd's *Sign of Angelica.*

17. Catharine Macaulay, *Letters on Education,* p. 208.

18. Ibid., p. 50.

19. *Analytical Review,* 11/1790, p. 309.

20. See Fraise, *Reason's Muse,* chap. 1.

21. Rousseau, *Émile,* p. 322.

22. See the excellent chapter "The Rhetoric of Revolution" in Hunt, *Politics, Culture, and Class in the French Revolution.*

23. *Vindication,* p. 109.

24. Ibid., p. 165.

25. Ibid., p. 237.

26. Ibid., p. 155.

27. Ibid., p. 237.

28. Mary has mixed feelings on both Rousseau and Gregory. Earlier she recommended Gregory's *Legacies to his Daughters* in the *Analytical Review.*

29. *Vindication,* p. 199.

30. Ibid., p. 273.

31. Ibid., p. 286.

32. Ibid., chap. 12.

33. Ibid., p. 296.

34. *Thoughts,* p. 32.

35. *Vindication,* pp. 222–223.

36. Ibid., p. 110.

37. Letter from Horace Walpole to Hannah More, 1/24/1795. He writes to conservative More: "Thou excellent woman! The reverse of the hyena in petticoats, Mrs. Wollstonecraft, who to this day discharges her ink and gall on Marie Antoinette. . . ."

38. More, *Strictures*, p. 147.

39. *Memoirs*, p. 56.

40. Letter from Eliza to Everina, 1/29/1792, Pforzheimer Collection, reel 9.

41. Barbauld, *Works*, p. 165.

42. Paul C. Nagel, *The Adams Women* (New York: Oxford University Press, 1987), p. 57.

43. Letter from Joel Barlow to Abraham Baldwin, 10/17/1791, Houghton Library, Harvard.

44. Letter from MW to Everina, 6/20/1792, Wardle, pp. 211–214.

45. See Mary's observations on America in the 9/1791 issue of the *Analytical Review*, in Wollstonecraft, *Works*, vol. 7, p. 391.

46. Letter from MW to Everina, 2/23/1792, Wardle, pp. 209–210.

47. Letter from MW to Everina, 9/14/1792, Wardle, pp. 214–216.

48. Letter from MW to William Roscoe, 1/3/1792, Wardle, pp. 205–206.

49. *Analytical Review*, 4/1792, in Wollstonecraft, *Works*, vol. 7, pp. 424–430.

50. Letter from MW to William Roscoe, 2/14/1792, Wardle, pp. 206–209.

51. Letter from MW to Everina, 6/20/1792, Wardle, pp. 211–214.

52. Knowles, *Fuseli's Life*, p. 167.

53. Ibid.

54. Letter from MW to JJ, Saturday night, late 1792, Wardle, pp. 220–221.

55. Ibid.

56. Letter from MW to William Roscoe, 11/12/1792, Wardle, pp. 216–218.

CHAPTER SIX

1. It is now the Rue Meslay in the Third Arrondissment.

2. Letter from MW to Everina, 12/24/1792, Wardle, pp. 225–226.

3. *French Revolution*, p. 19.

4. Letter from MW to Everina, 12/24/1792, Wardle, pp. 225–226.

5. *French Revolution*, p. 216.

6. Wollstonecraft, "Letter on the Present Character," p. 443.

7. *French Revolution*, p. 76.

8. Ibid., pp. 25–26.

9. Letter from MW to Everina, 12/24/1792, Wardle, pp. 225–226.

10. Letter from Eliza to Everina, 2/29/1793, Pforzheimer Collection, reel 9.

11. Letter from MW to Everina, 12/24/1792, Wardle, pp. 225–226.

12. Letter from Eliza to Everina, 1/29/1792, Pforzheimer Collection, reel 9.

13. Letter from Eliza to Everina, 6/12/1791, Pforzheimer Collection, reel 9.

14. *Le Patriote Français,* 12/12/1792.

15. "Social Contract," pp. 159–160.

16. Ibid., p. 188.

17. *Vindication,* p. 117.

18. Schama, *Citizens,* pp. 644–646.

19. Letter from Eliza to Everina, 1/20/1793, Pforzheimer Collection, reel 9.

20. Letter from MW to Joseph Johnson, 12/26/1792, Wardle, pp. 226–227.

21. Most of my information on this opening day of the trial comes from an article by J. M. Girey in *Le Patriote Français,* 12/27/1792.

22. For an insightful discussion of this subject, see Lynn Hunt's *Family Romance of the French Revolution.*

23. Letter from MW to JJ, 12/26/1792, Wardle, pp. 226–227.

24. Letter from MW to Eliza, 1/20/1793, Wardle, p. 228.

25. Young, *Arthur Young's Travels,* p. 104.

26. The guest was America's Gouverneur Morris. L. Kelly, *Women,* p. 7.

27. Ibid., p. 35.

28. My translation of Condorcet, *Oeuvres Complètes,* vol. 12, p. 20.

29. It is appealing to imagine these two strong-minded women palavering over a glass of wine or a kitchen table in some mixture of English and French; and an aquaintance of Mary's from the time does claim that she and Madame Roland met in Paris. But the acquaintance is less persuasive than Mary Hays, who writes in her obituary of Wollstonecraft that "various accidents, which [Mary] was accustomed to mention with regret," prevented her from meeting Madame Roland.

30. Doyle, *The Oxford History of the French Revolution,* p. 90.

31. de Gouges, *Écrits Politiques,* p. 206.

32. Ibid.

33. Kelly, *Women,* p. 49.

34. The books I found most informative about women during the Revolution were L. Kelly, *Women of the French Revolution;* Applewhite and Levy, eds., *Women and Politics in the Age of the Democratic Revolution;* Spencer, ed., *French Women and the Age of Enlightenment;* Doyle, *The Oxford History of the French Revolution;* Tomalin, *The Life and Death of Mary Wollstonecraft;* and Schama, *Citizens.*

35. Letter from MW to Eliza, 1/20/1793, Wardle, pp. 228–229.

36. Tomalin, *Life and Death,* pp. 167–168; see esp. p. 168n.

37. Williams, *Letter from France*, vol. 2, p. 4.

38. Letter from MW to Everina, 12/24/1792, Wardle, pp. 225–226.

39. "I am without voice," *Le Patriote Français*, 1/20/1793.

40. *Le Patriote Français*, 1/20/1793.

41. Letter from MW to Eliza, 1/20/1793, Wardle, p. 228.

42. Ibid.

43. Letter from Eliza to Everina, 1/20/1793, Pforzheimer Collection, reel 9.

44. Letter from Eliza to Everina, 6/12/1791, Pforzheimer Collection, reel 9.

CHAPTER SEVEN

1. It is now Place de la Concorde.

2. *Révolution de Paris*, no. 186, 1/26–2/2/1793, p. 206.

3. *Le Patriote Français*, 1/30/1793.

4. Letter from Eliza to Everina, 2/10/1793, Pforzheimer Collection, reel 9.

5. Letter from MW to Ruth Barlow, 2/1–2/15/1793, Wardle, pp. 229–230.

6. "Letter on the Present Character," in Wollstonecraft, *Works*, vol. 6, p. 445.

7. Letter from Eliza to Everina, 2/29/1793, Pforzheimer Collection, reel 9.

8. Letter from MW to Ruth Barlow, 1/1–1/15/1793, Wardle, pp. 229–230.

9. Letter from Mary to Eliza, 1/20/1793, Wardle, pp. 228–229.

10. For particular speculation on Imlay's date of birth, see Rusk, "Adventures," pp. 4–5.

11. Monmouth County War Records, on microfilm at the New Jersey State Archives, MSS no. 4126.

12. Casualty book on microfilm, New Jersey State Archives, MSS no. 3777.

13. Bond from Gilbert Imlay to Daniel Boone, 3/15/1783, Draper Collection from the Wisconsin Historical Society, on microfilm in the New York Public Library.

14. Rusk, "Adventures," pp. 8–11.

15. Ibid., p. 11.

16. Ibid.

17. Ibid., p. 39.

18. Ibid., pp. 184–185.

19. Ibid., p. 194.

20. Ibid., p. 181.

21. Ibid., 1797 ed., pp. 198–199.

22. Ibid., pp. 177–178.

23. Ibid., pp. 17–18.

24. See Schama, *Citizens*, pp. 705–725.

25. Letter from MW to Everina, 3/10/1794, Wardle, pp. 250–251.

26. Letter from I. B. Johnson to William Godwin, 11/13/1797, Bodleian Library, Dep. b. 214/3.

27. Letter from Joel Barlow to Ruth Barlow, 4/19/1793, Barlow Collection, Harvard University.

28. Letter from MW to GI, c. 12/1793, Wardle, pp. 238–239.

29. Letter from MW to GI, c. 9/1793, Wardle, pp. 236–237.

30. Letter from MW to GI, c. 12/1793, Wardle, pp. 238–239.

31. This story is recounted in Morley, ed., *Henry Crabb Robinson*, vol. 1, p. 209.

32. *Memoirs*, p. 74.

33. Letter from MW to GI, 1/9/1795, Wardle, p. 274.

34. *French Revolution*, p. 215.

35. Ibid., p. 216.

36. Letter from Eliza to Everina, 5/13/1793, Pforzheimer Collection, reel 9.

37. Ibid.

38. Letter from MW to Eliza, 6/13/1793, Wardle, pp. 231–232.

39. Schama, *Citizens*, p. 723.

40. Imlay, *Emigrants*, p. 293.

41. In his 1957 master's thesis, "The Base Indian: A Vindication of the Rights of Mary Wollstonecraft," Robert R. Hare argues that Wollstonecraft actually "wrote" Imlay's book, and his argument has been taken so seriously that prestigious international libraries still catalogue *The Emigrants* under both of their names. Hare's thesis is in my opinion entirely misguided. His theory that Mary met and wrote pseudonymously for Imlay in London defies all the facts we know about both of them in 1792; and even more fruitless is his attempt to prove that *The Emigrants* is written with Mary Wollstonecraft's style and sensibility. Any competent reader will immediately distinguish Mary's convoluted, intellectualized sentences from *The Emigrants'* flowery, narrative-driven counterparts. Besides, as Godwin perceived, Mary's greatest difficulty was creating the sort of strong plot that is *The Emigrants'* chief virtue. From Mary's letters (see particularly letter from MW to GI, 2/10/1795, Wardle, pp. 278–279), we can see that she believed Imlay wrote *The Emigrants* on his own. However, the style of *The Emigrants* does differ quite markedly from that of *A Topographical Description*; so it's possible, as some biographers have speculated, that an author other than Wollstonecraft, perhaps Helen Maria Williams, assisted Imlay in the writing of his novel. It is even more plausible that Imlay himself assumed a different style in his second book.

42. Imlay, *Emigrants*, p. 319.

43. Ibid., p. 318.

44. *French Revolution*, p. 46.

45. St. Clair, *Godwins*, p. 73.

46. *French Revolution*, p. 34.

47. Letter from MW to Everina, 3/10/1794, Wardle, pp. 250–251.

48. *Memoirs*, p. 69.

49. Letter from MW to GI, 6/1793, Wardle, pp. 230–231.

50. Letter from MW to Everina, 12/9/1792, Wardle, pp. 222–223.

51. *Vindication*, p. 296.

52. Letter from MW to GI, 1/14/1794, Wardle, p. 248.

53. Letter from MW to Ruth Barlow, mid-1793, Wardle, p. 234.

54. See letter from MW to GI, 8/1793, Wardle, p. 233.

55. *Memoirs*, p. 77.

56. For all her skepticism about revolutionary rhetoric in general, Mary accepted the most outlandish accusations against Marie Antoinette. Significantly, Imlay did not ascribe to the demonizing of the queen and instead attacked her "execrable" accusors. Marie Antoinette was "unfortunate," he wrote. Her "crimes were the crimes of the age and the national rather than the individual." Imlay, *A Topographical Description*, pp. 198–199.

57. Ibid. The information on Mary's visit to Versailles is on pp. 84–85.

58. Letter from MW to GI, c. 8/1793, Wardle, pp. 233–234.

59. Ibid.

CHAPTER EIGHT

1. All that remained of the church was its nave, which had been converted into a saltpeter factory.

2. Letter from MW to GI, 8/1793, Wardle, p. 233.

3. *French Revolution*, p. 106.

4. Ibid.

5. London *Times*, 9/23/1793, reporting on a 9/10 session at the Convention.

6. Letter from Eliza to Everina, 4/24/1793, Pforzheimer Collection, reel 9.

7. Letter from Eliza to Everina, 1/14/1794, Pforzheimer Collection, reel 9.

8. An example can be found in the London *Times*, 9/19/1793.

9. Letter from Eliza to Everina, 5/13/93, Pforzheimer Collection, reel 9.

10. French farmers were withholding their corn, for instance, to defy price regulations.

11. Letter from MW to GI, 8/1793, Wardle, p. 235.

12. Letter from MW to GI, 8/1793, Wardle, p. 233.

13. Letter from MW to GI, 11/1793, Wardle, p. 237.

14. Letter from MW to GI, 9/1793, Wardle, p. 236.

15. Ibid.

16. Ibid., pp. 236–237.

17. Letter from MW to GI, Sunday night, 11/1793, Wardle, pp. 237–238.

18. Durant, *Memoirs*, p. 251.

19. Letter from MW to GI, 1/1/1794, Wardle, pp. 242–243.

20. Letter from MW to GI, 1/6/1794, Wardle, p. 243.

21. Letter from MW to GI, 12/31/1793, Wardle, p. 241.

22. Letter from MW to GI, 1/1/1794, Wardle, p. 242.

23. Letter from MW to GI, 1/1/1794, Wardle, pp. 242–243.

24. Letter from MW to GI, c. 12/1793, Wardle, p. 238.

25. Letter from MW to GI, 1/1/1794, Wardle, pp. 242–243.

26. *Révolutions de Paris*, no. 215, New York Public Library. The italics are mine.

27. L. Kelly, *Women*, pp. 122–123.

28. Ibid., p. 122.

29. Durant, *Memoirs*, p. 77.

30. G. Kelly, *Women, Writing, and Revolution*, pp. 55–56.

31. Letter from MW to GI, 12/30/1793, Wardle, pp. 240–241.

32. Letter from MW to GI, 12/29/1793, Wardle, pp. 239–240.

33. Letter from MW to GI, 12/31/1794, Wardle, p. 241.

34. Letter from MW to GI, 1/1/1794, Wardle, pp. 242–243.

35. Letter from MW to GI, 1/8/1794, Wardle, pp. 244–245.

36. Letter from MW to GI, 1/11/1794, Wardle, pp. 246–247.

37. Letter from MW to Ruth Barlow, 2/3/1794, Wardle, pp. 249–250.

38. This mansion has been restored and is now a historical museum.

39. Letter from MW to Everina, 3/10/1794, Wardle, pp. 250–251.

40. Letter from MW to GI, 1/15/1794, Wardle, p. 249.

41. Letter from MW to Ruth Barlow, 2/3/[1794], Wardle, pp. 249–250.

42. Letter from MW to Ruth Barlow, 5/20/1794, Wardle, pp. 255–256.

43. Letter from MW to Ruth Barlow, 4/27/1794, Wardle, pp. 253–255.

44. Letter from MW to GI, 1/8/1794, Wardle, pp. 244–245.

45. Letter from MW to Everina, 3/10/1794, Wardle, pp. 250–251.

46. Letter from MW to Ruth Barlow, 4/27/1794, Wardle, p. 253.

47. Letter from MW to GI, 3/1794, Wardle, p. 252.

48. She gleaned most of her facts from the National Convention journals, the *New Annual Register*, and Mirabeau's letters.

49. *French Revolution*, p. 28.

50. Ibid., p. 42.

51. *French Revolution*, pp. 147–148.

52. Ibid., p. 141.

53. Letter from MW to William Roscoe, 11/12/1792, Wardle, pp. 216–218.

54. *French Revolution*, p. 141.

55. Ibid., p. 222.

56. Doyle, *Oxford History of the French Revolution*, p. 274.

57. Kurtz and Autrey, eds., *Four New Letters*, pp. 45–46.

58. Letter from MW to Ruth Barlow, 4/27/1794, Wardle, pp. 253–254.

59. Letter from MW to Ruth Barlow, 7/8/1794, Wardle, pp. 255–256.

60. Ibid.

61. Ibid.

62. Letter from MW to Ruth Barlow, 7/8/1794, Wardle, pp. 256–257.

63. Ibid.

64. Rowan, *Autobiography*, pp. 237–238.

65. Williams, *Letters Containing a Sketch*, p. 10.

66. Letter from MW to Everina, 9/22/1794, Wardle, pp. 261–262.

CHAPTER NINE

1. Letter from MW to GI, 8/20/1794, Wardle, pp. 260–261.

2. Letter from MW to GI, 2/10/1795, Wardle, pp. 278–279.

3. Letter from MW to GI, 8/20/1794, Wardle, pp. 260–261.

4. L. Kelly, *Women*, p. 149.

5. Letter from MW to GI, 8/17/1794, Wardle, pp. 258–259.

6. Letter from MW to GI, 8/19/1794, Wardle, pp. 259–260.

7. Letter from MW to GI, 10/1/1794, Wardle, pp. 266–267.

8. Letter from MW to GI, 8/19/1794, Wardle, pp. 259–260.

9. *Vindication*, p. 168.

10. Letter from MW to GI, 9/22/1794, Wardle, pp. 262–263.

11. Letter from MW to GI, 2/9/1795, Wardle, pp. 277–278.

12. Letter from MW to GI, 9/28/1794, Wardle, pp. 265–266.

13. L. Kelly, *Women*, p. 153.

14. Williams, *Letters Containing a Sketch*, p. 2.

15. L. Kelly, *Women*, p. 153.

16. Letter from MW to GI, 9/23/1794, Wardle, pp. 264–265.

17. Letter from MW to GI, Wardle, pp. 271–272.

18. Durant, *Memoirs*, p. 247, from Madeleine Schweizer's 1794 journal.

19. London *Times*, 7/31/94 and 8/4/94.

20. A. Rowan, *Autobiography*, p. 253.

21. Ibid., p. 254.

22. Durant, *Memoirs*, p. 255.

23. Rowan, *Autobiography*, p. 254.

24. Letter from Eliza to Everina, 7/4/1794, Pforzheimer Collection, reel 9.

25. This was copied out by Eliza in her letter to Everina, 8/15/1794, Pforzheimer Collection, reel 9.

26. Letter from Eliza to Everina, 11/17/1794, Pforzheimer Collection, reel 9.

27. Letter from Eliza to Everina, 2/1/1794, Pforzheimer Collection, reel 9.

28. Letter from MW to GI, 2/10/1795, Wardle, pp. 278–279.

29. Letter from MW to GI, Wardle, pp. 274–275.

30. Letter from MW to GI, 12/29/1794, Wardle, pp. 271–272.

31. Letter from MW to GI, 2/9/1795, Wardle, pp. 277–278.

32. Letter from MW to GI, 1/15/1795, Wardle, pp. 275–276.

33. Letter from MW to GI, Wardle, pp. 278–279.

34. Letter from MW to GI, 2/19/1795, Wardle, pp. 279–281.

35. Ibid.

36. Letter from MW to GI, 12/1795, Wardle, pp. 323–324.

37. Letter from MW to GI, 4/7/1795, Wardle, pp. 181–182.

38. Letter from MW to Archibald Hamilton Rowan, 4/9/1795, Wardle, pp. 282–283.

CHAPTER TEN

1. Letter from JJ to Joseph Priestley, 9/25/1795, Joseph Johnson's journal and correspondence in Pforzheimer Collection.

2. Isaac Kramnick, Introduction by Isaac Kramnick to *Political Justice*.

3. Ibid.

4. Porter, *English Society*, pp. 311–339.

5. More, *Strictures*, p. 100.

6. Edgeworth, *Letters for Literary Ladies,* pp. 4–5.

7. Ibid.

8. Barbauld, *Works*, p. 319.

9. Letter from MW to GI, 4/11/1795, Wardle, p. 285.

10. Letter from MW to GI, 6/12/95, Wardle, pp. 290–293.

11. Letter from MW to GI, 11/27/95, Wardle, pp. 320–322.

12. Letter from MW to GI, 8/26/1795, Wardle, p. 310.

13. *Memoirs*, p. 81.

14. Letter from MW to GI, 6/12/1795, Wardle, pp. 290–293.

15. Letter from MW to GI, 6/3/1795, Wardle, pp. 301–303.

16. Letter from Eliza to Everina, 3/8/1795, Pforzheimer Collection, reel 9.

17. Letter from Eliza to Everina, 3/4/1795, Pforzheimer Collection, reel 9.

18. Letter from Eliza to Everina, marked Thursday 10th 1795. This seems to be March 10. Pforzheimer Collection, reel 9.

19. Letter from MW to Eliza, 4/23/1795, Wardle, pp. 285–286.

20. Letter from Eliza to Everina, 4/29/1795! (Eliza's exclamation point), Pforzheimer Collection, reel 9.

21. Letter from Eliza to Everina, 6/13/1795, Pforzheimer Collection, reel 9.

22. Letter from Eliza to Everina, 4/29/1795, Pforzheimer Collection, reel 9.

23. Letter from Eliza to Everina, 5/8/1795, Pforzheimer Collection, reel 9.

24. Letter from Mary Hays to John Eccles, 8/13/1779, Hays, *Love Letters*, p. 46.

25. Letter from Mary Hays to John Eccles, 8/7/1780, Hays, *Love Letters*, p. 200.

26. Hays, *Love Letters*, p. 5.

27. Letter from MW to Mary Hays, 11/12/1792, Wardle, pp. 219–220.

28. Mary Hays, *The Annual Necrology for 1797–8*, London, 1798.

29. Letter from MW to GI, 2/10/1795, Wardle, pp. 278–279.

30. Letter from MW to GI, 5/22/1795, Wardle, pp. 287–289. Since this letter is dated three days later than Imlay's letter empowering Mary to act as his agent in Scandinavia, it was probably written after her suicide attempt. Still, the mood of the letter is indicative of Mary's frame of mind when she swallowed the laudanum.

31. MacDonald and Murphy, *Sleepless Souls*, p. 191.

32. See Porter, *English Society*, and MacDonald and Murphy, *Sleepless Souls*.

33. Letter from MW to GI, 6/12/1795, Wardle, pp. 290–293.

34. *Memoirs*, p. 83.

35. Letter from GI to MW, 5/19/1795, Pforzheimer Collection, reel 9.

36. Letter from Eliza to Everina, June 1795, Pforzheimer Collection, reel 9.

37. Letter from MW to GI, 12/8/1795, Wardle, pp. 322–323. After her final break with Imlay, Mary chastises him: "Whilst I was with you, I restrained my natural generosity, because I thought your property in jeopardy.— When I went to [Scandinavia], I requested you, *if you could conveniently*, not to forget my father,

sisters, and some other people, whom I was interested about.— Money was lavished away, yet not only my requests were neglected, but some trifling debts were not discharged, that now come on me— Was this friendship—or generosity?"

CHAPTER ELEVEN

1. Letter from GI, 5/19/1795, Pforzheimer Collection, reel 9. The writing is scrawled and very difficult to read.

2. Letter from MW to GI, 6/10/1795, Wardle, pp. 289–290.

3. Ibid.

4. *Letters*, pp. 243–247.

5. Letter from MW to GI, 6/27/1795, Wardle, pp. 299–300.

6. Letter from MW to GI, Wardle, p. 301.

7. Letter from MW to GI, 7/4/1795, Wardle, pp. 303–304.

8. *Letters*, p. 248.

9. Letter from MW to GI, 7/3/1795, Wardle, pp. 301–303.

10. *Letters*, p. 269.

11. Ibid., p. 274.

12. Author's interview with Ursula Houge.

13. *Letters*, p. 271.

14. Ibid., p. 288.

15. Ibid., p. 289.

16. Ibid., p. 280.

17. Townspeople still travel to this spot because of the excellence of the drinking water.

18. *Letter*, p. 281.

19. Ibid., pp. 282–283.

20. Ibid., p. 280.

21. Ibid., p. 294.

22. Ibid., p. 297.

23. Ibid., p. 305.

24. Ibid., pp. 308–309.

25. Letter from MW to GI, 9/6/1795, Wardle, pp. 311–312.

26. *Letters*, pp. 319–322.

27. *Vindication*, pp. 113–114.

28. Letter from MW to GI, 9/27/1795, Wardle, pp. 312–314.

29. Letter from MW to GI, 9/25/1795, Wardle, p. 312.

30. Letter from MW to GI, 10/10/1795, Wardle, pp. 316–317.

31. Ibid.

32. Ralph Wardle quotes an item in an October 1795 issue of the London *Times* that describes how an "elegantly dressed" woman, presumably Mary, jumped from Putney Bridge in an attempt to drown. Wardle, p. 317, n. 1.

33. The information about this suicide comes mostly from the *Memoirs*, pp. 86–90.

34. Letter from MW to GI, 11/1795, Wardle, pp. 317–318.

35. Ibid.

36. Ibid.

37. Letter from MW to GI, 11/1795, Wardle, pp. 319–320.

38. Letter from MW to GI, 11/27/1795, Wardle, pp. 320–322.

39. Letter from MW to GI, 12/8/1795, Wardle, p. 322.

40. Godwin imagines Mary's thoughts in *Memoirs*, pp. 90–91.

41. Letter from MW to JJ, late 1795, Wardle, pp. 325–326.

42. Letter from JJ to Charles Wollstonecraft, 11/15/1795, Johnson's letters, Pforzheimer Collection.

43. *Letters*, p. 325.

44. Letter from MW to Archibald Hamilton Rowan, 1/26/1796, Wardle, pp. 328–329.

45. Letter from WG to Mary Hays, 1/1796, Durant, *Memoirs of Mary Wollstonecraft*, p. 311.

CHAPTER TWELVE

1. Kegan, *William Godwin*, p. 26. This is a direct quote from WG's autobiographical writing.

2. Letter from Amelia Alderson to WG ?/28/1795, Pforzheimer Collection, reel 9. At this time, Amelia Alderson was visiting Mrs. Sothren on Godwin's account. She wrote Godwin (floridly) that she admired this woman "to whom the world is as much indebted as you are—for she watched over your childhood and [provided] you the means of that improvement by which you will be immortalized."

3. Letter from WG to Mr. Cole, 3/2/1802, Pforzheimer Collection, reel 8.

4. *SHC*, vol. 1, p. 6.

5. Kegan, *William Godwin*, p. 7.

6. Letter from WG to Mary Jane Godwin, 5/30/1811, Pforzeimer Collection, reel 4.

7. St. Clair, *Godwins*, p. 32.

8. Letter from Charles Lamb to Thomas Manning, 2/13/1800, *Letters of Charles and Mary Lamb*, p. 174.

9. This is how Mary Hays describes the very Godwin-like philosopher in her 1796 novel *Memoirs of Emma Courtney*.

10. Godwin, *St. Leon*, p. 165.

11. Undated letter from WG to Mrs. Godwin, Pforzheimer Collection, reel 7.

12. Elbridge Colby, Introduction to Holcroft's *Memoirs*.

13. Kegan, *William Godwin*, pp. 25–26.

14. Holcroft, *Memoirs*, pp. 122–129. This portion of Holcroft's *Memoirs* was written, after his death, by William Hazlitt.

15. Ibid., pp. 45–46.

16. Coleridge, *Collected Letters,* pp. 830–831.

17. Holcroft's radicalism does appear briefly (almost apologetically) in the prologue to his spoof of spoiled heirs, *Road to Ruin*. Diverging entirely from the main plot, the prologue hails the French Revolution and invites universal brotherhood and freedom for black slaves.

18. Kegan, *William Godwin*, p. 25.

19. Godwin, *St. Leon*, p. 153.

20. Letter from Thomas Holcroft to WG, 7/19/99, Pforzheimer Collection, reel 6.

21. Hazlitt, *Spirit of the Age*, pp. 125–126.

22. Letter from WG to Mary Jane Godwin, 4/5/1805, Bodleian Library, Dep. c. 523.

23. Kegan, *William Godwin*, p. 79.

24. *Memoirs*, pp. 62–63.

25. See Godwin's diary, 11/13/1791.

26. *Memoirs*, p. 64.

27. Quoted from St. Clair, *Godwins*, p. 53.

28. *Political Justice*, p. 175.

29. Ibid., p. 198.

30. Godwin qualifies himself a bit in a later passage where he admits, on pp. 280–281: "Yet, after all, it ought not to be forgotten that, though the connection be not essential or requisite, revolutions and violence have too often been coeval with important changes of the social system. What has so often happened in time past is not unlikely occasionally to happen in future."

31. *Political Justice*, p. 335.

32. Ibid., p. 763.

33. Ibid., p. 762.

34. Hazlitt, *Spirit of the Age*, p. 182.

35. Ibid., pp. 133–134.

36. "Called on Inchbald," Godwin records in his diary on May 6, 1793.

37. Letter from Coleridge to WG, 5/21/1800, Pforzheimer Collection, reel 6.

38. This unnamed writer is quoted in Ford K. Brown, *The Life of William Godwin* (London: J. M. Dent & Sons, 1926), p. 78.

39. C. L. Brightwell, ed., *Memorials of the Life of Amelia Opie* (London: Longman, Brown, 1854), pp. 59–60.

40. Brown, *Life*, p. 75.

41. *Caleb Williams*, p. 336.

42. Maurice Hindle quotes this passage in his Introduction to *Political Justice*, p. 9.

43. Hazlitt, *Spirit of the Age*, p. 190.

44. Letter from WG to Maria Reveley, 8/25/1799, Pforzheimer Collection, reel 6.

45. Ibid.

46. *Memoirs*, pp. 84–85.

47. Letter from MW to Archibald Hamilton Rowan, 1/26/1796, Wardle, pp. 328–329.

48. Letter from MW to GI, 3/1796, pp. 329–330.

49. *Memoirs*, p. 95.

50. Letter from MW to Gustav, Graf von Schlabrendorf, 5/13/1796, Wardle, pp. 330–331.

CHAPTER THIRTEEN

1. May 1796 issue of the *Analytical Review*, in Wollstonecraft, *Works*, vol. 7, pp. 462–464.

2. It is impossible to be positive that the unsigned letter declaring love for Mary came from Holcroft, but I have compared the handwriting here to the handwriting in Holcroft's letters to Godwin and found it remarkably similar. William St. Clair makes a convincing case for Holcroft's authorship in *The Godwins and the Shelleys*, p. 162.

3. Letter addressed to "Mrs. Imlay" at Finsbury Place and postmarked 1/2/1796, Bodleian Library, Dep. b. 214/3.

4. Letter from Amelia Alderson to MW, 8/28/1796, Pforzheimer Collection, reel 6.

5. Letter from Amelia Alderson to WG, 11/16/1796, Pforzheimer Collection, reel 6.

6. Letter from Amelia Alderson to WG, 11/18/1796, Pforzheimer Collection, reel 6.

7. *Memoirs*, p. 96.

8. Wardle, *Godwin and Mary* (hereafter, *G&M*), pp. 4–5, dated 7/1/1796.

9. Letter from Amelia Alderson to MW, 8/28/1796, Pforzheimer Collection, reel 6.

10. Letter from Robert Southey to Joseph Cottle, 3/13/1787, reprinted in *Life and Correspondence of Robert Southey*, p. 95.

11. See St. Clair, *Godwins*, pp. 164, 536n.

12. *Memoirs*, pp. 99, 100.

13. Letter from MW to WG, 7/21/1796, *G&M*, p. 10.

14. Letter from MW to WG, 8/2/1796, *G&M*, p. 11.

15. William St. Clair, *Godwins*, elaborately illustrates his methods of decoding Godwin's diary in his appendix 1, pp. 497–503.

16. Letter from MW to WG, 8/17/1796, *G&M*, pp. 14–15.

17. Letter from WG to MW, 8/17/1796, *G&M*, pp. 16–17.

18. Letter from MW to WG, 8/17/1796, *G&M*, pp. 18–19.

19. Letter from MW to WG, 8/22/1796, *G&M*, p. 23.

20. Letter from WG to MW, 8/22/1796, *G&M*, p. 23.

21. Letter from MW to WG, 8/24/1796, *G&M*, p. 23.

22. Letter from WG to MW, undated, *G&M*, p. 24.

23. Letter from MW to WG, 11/3/1796, *G&M*, pp. 45–46.

24. Letter from MW to WG, 11/4/1796, *G&M*, pp. 29–30.

25. Letter from WG to MW, undated, *G&M*, p. 44.

26. Letter from MW to WG, 11/13/1796, *G&M*, pp. 46–47.

27. Letter from WG to MW, undated, *G&M*, p. 47.

28. Letter from MW to WG, 10/4/1796, *G&M*, pp. 41–42.

29. Letter from MW to WG, 9/13/1796, *G&M*, p. 33.

30. Letter from MW to WG, 9/28/1796, *G&M*, p. 38.

31. Letter from MW to WG, 11/10/1796, *G&M*, p. 46.

32. Letter from MW to WG, 9/10/1796, *G&M*, pp. 30–32.

33. Wollstonecraft, *Works*, vol. 7, pp. 467–472.

34. Letter from MW to WG, 9/4/1796, *G&M*, pp. 29–30.

35. Letter from MW to WG, 8/31/1796, *G&M*, pp. 26–27.

36. Letter from MW to WG, 7/4/1797, *G&M*, pp. 110–112.

37. Letter from MW to WG, 11/18/1796, *G&M*, p. 48.

38. Letter from WG to MW, undated, *G&M*, p. 49.

39. Letter from MW to WG, 11/28/1796, *G&M*, p. 53.

40. Letter from WG to MW, 8/22/1796, *G&M*, p. 23.

41. Letter from MW to WG, 8/26/1796, *G&M*, p. 24.

42. Abinger Microfilm, Duke University, reel 3.

43. Letter from MW to WG, 9/4/1796, *G&M*, pp. 27–29.

44. Letter from MW to WG, 9/4/1796, *G&M*, pp. 29–30.

45. Letter from MW to WG, 9/15/1796, *G&M*, p. 35.

46. Letter from MW to WG, 9/17/1796, *G&M*, p. 36.

47. Letter from MW to WG, 9/23/1796, *G&M*, p. 52.

48. Letter from MW to WG, 12/6/1796, *G&M*, pp. 53–54.

49. Letter from MW to WG, 12/7/1796, *G&M*, p. 54.

50. Letter from MW to WG, 12/20/1796, *G&M*, p. 57.

51. Letter from MW to WG, 12/23/1796, *G&M*, p. 57.

52. Letter from WG to MW, 12/31/1796, *G&M*, pp. 59–60.

53. Letter from MW to WG, 12/31/1796, *G&M*, p. 60.

54. Letter from MW to WG, 1/1/1797, *G&M*, pp. 60–61.

55. Letter from MW to Everina, 3/22/1796, Wardle, pp. 384–385.

56. Letter from MW to WG, 1/12/1797, *G&M*, p. 62.

57. Letter from MW to WG, undated, *G&M*, p. 64.

58. Letter from MW to WG, 2/21/1797, *G&M*, pp. 69–70.

CHAPTER FOURTEEN

1. Letter from WG to ?, 8/29/1801, Pforzheimer Collection, reel 8.

2. Marshall, *Life and Letters of Mary Shelley*, p. 33. The visitor is Christy Baxter, the sister of Mary Godwin's close friend.

3. Letter from MW to WG, *G&M*, p. 74.

4. *Memoirs*, p. 108.

5. Godwin, *St. Leon*, p. 41.

6. Sunstein, *A Different Face*, p. 336.

7. Quoted in Brown, *Life*, pp. 118–119.

8. Letter from Thomas Holcroft to WG, 4/6/1797, Pforzheimer Collection, reel 6.

9. Letter from MW to Amelia Alderson, 4/11/1797, Wardle, pp. 389–390.

10. Ibid.

11. Letter from JJ to Charles Wollstonecraft, 7/15/1797, Johnson's letters, Pforzheimer Collection.

12. Letter from Elizabeth Inchbald to WG, 11/1/1816, Pforzheimer Collection, reel 6.

13. Letter from Everina to Eliza, undated, Pforzheimer Collection, reel 6.

14. Letter from MW to Maria Reveley, 6/26/1797, Wardle, pp. 400–401.

15. Letter from MW to WG, 7/4/1797, *G&M*, pp. 110–112.

16. Letter from WG to MW, 8/9/1797, *G&M*, p. 119.

17. Letter from N. Pinkerton to MW, *G&M*, p. 118.

18. *Maria*, p. 75.

19. Ibid., p. 88.

20. Ibid., p. 90.

21. Ibid., p. 88.

22. Ibid., p. 141.

23. Ibid., p. 122.

24. Ibid., p. 67.

25. Letter from MW to George Dyson, 5/15/1797, Wardle, pp. 391–392.

26. *Vindication*, p. 114.

27. *Maria*, p. 96.

28. Letter from MW to WG, 6/6/1797, *G&M*, pp. 82–84.

29. Letter from WG to MW, 6/10/1797, *G&M*, pp. 89–92.

30. Letter from MW to WG, 6/19/1797, *G&M*, pp. 106–107.

31. *Lessons*, pp. 471–472.

32. Ibid.

33. *Memoirs*, p. 113.

34. Ibid.

35. Ibid., p. 116.

36. Ibid.

37. Ibid., p. 118.

38. Letter from Elizabeth Fenwick to Everina, 9/12/1797, Pforzheimer Collection, reel 9.

39. *Memoirs*, p. 118.

40. Ibid., p. 122.

41. Letter from MW, probably to Mary Hays, summer 1797, Wardle, p. 413.

EPILOGUE

1. Letter from JJ to WG, 9/10/1797, Pforzheimer Collection, reel 8, file 39.

2. Letter from Hamilton Rowan to MW, 9/15/1797, Pforzheimer Collection, reel 6, file 31.

3. Johnson sent this letter from Imlay to Godwin, who returned the original and

in his own hand copied Imlay's words on the back of Johnson's request for the "Trust Deed." Bodleian Library, Dep. 229(a)–(b).

4. Mary Hays, *The Annual Necrology for 1797–8*, London, 1798, p. 426.

5. Letter from WG to ?, 1/2/179?, Bodleian Library, Dep. b. 227/8.

6. Letter from WG to ?, 8/29/1801, Pforzheimer Collection, reel 8.

7. Letter from WG to William Cole, 3/2/1802, Pforzheimer Collection, reel 8.

8. Letter from WG to James Marshall, 7/1/1800, Pforzheimer Collection, reel 6.

9. Letter from WG to James Marshall, 8/2/1800, Pforzheimer Collection, reel 6.

10. Letter from WG to Maria Reveley, 8/25/1799, Pforzheimer Collection, reel 6.

11. Marshall, *Life and Letters,* p. 165.

12. St. Clair, *Godwins,* p. 243.

13. Unaddressed letter from Godwin, undated, Pforzheimer Collection, reel 4.

14. Letter from Margaret Mountcashell to Mary Shelley, undated, Pforzheimer Collection, reel 7.

15. Letter from WG to E. Fordham, 11/13/1811, Pforzheimer Collection, reel 6.

16. Ibid.

17. Marshall, *Life and Letters,* p. 164.

18. Ibid., p. 163.

19. Letter from Fanny Imlay to Mary Godwin, 5/29/1816, Marshall, *Life and Letters,* pp. 23–24.

20. *Cambrian*, 10/12/1816, p. 3, in Swansea Library.

POSTSCRIPT

1. Letter from Everina to Elizabeth Berry, July 17, 1839, Mitchell Collection, State Library of New South Wales, Australia, pp. 55–57.

2. Ibid.

3. Joseph Johnson's will, London Public Record Office.

4. The book can be read in the Pforzheimer Collection.

5. Tomalin, *Life and Death,* p. 287.

6. Ibid. She uses a copy of the gravestone made in 1833 and cited in 1903 by Richard Garnett.

SELECT BIBLIOGRAPHY

Abbott, John S. A. *History of Madame Roland*. New York: Harper & Row, 1856.

Aikin, John. "Biographical Account of the Late Joseph Johnson." *Gentleman's Magazine* 106 (1809).

Alger, John G. *Englishmen in the French Revolution*. London: Sampson, Low, Marston, Searle & Rivington, 1889.

Applewhite, Harriet B., and Darline G. Levy, eds., *Women and Politics in the Age of the Democratic Revolution*. Ann Arbor: University of Michigan Press, 1993.

Astell, Mary. *A Serious Proposal to the Ladies*. New York: Source Book Press, 1970.

Barbauld, Anna Laetitia. *The Works of Anna Laetitia Barbauld with a Memoir by Lucy Aikin*. London: Longman, Hurst, Rees, Orme, Brown & Green, 1825.

Barlow, Joel. Correspondence in the Houghton Library, Harvard.

Brewer, John. *The Pleasures of the Imagination*. New York: Farrar, Straus & Giroux, 1997.

Burgh, James. *The Dignity of Human Nature*. London, 1754.

Burke, Edmund. *Reflections on the Revolution in France*. Harmondsworth, England: Penguin Books, 1986.

Chard, Leslie F. "Joseph Johnson: Father of the Book Trade." *Bulletin of the New York Public Library*, Autumn 1975.

Coleridge, Samuel. *Collected Letters of Coleridge*. Edited by E. L. Griggs. New York: Oxford University Press, 1956.

Condorcet, Marie-Jean-Antoine-Nicolas Caritat, Marquis de. *Oeuvres Complètes de Condorcet*. Paris: Chez Henrichs; Fuchs; Koennig; Levrault, Schoell et Cnie, 1804.

Coombs, Tony. *Tis a Mad World at Hogsdon: A Short History of Hoxton and Surrounding*

Area. London: Hoxton Hall in association with the London Borough of Hackney, 1995.

Doyle, William. *The Oxford History of the French Revolution*. New York: Oxford University Press, 1989.

Durant, W. Clark, ed. *Memoirs of Mary Wollstonecraft . . . with a Preface, a Supplement Chronologically Arranged and Containing Hitherto Unpublished or Uncollected Material and a Bibliographical Note*. New York: Haskell House Publishers, 1969.

Edgeworth, Maria. *Letters for Literary Ladies*. New York and London: Garland Publishing, 1974.

Edgeworth, Maria, and R. L. Edgeworth. *Practical Education*. London: Routledge/Thoemmes Press, 1992.

Fraisse, Geneviève. *Reason's Muse: Sexual Difference and the Birth of Democracy*. Chicago and London: University of Chicago Press, 1994.

Gay, Peter. *The Enlightenment: An Interpretation*. Vol. 2: *The Science of Freedom*. New York and London: W. W. Norton & Company, 1969.

Genlis, Madame la Comtesse de. *Adelaide and Theodore; or, Letters on Education*. London: C. Bathurst, 1784.

George, M. Dorothy. *London Life in the Eighteenth Century*. New York: Capricorn Books, 1965.

Godwin, William. Diary, in the Bodleian Library at Oxford, and there is a copy in the Pforzheimer Collection, New York Public Library.

———. *An Enquiry Concerning Political Justice*. Harmondsworth, England, and Baltimore: Penguin Books, 1976.

———. *Memoirs of Mary Wollstonecraft*. Edited and with a biographical note by W. Clark Durant. New York: Haskell House Publishers, 1969.

———. *St. Leon*. Oxford and New York: Oxford University Press, 1994.

———. *Things as They Are; or, The Adventures of Caleb Williams*. Harmondsworth, England: Penguin Books, 1988.

Gouges, Olympe de. *Écrits Politiques*. Paris: Côté-Femmes, 1993.

Gregor-Dellin, Martin. *Schlabrendorf oder Die Republik*. Munich: R. Piper & Co., 1982.

Halsband, Robert, ed. *The Selected Letters of Lady Mary Wortley Montagu*. New York: St. Martin's Press, 1970.

Hamilton, Elizabeth. *Letters on Education*. London: G. G. & J. Robinson, 1801.

———. *Memoirs of Modern Philosophers*. London: G. G. & J. Robinson, 1800.

Handlin, Oscar, and Mary Handlin. *James Burgh & American Revolutionary Theory*. Massachusetts Historical Society, *Proceedings* 73 (January–December 1961): 38–57.

Hare, Robert R. "The Base Indian: A Vindication of the Rights of Mary Wollstonecraft." Master's thesis, University of Delaware, 1957.

Hays, Mary. *Appeal to the Men of Great Britain in Behalf of the Women*. London: Joseph Johnson, 1798.

———. *The Love Letters of Mary Hays*. Edited by A. F. Wedd. London: Methuen, 1925.

———. *Memoirs of Emma Courtney*. London: G. G. & J. Robinson, 1796.

Hazlitt, William. *The Spirit of the Age*. New York: E. P. Dutton, 1955.

Holcroft, Thomas. *Memoirs of the Late Thomas Holcroft, Written by Himself*. Edited by William Hazlitt. London, 1852.

Holmes, Richard. *Footsteps: Adventures of a Romantic Biographer*. New York: Viking Press, 1985.

Hunt, Lynn. *The Family Romance of the French Revolution*. Berkeley and Los Angeles: University of California Press, 1992.

———. *Politics, Culture, and Class in the French Revolution*. Berkeley and Los Angeles: University of California Press, 1984.

Imlay, Gilbert. *The Emigrants*. Gainesville, Florida: Scholars' Facsimiles & Reprints, 1964.

———. *A Topographical Description of the Western Territory of North America*. London: J. Debrett, 1792.

Johnson, Joseph. Letter book in the Pforzheimer Collection, New York Public Library.

Kegan, Paul. *William Godwin: His Friends and Contemporaries*. London: Henry S. King & Co., 1876.

Kelly, Gary. *Women, Writing, and Revolution, 1790–1827*. Oxford: Clarendon Press, 1993.

Kelly, Linda. *Women of the French Revolution*. Harmondsworth, England: Penguin Books, 1989.

Knowles, John. *Fuseli's Life and Lectures*. London: Henry Colburn & Richard Bentley, 1831.

———. *The Life and Writings of Henry Fuseli*. London, 1831.

Kurtz, Benjamin P., and Carrie C. Autrey, eds. *Four New Letters of Mary Wollstonecraft and Helen Maria Williams*. Berkeley: University of California Press, 1937.

Lamb, Charles, and Mary Lamb. *The Letters of Charles and Mary Lamb*. London: J. M. Dent & Sons & Methuen, 1935.

Lefebre, Georges. *The French Revolution from 1793 to 1799*. Vol. 2. New York: Columbia University Press, 1964.

Select Bibliography

Macaulay, Catharine. *Letters on Education*. New York and London: Garland Publishing, 1974.

MacDonald, Michael, and Terrence R. Murphy. *Sleepless Souls: Suicide in Early Modern England*. Oxford: Clarendon Press; New York: Oxford University Press, 1990.

Marshall, Mrs. Julian. *The Life and Letters of Mary Wollstonecraft Shelley*. London: Richard Bentley & Sons, 1889.

McAleer, Edward C. *The Sensitive Plant: A Life of Lady Mount Cashell*. Chapel Hill: University of North Carolina Press, 1958.

More, Hannah. *Strictures on the Modern System of Female Education*. London: T. Cadell & W. Davies, 1799.

Nyström, Per. *Mary Wollstonecraft's Scandinavian Journey*. Gothenburg: Kungl. Vetenskaps och Vitterhets-Samhället, 1980.

Paine, Thomas. *The Rights of Man*. Harmondsworth, England: Penguin Books, 1985.

Porter, Roy. *English Society in the Eighteenth Century*. Harmondsworth, England: Penguin Books, 1990.

Price, Richard. *A Discourse on the Love of Our Country*. Delivered 11/4/1789; published London, 1790.

Robinson, Henry Crabb. *Books and Their Writers*. Edited by Edith Morley. London: J. M. Dent & Sons, 1938.

Roche, Daniel. *The People of Paris: An Essay in Popular Culture in the Eighteenth Century*. Berkeley: University of California Press, 1987.

Roland, Manon. *The Private Memoirs of Madame Roland*. Edited by Edward Gilpin Johnson. Chicago: A. C. McClurg & Co., 1901.

Roland, Thomas. *Richard Price: Philosopher and Apostle of Liberty*. London: Oxford University Press, 1924.

Rousseau, Jean-Jacques. *Émile*. London: J. M. Dent & Sons, 1974.

———. "The Social Contract." In *Basic Political Writings*. Edited by Donald A. Cress. Indianapolis: Hackett Publishing Co., 1987.

Rowan, Archibald Hamilton. *Autobiography of Archibald Hamilton Rowan*. Dublin: Thomas Tegg & Co., 1840.

Rusk, Ralph Leslie. "The Adventures of Gilbert Imlay." *Indiana University Studies* 10, no. 57 (March 1923).

St. Clair, William. *The Godwins and the Shelleys*. London and Boston: Faber & Faber, 1991.

Schama, Simon. *Citizens: A Chronicle of the French Revolution*. New York: Vintage Books, 1989.

Shelley and His Circle. 8 vols. Edited by Kenneth Neill Cameron. Cambridge, Mass.: Harvard University Press, 1961.

Southey, Robert. *Life and Correspondence of Robert Southey.* Edited by Charles Cuthbert Southey. New York: Harper & Brothers, 1851.

Spencer, Samia I., ed. *French Women and the Age of Enlightenment.* Bloomington: Indiana University Press, 1984.

Sunstein, Emily W. *A Different Face: The Life of Mary Wollstonecraft.* New York: Harper & Row, 1975.

Todd, Janet. *The Sign of Angelica.* New York: Columbia University Press, 1989.

Tomalin, Claire. *The Life and Death of Mary Wollstonecraft.* Harmondsworth, England: Penguin Books, 1985.

Trimmer, Sarah. *The History of the Robins.* London: Griffith & Farran, 1869.

Trimmer, Sarah, and "A Lady." Contributors to *Easy Lessons; or, Leading Strings to Knowledge.* Boston: Munroe & Francis, 1839.

Tyson, Gerald P. *Joseph Johnson: A Liberal Publisher.* Iowa City: University of Iowa Press, 1979.

Wakefield, Priscilla. *Reflections on the Present Condition of the Female Sex with Suggestions for Its Improvement.* London: Joseph Johnson, 1798.

Walker, George. *The Vagabond.* London: G. Walker, 1799.

Wardle, Ralph M., ed. *Collected Letters of Mary Wollstonecraft.* Ithaca, N.Y., and London: Cornell University Press, 1979.

———. *Godwin and Mary: Letters of William Godwin and Mary Wollstonecraft.* Lincoln and London: University of Nebraska Press, 1977.

West, Jane. *Letters to a Young Lady in Which the Duties and Character of Women Are Considered Chiefly with a Reference to Prevailing Opinions.* London: Longman, Hurst, Rees & Orme, 1806.

Williams, Helen Maria. *Letters Containing a Sketch of the Politics of France from the Thirty-first of May, 1793, till the Twenty-eighth of July, 1794 and of the Scenes Which Have Passed in the Prisons of Paris.* London: G. G. & J. Robinson, 1795.

———. *Letters from France: Containing Many New Anecdotes Relative to the French Revolution and the Present State of French Manners.* London: G. G. & J. Robinson, 1792.

———. *Memoirs of the Reign of Robespierre.* London: John Hamilton, 1929.

Wollstonecraft, Mary. *The Cave of Fancy.* In *Posthumous Works.* London: Joseph Johnson, 1798. Reprint, edited by Janet Todd and Marilyn Butler, *The Works of Mary Wollstonecraft.* Vol. 1. New York: New York University Press, 1989.

———. *An Historical and Moral View of the Origins and Progress of the French Revolution; and the Effect It Has Produced in Europe.* London: Joseph Johnson, 1794. Reprint, edited by Janet Todd and Marilyn Butler, *The Works of Mary Wollstonecraft*. Vol. 6. New York: New York University Press, 1989.

———. *Lessons*. In *Posthumous Works*. London: Joseph Johnson, 1798. Reprint, edited by Janet Todd and Marilyn Butler, *The Works of Mary Wollstonecraft*. Vol. 4. New York: New York University Press, 1989.

———. "Letter on the Present Character of the French Nation." In *Posthumous Works*. London: Joseph Johnson, 1798. Reprint, edited by Janet Todd and Marilyn Butler, *The Works of Mary Wollstonecraft*. Vol. 6. New York: New York University Press, 1989.

———. *Letters Written During a Short Residence in Sweden, Norway, and Denmark*. London: Joseph Johnson, 1796. Reprint, edited by Janet Todd and Marilyn Butler, *The Works of Mary Wollstonecraft*. Vol. 6. New York: New York University Press, 1989.

———. *Maria; or, The Wrongs of Woman*. In *Posthumous Works*. London: Joseph Johnson, 1798. Reprint, New York and London: W. W. Norton & Company, 1974.

———. *Mary*. London: Joseph Johnson, 1788. Reprint, with Mary Shelley, *Mary, Maria, & Matilda*. Harmondsworth, England: Penguin Classics, 1992.

———. *Original Stories from Real Life: With Conversations Calculated to Regulate the Affections and Form the Mind to Truth and Goodness*. London: Joseph Johnson, 1791. Reprint, edited by Janet Todd and Marilyn Butler, *The Works of Mary Wollstonecraft*. Vol. 4. New York: New York University Press, 1989.

———. *Thoughts on the Education of Daughters; with Reflections on Female Conduct, in the More Important Duties of Life*. London: Joseph Johnson, 1787. Reprint, edited by Janet Todd and Marilyn Butler, *The Works of Mary Wollstonecraft*. Vol. 4. New York: New York University Press, 1989.

———. *A Vindication of the Rights of Men in a Letter to the Right Honourable Edmund Burke Occasioned by His Reflections on the Revolution in France*. London: Joseph Johnson, 1790. Reprint, edited by Janet Todd and Marilyn Butler, *The Works of Mary Wollstonecraft*. Vol. 5. New York: New York University Press, 1989.

———. *A Vindication of the Rights of Woman with Strictures on Political and Moral Subjects*. London: Joseph Johnson, 1792. Reprint, Harmondsworth, England: Penguin Classics, 1992.

Woodress, James. *A Yankee's Odyssey: The Life of Joel Barlow*. Philadelphia and New York: J. Lippincott Co., 1958.

Young, Arthur. *Arthur Young's Travels in France During the Years 1787, 1788, 1789*. London: George Bell & Sons, 1892.

ACKNOWLEDGMENTS

First and foremost, I am grateful to Lord Abinger, who through Bruce Barker-Benfield at the Bodleian Library gave me access to his magnificent collection of papers relating to Mary Wollstonecraft, her family, and her friends. These I read both at the Carl H. Pforzheimer Collection in the New York Public Library and at the Bodleian in Oxford. I can never sufficiently thank the Pforzheimer's valiant Stephen Wagner, who was as ingenious at ferreting out obscure material (particularly on the education of eighteenth-century women) as he was unfailingly helpful in providing the microfilms, manuscripts, and photographs so crucial to this book. Bruce Barker-Benfield was also of great help during my shorter stay at the Bodleian.

Many thanks go to the cheerful, informative staffs of the libraries I visited: the Allentown, New Jersey Library; the Beverley Library; the Bobst Library at New York University; the British Library; the Carl H. Pforzheimer Collection of Shelley and His Circle; the Houghton Library at Harvard; the London Guildhall; the Library of London Public Record Office; the Mid-Manhattan Library; the New Jersey State Archives in Trenton; the New York Public Library Astor, Lenox, and Tilden Foundations; the Spitalfields Library; the State Library of New South Wales (which permitted me to use its original manuscript of Everina's letter about Fanny Godwin in the Mitchell Library), and the Swansea Library. I am grateful to Dr. Ina Cholst for explaining the causes of Mary's death to me. Janet Todd and Marilyn Butler's comprehensive *The Works of Mary Wollstonecraft* and Ralph M. Wardle's *Collected Letters of Mary Wollstonecraft* were constant reference points, and I am indebted to Emily Sunstein, Claire Tomalin, and Janet Todd not only for their earlier works on my subject, but for cheering this project on. The scholars at the Shelley and His Circle office at the New York Public

Acknowledgments

Library, especially Doucet Devin Fischer, plied me with information, as did my Australian researcher Leona Geeves.

I want to thank my agent, Kim Witherspoon, whose unfailing support saw me through difficult moments, and my editor, Alice Mayhew, whose rigor and high standards made this a better book. Many thanks go also to Alice's colleagues Anja Schmidt and Ana Debevoise and to my first editor, Rebecca Salatan, and my first agent, Dona Chernoff. I thank Gideon Weil for personal attention far beyond the call of duty and am, indeed, grateful to all the extraordinary professionals at Simon & Schuster and in Kim Witherspoon's office who made my life easier during this time. I want to thank Carol Agboti, Martha and John Caute, Françoise, Peter, and Robin Cowie, and Carol and Ian Jewel for enlivening my London visits. And thanks to Michel Vale for lending me his Paris apartment while I was imagining Mary's adventures in revolutionary France. I am most deeply grateful to Anne Yarowsky and Gerry Rabkin for their keen comments on early drafts of my manuscript and to my wonderful daughter, Masha, whose life is so much freer because Mary Wollstonecraft lived.

INDEX

Adams, John and Abigail, 108
Alderson, Amelia, 233–34, 242, 243,
    244, 245, 259, 279
American Revolution, 79, 80, 103,
    138–39
Analytical Review:
    contributors to, 72
    editors of, 71–72
    Johnson and, 71–72, 73, 82, 226
    Mary's articles for, 71–73, 81–82, 87,
        88, 89, 101, 111, 118, 241, 251
Arden, Jane:
    biography of, 31
    marriage of, 31
    Mary's letters to, 21–25, 27, 28, 29,
        31
Arkwright, Richard, 191
Astell, Mary, 39, 99–100, 101–2
Austen, Jane, 38

Barbauld, Anna Laetitia, 39, 42, 45, 47,
    58, 63, 107–8, 192, 229, 233
Barlow, Joel, 108–10, 113, 137, 141,
    142, 148, 150, 156, 164, 178
Barlow, Ruth, 108–10, 113, 135,

136–37, 149–50, 156, 164, 165,
    169, 171, 178, 242
Behn, Aphra, 39, 57, 100
Bishop, Elizabeth Mary Francis, 32, 33,
    35
Bishop, Eliza Wollstonecraft (sister):
    discontent of, 63, 107, 118–19, 131,
        144, 155, 194, 196–97, 203–4,
        242
    escape of, 33–36, 99, 265
    as governess, 98
    and Imlay, 194–95, 204
    job options of, 37, 60, 118, 204, 261
    madness of, 32–33, 44, 50, 82, 93,
        113
    marriage of, 31, 32–36
    Mary's concerns for, 62–63, 75,
        95–96, 113, 119, 130–31,
        144–45, 195, 204
    as teacher, 37–39, 46, 63, 71, 75, 81,
        88, 280
    and visit to France, 119, 144, 156,
        180
    see also Wollstonecraft, Eliza
Bishop, Meredith, 31, 32–36

Index

Blackburn, Mrs. (neighbor), 46
Blackman, Elias, 206, 209
Blake, William, 45, 58, 59, 68, 71
Blenkinsop, Mrs. (midwife), 270, 271
Blood, Fanny, 26–29, 31, 42
    death of, 41, 44, 60, 81, 269
    illness of, 39
    marriage of, 39–40
    and Mary's family, 28, 33, 34
    "romantic friendship" of Mary and,
        27–29, 31, 40, 89
    and school, 38
Blood, George, 29
    gift from, 46
    and Mary's family, 82, 83–84, 98,
        284
Blood, Mr. and Mrs., 26, 27, 28–29, 41,
    44, 45, 47, 218
Bonnycastle, John, 68–69
Bowdler, Henrietta, 27–28
Bregantz, Mrs. (headmistress), 81, 88,
    116
Brissot, J.-P., 137, 141, 145, 160
Brooks, Mrs. (friend), 37
Burgh, James, 37
Burgh, Mrs. (friend), 37–40, 46, 50, 63
Burke, Edmund, 80, 91–92, 93, 94, 112,
    121, 155, 226–27, 230, 232
Burney, Fanny, 52
Butler, Eleanor, 27
Buzot, François, 127

Caleb Williams (Godwin), 224, 234–36,
    262
Carlisle, Anthony, 229, 252
Cartwright, Edmund, 190–91
Cave of Fancy, The (Wollstonecraft),
    60–61

Chapone, Hester, 20
Chapter Coffee House, 57
Christie, Rebecca, 129, 141, 151, 178,
    197, 219, 222, 239, 243
Christie, Thomas, 71–72, 87, 129, 142,
    151, 178, 243
Church, Mr. ("Friendly Church"), 38
Clare, Mr. and Mrs., 26, 37, 225
Club des Amis de la Loi, 128
Club des Tricoteuses, 128
Cockburn, Mrs. (neighbor), 40, 41, 47
Codman, Richard, 164–65
Coleridge, Samuel Taylor, 198, 227–28,
    258, 281
Committee of Public Safety, Paris, 145
Condorcet, Marquis and Marquise de,
    126, 127, 130, 136, 145, 159, 177
Confédération des Amis de la Vérité,
    127
Cordeliers, 127
Cort, Henry, 190
Cowper, William, 58, 72, 202
Croft, Herbert, 201
Curran, John, 280
Curwen, John Christian, 191

Danton, Georges-Jacques, 121, 122,
    156, 168–69, 171
Dawson, Mrs., Mary as companion to,
    29, 44, 225
Declaration of the Rights of Man, 87
Defoe, Daniel, 100
Different Face, A (Sunstein), 31
Dilly, Charles and Edward, 56
Dissidents, 25, 44, 103, 192, 199
    academies of, 38
    and French unrest, 80
    and Godwin, 223, 225, 226

and Johnson, 45, 56–57, 72
and Revolution Society, 85–87
Dürer, Albrecht, 69
Dyer, George, 199
Dyson, George, 266, 272

Easy Lessons ("a Lady"), 64–65
Eccles, John, 198–99
Edgeworth, Maria, 191, 279
Ellefsen, Peder, 205–6, 210, 214
Emigrants, The (Imlay), 142, 145–46, 147
Émile (Rousseau), 50, 103, 121
England:
   circulating libraries in, 56
   Dissidents in, 25, 38, 80, 85–87
   divorce in, 34, 264
   and French unrest, 80, 87, 91–92,
      109, 112, 114, 129, 135, 155,
      279
   industrialization in, 57, 100, 190–91
   marital rights in, 33–34, 261
   Mary's return to, 189–200
   primogeniture in, 16–17, 18
   publishing in, 55–57, 63
   religion in, 56
   suicides in, 201–2
   war with France, 131, 137, 154–56,
      163, 165, 189, 236–37, 243
England, Church of, 91
English Review, 226
Enlightenment, 68, 102, 201, 225, 226,
   231

Fénelon, François, 232
Fenwick, Eliza, 242, 260, 272–73
Fenwick, John, 272
Filliettaz, Aline, 116, 148
Fordyce, George, 58, 69

Fordyce, James, 192
Fouché, Joseph, 171
Fox, Charles James, 91, 135, 230
France, 133–52, 153–65
   Catholic Church in, 91, 159, 171, 182
   Mary's arrival in, 115–32
   Mary's desire to visit, 80–81, 112,
      113–14, 119
   Mary's return to, 231
   militant women of, 128–29, 177
   Reign of Terror in, 145, 148, 151,
      154–56, 163–64, 168–69,
      171–72, 173, 177, 179, 182, 208,
      219–20, 232, 279
   revolutionary clubs in, 127
   social life in, 125–29, 176–77
   social unrest in, 79–81, 83, 86, 93,
      112, 120, 122–23, 154; *see also*
      French Revolution
   Versailles Palace, 150–51
   war with England, 131, 137, 154–56,
      163, 165, 189, 236–37, 243
   war with Europe, 137, 197–98
Frankenstein (M. W. Shelley), 286
Franklin, Benjamin, 45
French Republic, 154–55
French Revolution, 83, 88, 89, 103,
   109, 110, 129, 232
   and civil rights, 87, 91–92, 101, 126,
      145, 159–60, 172, 174
   individuals swallowed up by, 127,
      154–55, 160–61, 171–72
   Mary's writings about, 86–87, 111,
      114, 116, 145, 146–47, 163, 165,
      166–68, 192, 222, 251
   and violence, 112, 124, 129, 131, 135,
      142, 145, 148, 150, 151, 155–56,
      163–64, 171, 220

Fuseli, Henry, 71, 72
    and French Revolution, 88, 112
    and Johnson, 58, 69, 96
    Mary's relationship with, 88, 89, 90,
        93, 98, 106, 109, 111, 112–14,
        124, 142, 197
    as painter, 69–70, 88–89
    and Sophie, 70, 88, 112–13

Gabell, Ann, 90–91
Gabell, Henry, 47, 49, 52, 90
Genlis, Madame de, 49
Gentleman's Magazine, 72
George III, king of England, 18, 82,
        85–86, 91, 93, 100, 135, 189
Girondists, 122, 123, 127, 129, 130, 137,
        141, 142, 145, 148, 150, 154,
        160–61, 169, 189
Godwin, Fanny (daughter), 258, 280,
        283–86
    career options of, 284–85
    early years of, *see* Imlay, Fanny
    and Godwin as "Papa," 267, 278,
        282, 283
    and mother's death, 272, 273, 278
    and sister, 280, 283–84
    and stepmother, 281, 284
    suicide of, 285–86
Godwin, Mary (daughter), *see* Shelley,
        Mary Wollstonecraft Godwin
Godwin, Mary Jane Clairmont (second
        wife), 229, 281, 282
Godwin, William, 69, 223–38, 287
    birth and childhood of, 223–24
    daughter Mary, *see* Shelley, Mary
        Wollstonecraft Godwin
    education of, 224, 225
    and Fanny, 249, 257, 267, 278, 282,
        283

and fatherhood, 279–80, 281–82
first meetings of Mary and, 230–31,
        238
and Hays, 200–201, 222, 233, 238
and Holcroft, 222, 227–29, 230, 236,
        241, 259
and Johnson, 58, 230, 260, 277
and Juvenile Library, 281
literary career of, 83, 226–27, 229,
        231–33, 234–36, 260, 284; *see
        also specific titles*
marriage of Mary and, 256, 257–61
and Mary's death, 271–74, 277–79
and Mary's family, 255–56, 280
Mary's friendship with, 241–56
and Mary's work, 107, 238, 243–44,
        252–53, 263–64, 266, 274, 279
ministerial posts of, 225–26
personal traits of, 224–25, 228
political views of, 83, 109, 147, 190,
        229–30, 231–32, 236–37
and Shelley, 282–84
walking tour of, 267–68
Godwins and the Shelleys, The (St. Clair),
        245
Goethe, Johann Wolfgang von, 73, 201
Gouges, Olympe de, 128, 150, 160
Gregory, John, 104, 192

Hamilton Rowan, Archibald, 179, 185,
        222, 238, 277
Hardy, Thomas, 109
Hayes, Samuel, 82
Hays, Mary, 198–201
    and Eccles, 198–99
    and Godwin, 200–201, 222, 233,
        238
    and Godwins' marriage, 258–59
    and Mary's death, 201, 272, 278–79

Mary's friendship with, 198, 199, 200, 201, 222, 238, 248, 250, 251
and Mary's work, 107, 199
writings of, 107, 192, 199, 243
Hazlitt, William, 227, 232, 236, 258
Hébert, Jacques-René, 153, 168–69, 171
Helvétius, 225
Henry, Mademoiselle, 70, 79
Hewlett, John, 38, 39, 41, 45, 47, 72
History of the Robins (Trimmer), 64
Holcroft, Thomas, 222, 227–29, 230, 234, 236, 241–42, 259
Homer, 69

Imlay, Fanny (daughter):
birth of, 169–70
and father, 239, 255, 261, 278
and Godwin, 249, 257; *see also* Godwin, Fanny
illness of, 253–54
infancy and childhood of, 172, 175, 176, 178, 179, 183–85, 192–95, 222
and Mary's sisters, 256, 280, 285
and Mary's suicide attempts, 217, 218, 219
in Scandinavia with Mary, 206, 207, 208, 209, 215
Imlay, Gilbert, 138–49, 288
affair of Mary and, 142–44, 148–49, 150, 152, 158, 164, 174–75, 193–94, 197, 208, 216–18, 219–20, 233, 238–40, 261, 283
birth and background of, 138–41
business affairs of, 148, 156–57, 159, 161, 164, 165, 170, 172, 173–75, 183, 203–4, 205–10, 214, 215–16, 243

and daughter, 239, 255, 261, 278
debts of, 139–40, 141
financial prospects of, 195–96
first meeting of Mary and, 141–42
Mary registered as wife of, 151–52
and Mary's family, 180–82, 194–95, 204
Mary's financial dependence on, 165, 174, 182, 183, 193, 217, 219, 255
and Mary's pregnancy, 157
and Mary's suicide attempts, 203, 219
mistresses of, 193, 217, 218, 220
and politics, 137, 142
as writer, 140–41, 142, 145–46, 147, 182
Inchbald, Elizabeth, 233, 234, 241, 254, 260
Industrial Revolution, 57, 100, 190–91

Jacobins, 122, 123, 127, 137, 141, 145, 150, 151, 153, 154–55, 160, 168–69, 177, 189, 192, 198, 243
Jefferson, Thomas, 140–41
Johnson, Joseph, 57–63, 127, 189, 287–88
and *Analytical Review,* 71–72, 73, 82, 226
birth and early years of, 57–58
as Dissident, 45, 56–57, 72
and Godwin, 58, 230, 260, 277
health of, 95
and Mary's death, 272, 277
as Mary's friend, 47, 60, 61–62, 63, 70, 74, 87–88, 95, 97, 109, 113, 129, 149, 161, 180, 196, 197, 198, 199, 220–21, 243, 255
Mary's meetings with, 47, 60

Johnson, Joseph *(cont.)*
 personality traits of, 45, 58–59,
  61–62, 70, 73
 physical appearance of, 45, 47, 58
 as publisher, 45, 56–57, 59–60, 68,
  71, 86, 92, 94, 96, 107, 113, 165,
  192, 200, 202, 253, 279
Johnson, Dr. Samuel, 39, 57, 73
Jones, Louisa, 273, 279, 280
Julia (Williams), 89, 118

Kingsborough, Margaret, 60, 68, 81
 as Lady Mountcashell, 280, 281, 288
 as Mary's pupil, 48–50, 53–54, 98
Kingsborough, Lord Robert and Lady
  Caroline, 46, 47–50, 53, 61
Knights Templar, 115–16

"a Lady" (author), 64–65
Lamb, Charles and Mary, 32, 281
Lavater, Anna, 70
Lavater, Johann, 70
Leavenworth, Mark, 164
Le Havre:
 Imlay family in, 172, 175
 Imlay in, 156–57, 159, 161–62
 Mary's travel to, 163–66, 184
Léon, Paulie, 145
Lessons (Wollstonecraft), 268–69
Letters for Literary Ladies (Edgeworth),
 191
Letters on Education (Macaulay), 101
*Letters Written During a Short Residence in
 Sweden, Norway, and Denmark*
 (Wollstonecraft), 207–16, 221–22,
 238, 242
Lettsome, John Coakley, 38
Locke, John, 26, 29, 38, 42, 147, 198,
 201, 231

London Corresponding Society (LCS),
 189–90
Louis XVI, king of France, 122
 execution of, 130, 132, 133–35, 136,
  137, 141, 232
 in Mary's book, 166, 167
 and social unrest, 79–80, 83, 112,
  117, 124, 128
 trial of, 115–16, 120, 121, 123, 130,
  131

Macaulay, Catharine, 39, 99, 100–102,
 105, 130
Marat, Jean–Paul, 142, 145, 150, 177
Marguerite (nursemaid), 177, 179, 183,
 192, 201, 206, 207, 209, 218, 219,
 251, 272
Maria (Wollstonecraft), 202, 252–53,
 261–67, 268, 279
Marie Antoinette, queen of France,
 154, 159, 166, 167
"Marseillaise," 179
Marshall, James, 224, 226, 256, 272,
 277, 280
Mary (Wollstonecraft), 50–53, 61, 68,
 71, 265
Memoirs of Mary Wollstonecraft, The
 (Godwin), 143–44, 243–44, 278,
 279
Mericourt, Théroigne de, 128, 145
Merry, Robert, 245
Milton, John, 26, 73
Mirabeau, Comte de, 128, 143, 154,
 167
Montagu, Lady Mary Wortley, 20, 28,
 57
Montague, Basil, 271
Moralisches Elementarbuch (Salzmann),
 74, 82–83

Index

More, Hannah, 64, 107, 191, 192
Mountcashell, Lord, 280

Narbonne, Comte de, 125
Necker, Jacques, 70, 71, 74, 81–82, 125, 166
New Annual Register, 83, 226, 229, 231
Newbery, John, 56
Newton, Samuel, 224
Nichols, John, 72
Noble, Frances, 56

Ogle, George, 48, 69
Opie, John, 88–89, 97, 111–12, 244–45, 261, 269
Original Stories (Wollstonecraft), 65–68, 70, 71, 88, 89, 92, 93, 252

Paine, Thomas, 58, 59, 80, 92, 109, 121–22, 129, 130, 155, 161, 163, 230, 232
Palm d'Aelders, Etta, 127–28
Paris, *see* France
patriarchy, 36
Pinkerton, Miss N., 261
Pitt, William, 189, 190, 236
Political Justice (Godwin), 107, 147, 190, 200, 229, 231–33, 234, 235, 236, 250, 261, 279, 282–83
Ponsonby, Sarah, 27
Posthumous Works (Wollstonecraft), 61
poverty:
    character built by, 44
    and expectations, 44
    literary depictions of, 52–53, 252
    and social unrest, 88, 93, 117, 154, 168, 182
Price, Richard, 38–39, 45, 46, 58, 80, 85–87, 91, 94, 96, 229

Priestley, Joseph, 45, 58, 80, 199
primogeniture, 16–17, 18
Prior, Mrs. (friend), 46

Radcliffe, Ann, 145, 198
Rawlins, Sophia, 70, 88, 112–13
Reflections on the Revolution in France (Burke), 91–92
Reveley, Maria, 237, 242, 260, 280–81
Revolution Society, 85–87, 91, 229
Reynold, Joshua, 88
Richardson, Samuel, 28, 52
Rights of Man, The (Paine), 59, 92, 121, 230
Rights of Woman, The (Barbauld), 107–8
Robespierre, Maximilien:
    and the Convention, 121, 122, 173
    and Danton, 121, 122, 156, 168–69
    death of, 171–72, 173, 177, 179
    and Jacobins, 122, 127, 150, 155, 168–69
    and Marat, 142
    and 22 Prairial, 171, 172
    on virtue, 163, 169
Robinson, George, 226, 229, 231, 232
Robinson, Mary, 233
Roland, Jean–Marie and Manon, 126–27, 145, 148, 161, 192
Roscoe, William, 97, 98, 111, 113–14
Rouget de l'Isle, Claude-Joseph, 179
Rousseau, Jean-Jacques, 64
    on child-rearing, 42, 175
    Émile by, 50, 103, 121
    and French unrest, 80, 123
    low opinion of women, 50, 103, 104
    Mary's appreciation of, 29, 42, 50, 52, 73, 102, 121, 125, 147, 198, 244
    Social Contract by, 120–21

Rousseau, Jean-Jacques *(cont.)*
  theories of, 29, 42, 69, 80, 102, 120,
    212, 225
Roux, Jacques, 153

St. Clair, William, 245
St. Leon (Godwin), 224, 226, 258,
    279
Salmon, Mrs., waxworks of, 63
Salzmann, Christian Gotthilf, 74,
    82–83
Scandinavia, Mary's trip to, 203–4,
    205–17
Schlabrendorf, Gustav Graf von, 154,
    158, 179
Schweizer, Madeleine, 178
Serious Proposal to the Ladies, A (Astell),
    99–100, 101
Seze, Romain de, 123
Shakespeare, William, 26, 69, 73
Shelley, Mary Wollstonecraft Godwin
    (daughter), 227, 229
  as "Baby William," 267, 269, 271
  birth of, 271
  early years of, 280
  Frankenstein by, 286
  and Percy, 260, 282–84
Shelley, Percy Bysshe, 260, 282–84
Siddons, Sarah, 260
Skeys, Hugh, 27, 33, 39–40, 41, 98
Smith, Charlotte, 58, 59, 73, 202
Smith, Elizabeth, 28
Social Contract (Rousseau), 120–21
Société des Républicaines-
    Révolutionnaires, 145
Society of the Thirty, 127
Sothren, Mrs. (Godwin's guardian),
    224

Southey, Robert, 225, 244, 279
Staël, Madame de, 125–26, 127–28,
    148, 176
Stone, John Hurford, 129, 155, 159
Sunstein, Emily, 31
Swift, Jonathan, 26

Talleyrand-Périgord, Charles-Maurice
    de, 102, 125
Tallien, Jean-Lambert, 171, 173, 176
Thelwall, John, 190
Thomson, James, 26
Thoughts on the Education of Daughters
    (Wollstonecraft), 42–44, 45, 46,
    49, 68, 89, 106
Times of London, 56, 80, 87, 88, 92,
    135, 155–56
Trimmer, Sarah, 48, 63–64, 65, 67, 83

United States:
  as democracy, 79
  Wollstonecraft's audience in, 108

Varlet, Jean, 153
Vindication of the Rights of Men, A (Woll-
    stonecraft), 92–95, 96, 97, 107,
    124, 125, 222
Vindication of the Rights of Woman, A
    (Wollstonecraft), 36, 74, 99,
    101–11, 112, 118, 119, 126, 127,
    175, 199, 209, 217, 233, 238, 264,
    266, 274, 284
Voltaire, 80, 174, 225, 230

Walker, George, 279
Walpole, Horace, 57, 107
Wedgwood, Josiah, 191
Wedgwood, Thomas, 255

Index

Wedgwood family, 233, 255, 267
Wheatcroft, John, 163
Wilkie, John, 56, 58
William of Orange, 85
Williams, Helen Maria, 126, 229
   and French Revolution, 129–30, 155,
     159, 161, 169, 172, 177
   Julia by, 89, 118
   personal traits of, 118, 129–30
   and Stone, 129, 155, 159
   as travel writer, 140
Wollstonecraft, Charles (brother), 71,
   287
   birth and childhood of, 18, 19, 20,
     25, 30
   and financial support, 119, 194, 221,
     260
   and George Blood, 82, 83–84
   idleness of, 84, 90, 98
   law career of, 60, 74, 81, 82
   and U.S., 110, 113, 161, 180, 197
Wollstonecraft, Edward (grandfather),
   15–17, 18, 265
Wollstonecraft, Edward John (father),
   16–17, 60, 99, 119–20, 287
   and family moves, 19, 25, 28
   jobs of, 17, 18
   and Lydia, 30, 132
   and money, 20, 25, 44, 74–75, 84,
     207
Wollstonecraft, Eliza (sister):
   birth and childhood of, 16, 18, 20,
     25, 28
   financial support of, 31, 81, 95
   marriage of, *see* Bishop, Eliza
     Wollstonecraft
Wollstonecraft, Elizabeth Dickson
   (mother), 17–19, 20, 23, 30, 99

Wollstonecraft, Everina (sister), 30,
   242–43, 287
   birth and childhood of, 18, 20, 25,
     28
   and Fanny Imlay/Godwin, 256, 280,
     285
   financial support of, 31, 81, 95
   and Godwin, 255–56, 280
   jobs of, 60, 88, 98, 118, 131, 179,
     197
   Mary's concerns for, 62, 95–96, 119
   in Paris, 70–71, 75, 79, 87
Wollstonecraft, Henry (brother), 16, 18,
   20, 25, 31, 82
Wollstonecraft, James (brother), 287
   birth and childhood of, 18, 20, 25
   financial support for, 83, 119
   as sailor, 31, 48, 60, 81, 98, 131, 194
Wollstonecraft, Jane (grandmother), 16
Wollstonecraft, Lydia (stepmother), 30,
   75, 132
Wollstonecraft, Mary:
   adolescent years of, 21–26, 27, 31
   as American citizen, 151–52
   birth of, 17
   Cave of Fancy by, 60–61
   celebrity of, 97–98
   childhood of, 18–20
   daughters of, *see* Imlay, Fanny; Shel-
     ley, Mary Wollstonecraft
     Godwin
   death in childbirth, 269–75, 277
   debts of, 45, 46, 50, 53, 63, 279
   depressions of, 26, 40, 106, 201–2,
     208, 238, 247, 254
   education manual written by, 41–42
   education of, 21, 24, 26
   family background of, 15–19, 24–25

Index

Wollstonecraft, Mary *(cont.)*
  and family finances, 74–75, 83, 84,
    90, 119–20
  family moves of, 18–19, 25, 28
  and Fanny Blood, *see* Blood, Fanny
  financial success of, 97–98, 118–19
  in France, *see* France
  on the French Revolution, 86–87,
    111, 114, 116, 145, 146–47, 163,
    165, 166–68, 192, 222, 251
  and Godwin, *see* Godwin, William
  ill health of, 50, 254, 255
  and Imlay, *see* Imlay, Gilbert
  independent nature and strong will
    of, 23, 29, 35–36, 41, 44, 54,
    60, 95
  intellect of, 29, 49, 73, 89
  jobs held by, 29–30, 37–39, 45–46,
    48–49, 53–54
  and Johnson, *see* Johnson, Joseph
  Lessons by, 268–69
  Letters by, 207–16, 221–22, 238, 242
  on madness, 93–94
  Maria by, 202, 252–53, 261–67, 268,
    279
  Mary by, 50–53, 61, 68, 71, 265
  and motherhood, 176, 178, 183
  obituary for, 201, 278–79
  Original Stories by, 65–68, 70, 71, 88,
    89, 92, 93, 252
  personal characteristics of, 52,
    61–62, 143–44, 158, 178, 200,
    278–79
  physical appearance of, 47, 55, 111,
    244
  portraits of, 97, 111–12, 261, 269
  pregnancies of, 157, 159, 161, 162,
    165, 254, 255–56, 267, 269
  relationships with men, 89, 93, 106,
    108, 109, 112–14, 143–44, 149,
    150, 157, 175
  and religion, 19, 25, 39, 44, 47, 73,
    93, 103, 201, 212, 273
  as resolved not to wed, 28
  Rights of Men by, 92–95, 96, 97, 107,
    124, 125, 222
  Rights of Women by, *see Vindication of*
    the Rights of Woman
  on romantic friendships between
    women, 27–28, 31
  Scandinavian trip of, 203–4, 205–17
  suicide attempts of, 201–3, 216–19
  Thoughts on Education by, 42–44, 45,
    46, 49, 68, 89, 106
  as translator, 70, 74, 81–83
  writing career of, 47, 49, 50, 54, 57,
    60–61, 63, 71–75, 87–88, 89,
    92, 96, 97, 98–99, 111, 118–19,
    203, 253, 260
Wollstonecraft, Ned (brother), 287
  birth and childhood of, 16, 18, 20,
    23, 99
  financial support from, 31, 33
  jobs of, 25, 30
  as less than supportive, 60, 74, 119
  and primogeniture, 16–17, 18
  sisters harbored by, 35, 46
women:
  bluestocking traditions, 99, 129
  and child custody, 33, 34, 126
  death in childbirth, 269, 274
  dependency of, 49, 106, 209, 254
  early marriages for, 42
  education of, 20–21, 25, 41–42, 47,
    52, 99–102, 105–6, 126, 192,
    200
  and imagination, 106–7, 175–76, 258
  industrialization and, 57, 100, 191

legal rights of, 45, 99, 101–2, 126, 127, 128, 191, 209
literary, 39, 63–64, 99–101, 118
in London clubs, 39
love between men and, 42–44, 89, 93, 106, 108
lowly status of, 47–48, 49, 100, 103, 264
and marital laws, 33–34, 260–61, 264
options open to, 29, 37, 44, 57, 99, 100, 204, 284

as property, 16
property of, 17, 126, 141, 264
qualities of ideal wives in, 37, 42, 100, 191
"romantic friendships" between, 27–28, 31
self-supporting, 57, 264
Wordsworth, William, 58, 211, 232
Wulfsberg, Jacob, 210, 213

Young, Arthur, 125
Young, Edward, 26